A PRIEST'S JOURNEY TO HELL AND BACK

By

PETER J. RIGA

AuthorHouse™
1663 Liberty Drive
Bloomington, IN 47403
www.authorhouse.com
Phone: 1-800-839-8640

Published by AuthorHouse 7/12/2013

ISBN: 978-1-4817-7897-8 (sc)
ISBN: 978-1-4817-7898-5 (e)

Library of Congress Control Number: 2013912776

CHAPTER I

CULTURE AND CHILD ABUSE: ONE MAN'S HISTORY

In a society and culture like ours child abuse is not only illegal but downright criminal. In Roman and Islamic law, children are property to do what parents wish with them. The paterfamilias had the power of life and death over every child born into his household. A child was not legitimate until the paterfamilias accepted him into the family and if he did not, the child was left to die or be exposed to be eaten by wild animals. (The early Christians rescued many of these children who were called appropriately, rescuers.) This Roman influence continued until well into the nineteenth century where infanticide for sick or unwanted children was widely practiced. Abortion was common in both East and West, particularly in eastern countries as a type of sex selection where girls were undesired and killed one way or another. India and China had to pass laws forbidding female genocide, that is, abortion as a form of sex selection (boys over girls). Ironically that is perfectly legal in American today. Today there is a great imbalance of boys/girls in China and India.

This cultural phenomenon has come down to us in modified forms until well into the twentieth century. As an Italian the first born son (primogenitor) had to be beaten to strengthen him to protect the family. This will help the reader understand why I want to communicate my history to you. I find fault with no one. It was simply the culture I grew up in descended from the Romans. If you have seen the films of "The Godfather" you will understand a little of what I am going to say.

In the Italian culture everything passes to the first born son who is like the godfather. From a very young age, he is to be hardened by severe discipline so that he can protect his family with everything he has, including his life if it comes down to that. That takes the form of physical beatings, not because parents enjoy beating their son but because they know that he had to be strong in order to protect the family. He must be strong and parents only want to toughen him up by physical discipline. That will make him strong against the enemies of the family which is first and most important in the opinion of that culture. That is the reality and history that is handed down to him from generations past. The examples in my case are numerous. If they were applied today, my parents would be in jail.

The toughening process starts very early. When I was about three to four years old, I was intrigued by the Iroquois gas containing tower that provided natural gas for the area of South Buffalo. It would go up and down as need was greater or lesser surrounded by a steel frame to strengthen the bubble gas within the frame. There were levels of stairs that went right to the top some hundreds of feet. I climbed the fence and made my way all the way to the top. The view was breathtaking. I had never seen anything so beautiful in my whole life. The countryside (it seemed to me) was in brilliant colors. Meanwhile the workers had called the police who were afraid that I would jump if they came too close. So they tried to coax me with candy but I wouldn't budge. Finally they called my parents who also came with my relatives. A police officer explained to me that my mother was waiting for me below. When I said that if I came down, she would beat me, the officer swore that she would not. So I climbed down with the officer and my mother took me home. When we got home she proceeded to beat the hell out of me for causing such a ruckus. From that moment, I never again trusted any adult when they told me anything. Never lie to a child. My distrust endures to this day. Never again! After I was ordained a priest, I had trouble with my religious superiors because I had not trusted them. That is not good for the smooth running of a religious organization. More on this later.

There were so many violent exchanges with my parents that it is difficult to pick and choose. Here are some others. I never liked school at the lower levels. I attended PS 70 near the East River in New York. My best friend was Billy Buffo who later was executed at Sing Sing prison for a shoot out where he killed three state troopers. He and I simply skipped school to go fishing. In fact, what happened was just down the East River. Two young boys had drowned while swimming and when they checked that we two were missing from school, they thought it was us. When I arrived home with my brilliant catch of four carp, I guessed something was wrong when I saw all the cars around the house. When I appeared it must have looked like Jesus after the crucifixion who appeared before the apostles. Happiness for Italians is expressed by blows. How many you can take, the better head of the family you are bound to be. The initial blows blew me into the kitchen where the women were and more blows. That really was an expression of their love (if you can believe that). My father then took me into the bathroom, grabbed his razor strap and started to beat me with blows with all his strength. In between blows he shouted, "Are you going to see Billy Buffo again?" I would and adamantly yelled, "Yes" followed by more blows until I passed out. I learned later that my uncles had broken down the bathroom door to take me away. But I did learn a valuable lesson that evening. If I really believed something, nothing would move me, not even death itself. It was a discovery that I was not a coward after all. I could stand up even to my father.

I do remember the time when I told my parents that I wanted to be a priest. Our family was not particularly religious and I still do now know where I got the idea of becoming a priest. I was no more than fifteen years old so I could no longer be beaten to bring me into line but they could do perhaps something worse. They simply threw me out of the house, clothes and all. The reason was clear. As a priest I could not continue the family line and I could not be around to defend the family from any and all harm which might befall it. Luckily, I had a pastor who was kind as he was intelligent. He got me a room next to the boiler room at the Mother's House of the Sisters of St. Francis in Williamsville, New York. My duties would be to serve Mass each morning at 6:00 AM and to serve the adoration of the Blessed Sacrament in the evening while I attended the minor seminary a few miles down the road on Bailey Avenue. It was then called the Little Seminary. That would go on for three years until I was sent to study in Europe. I am so very happy that all this was done without a beating. I did not reconcile with my parents until after I was ordained. I never saw them for ten long years.

To return to childhood days. When I was no more than seven years old, we lived in the Italian section of Buffalo, New York on Swan Street. Like all kids, I loved to play ball. Our neighbor had built a fence of no more than three feet tall with barbed wire over the top which was illegal even then. When I went to retrieve a ball, I fell on the barbed wire and cut my face badly. The scar on my face is still there. My father settled with the guy for fifty dollars and I had that reminder for the rest of my life. Moreover, what I got was yet another beating for going over the neighbor's fence in the first place. I was sold for a lot less than thirty pieces of silver which would have been worth something in those days. But I wasn't worthy of the payment of Judas for a scar that would be mine for the rest of my life.

That money meant more to my father than the maiming of his eldest son. I never did forgive him for that. The beatings were mostly administered by my mother but those of my father were more vicious and lasting. To this day I do not know where they found the courage to treat me so. It wasn't the feeling; it was the culture.

My father used to make his own wine from the California grapes we bought at the Niagara food terminal in Buffalo on Bailey Avenue. We would squeeze the grapes in the fall and put the juice in four large barrels and wait a few months as the grape juice fermented. My father thought that wine was pure Burgundy. I never drank the stuff because I thought it tasted like vinegar. But one day while squeezing the grapes, I managed to tip the press over and therefore, lost about five gallons of grape juice. My father was furious. He took up a board and beat me until I almost passed out. I spent the night in that cellar, chained to a post without supper for my punishment. For a pure accident, I received the equivalent of a gulag as punishment. My right shoulder became infected from the blows. When they took me to the emergency room of Mercy Hospital on Abbot Road, my parents told the doctor and nurses that I had taken a fall. No one investigated because there was no understanding in those days that a parent would lie about the bruises of a young child. We hadn't gotten to that kind of a realization in those days. It took about four weeks to heal and I almost developed blood poisoning. That was one of the few times I did not get a beating because my father had to pay out twenty dollars for emergency room payment which was a lot of money in those days. My father thought the wound would only get bigger if he beat me again and another twenty dollars for treatment in the emergency room. The money was more important to him than the hurt that was mine for many weeks. The healing had to take its own time. No more hospital if I died.

II

But I digress. I was quite precocious (or shall I say rebellious) at an early age which I remember clearly. These childhood recollections are so vivid to me as one who was hard headed, rebellious, disrespectful of authority even at a young age and how I got to be that way. I write these memoirs for my own self understanding and for my children rather than for any purpose of self aggrandizement. It is an endeavor of self understanding more than anything else. To be honest with myself it is terribly difficult. But I will try as I dwell deeper into my past.

The first acts of rebellion were (as I recalled them clearly) – while an infant. This may seem strange or perhaps unbelievable but it is as clear to me as day even after some seventy five years. I loved milk so much that my mother would fill up the old quart beer bottle rather than giving me a simple baby bottle. It was from Buffalo's finest Beck beer! She would fill it up, put a nipple on it and I'd be as happy as a puppy with two peters. One time I had emptied the bottle and I couldn't get the attention of my mother for a refill. So I took the bottle and threw it through the front window of the house which my mother and father rented. That got her attention but I was too young for an old fashioned beating. That would come later as one given to the primogenitor. I don't remember anything after that like the reaction of my parents that I would do such a thing.

The second episode happened when I was no older than three years. I simply had to have my way or there would be hell to pay. One Sunday afternoon I wanted my parents to stay with me for reasons I don't recollect. I cried and cried but they had to visit relatives and left me in the care of my older sister. To grab their attention as they left, I climbed up on the front porch (all homes in Buffalo had porches in those days) and threw myself down the concrete sidewalk head first. I bashed my head and it bled so hard that I had to be taken to the emergency room for stitches. My parents returned immediately to take care of me (they had walked only a few blocks when they heard the commotion). I still have the scar on the top of my forehead after that visit to Mercy Hospital. I had no other way to convince my parents not to leave me, so I did something that would force them to stay home with me. And you know what? I was happy to do it if it meant an afternoon with my parents. From that day I feared to be alone and that I would do anything not to be left alone. It was a wonder that I didn't received brain damage.

When I was four, we moved out to a suburb of Buffalo to West Seneca where my father bought a home and a plot of land next to the house to grow vegetables. My mother would preserve most of them for the winter. That would save a lot of money which, of course, we did not have. My mother and sister had to help in that garden along with feeding and cleaning the chickens, turkeys and a goat which we also raised for food during those long days of the Buffalo winter. We had fresh goat milk each morning.

The life of mischievousness continued in the gang I hung around with. We would go along the streets, pick up cigarette butts and roll them into "cigs". We would have contests on who would get most of the produce. In one game we all would like up at the drop of a stick and the boys would all start to masturbate. The one who came first got the lion's share and second place to the guy who could shoot his sperm the furthest. It was all measured. Pretty gross but believe it or not, I did not participate as I felt shame. I was assigned as the one who dropped the stick to start the contact and judge the winner by measuring rod. For that I'd get three to four "cigs". Cigar butts were the best. The winner would always be an older boy (I won't mention his name) who had a very large donnager. Usually he would come in both first and second place! He would then sell us a few for exorbitant prices. We were jealous of him because of his oversized instrument – envious really. According to the girls in the area, size does matter! We were called the "jerkoffers" of which we were proud. That was second to beating up the Irish and the Pollacks down the street.

Much more serious was our raids on the railroad cars at a junction near my home where freight cars would remain until they would be ready for further transport. It was during WWII so we didn't know what we would find. In addition, we needed a solid cover for the underground fortress we had built. Its entrance was some fifty yards away so we stole a number of iron barriers from the local wire factory on Indian Church Road. We placed them in the tunnel so that the earth would not crumble and perhaps bury us alive. So one night we broke into a freight car after we had broken the federal seal. It was loaded with guns and boxes of hand grenades. We took one crate of grenades and the door of the freight car for the roof of our underground hide-away which we covered with underbrush. For weeks on end, agents of the FBI searched for those grenades. No one ever ratted on us because of the deep distrust of government by the Italians at the time. It was enough that the government took their sons to die in a struggle they did not understand. So every once in a while we would go to the local swamp, hide behind railroad tiles, pull the pin and throw a grenade into the swamp. We'd catch a lot of fish which we cleaned and ate. The FBI never found the grenades which we left there after we all went to college or to work into the local factories. I still am concerned that the local build up of homes in that area would blow them up. Nothing about that in the newspapers.

Each summer my mother, sister and brother would become migrant farmers for our months. We got permission for an extended month from the school district to harvest the crops in late September. It was either that to pay the mortgage or we would be on the streets. I was much too young to really pick the strawberries, blackberries, green and wax beans, tomatoes and grapes so I played as best I knew how in the rows. One day I came up on an orchard full of apples and I picked up a stash for future eating. The farmer, who was one mean bitch, saw me, came up to me and gave me a blow so hard that she cut my face. When I arrived to where my mother was picking, she asked what had happened. When I told her, she said nothing until that farmer-boss came around to check whether the beans or berries were being picked clean. My mother confronted her and told her in no uncertain terms to leave her child alone. The farmer was so furious (she was the boss) that she went to hit my mother with a walking stick she used to walk and to examine the crops. My mother landed an uppercut to her jaw and down she went like a ton of bricks. She did the same thing to her older son who had come to help his mother. We gathered our things, walked back to the shack and took a Greyhound bus back to Buffalo. The next year we worked for a more decent farmer called George Leone in Brant, New York. I don't even remember the name of the other farmer bitch. I think it was Thomas. If she is dead, may she rest in peace. My mother was one tough dude.

When I was no more than seven or eight, one of my closest friends was a boy called Billy Buffo. His mother had left him and his father because of the brutality of her husband.

He would beat Billy mercilessly for any reason, mostly in a drunken stupor. Many times I would ask my mother to have Billy spend the night with us to avoid those brutal beatings. Later in life, I heard that Billy had gone on a rampage of crime and was executed at Sing Sing prison for the murder of three state troopers in a shootout. In those days in the neighborhood you became either a priest or a criminal. I chose one and Billy chose the other. Billy was executed after a long life of misery, poverty and pain. I pray for him every day. He was the original "Dead Man Walking" at Sing Sing.

Our parish in West Seneca was St. William Parish and altar boys started very early in life. The pastor, Francis A. Growney, was a bear of a man, strong, educated and a great public speaker. All I learned about public speaking I learned from him. Among so many memories as an altar boy, the one that stands out was the one on Holy Saturday morning when the Easter ceremonies were conducted in the morning and in the sacristy. It was only after Vatican II that the Easter Vigil was radically changed. In any case, "Pops" Growney (as we called the pastor), hated to get up early to say the 8:00 AM Mass but prudence had it that you simply stayed out of his way. Or else! The blessing of the new holy water was made at that liturgical time and the celebrant was to breathe gently on the water as symbolic of the Spirit over the waters in Genesis at the beginning of creation. Pops Growney gave such a guttural sound that I thought he had farted and I burst into uncontrollable laughter. He looked at me red faced and eyes bulging. "Peter" he exclaimed, and then he took me to hang me up on a coat hanger for the rest of the ceremony (I was not yet five years old). From there I witnessed the rest of the ritual until another altar boy at the end of the ceremony had to remind Pops that I was still hung up on the coat hanger. I was unceremoniously taken down and told never to laugh in church again. But how can you keep from laughing when you think the pastor farted big time right in church? I swear that it sounded like a big fart.

Christmas time was always a joyous time in our home. We had enough money to buy a tree and we would decorate it with ornaments that we had made. Each Christmas, my mother would bake Christmas cookies and it was my brother and I who would take these cookies to the neighbors and wish them a Merry Christmas. We had little else to give anyone. Our gifts at Christmas were mostly clothes and shoes that we needed any way. We were given one toy each. But we had one distasteful chore to bring those cookies next door to the Hegner's. Mrs. Hegner was a saint but Mr. Hegner was an SOB of the very first order. He would even keep the ball if we accidentally kicked it into his yard. Mrs. Hegner would give it back later. So my brother and I brought the cookies to wish them a Merry Christmas. Mr. Hegner took the cookies and for the first time in my life, I heard an adult say a real nasty word – "Merry kiss my ass" closing the door in our faces without even inviting us in. I had never heard such language before and any such language in our house was always given in Italian!

Another truly painful memory I had as a child and beyond the beatings I received from my parents. My brother and sister were never beaten mainly because they were good and followed the narrow path. I was rebellious which by now you must know. But more than that, I had to be beaten hard to prepare to suffer for the family. The family is everything and the first born (me) was to be toughened up to protect the family. Without family, we are lost and have no future. Without family, there is nothing to celebrate in life and there is only death to look forward to. I suppose such beatings today would be cruelty and they would be charged with child abuse from the authorities. But there was certain logic to this tradition but that logic was lost on me at the time. I only remember sometimes being tied up in the cellar there to remain alone without food for the night. But I never gave in when my parents would command me not to so such and such. If my mind was made up, no amount of beating would change my mind. My rebelliousness resided there in a very strong will.

There were other memories. Particularly of my first love, Doris Schellhamer. Doris was a nice girl and she allowed me to feel her breasts (bumps really at that time). I so wanted to put it into her (I had experienced erections with my gang friends) but she never allowed me to do so. So we would go to the Saturday matinees and see the adventures of Tom Sawyer or Tom Mix or Superman in a double feature movie. We would just feel each other up and go no further than "first base" as we called it then. No home run! I was a virgin until age thirty. I often wonder whatever happened to Doris who was really a sweet child.

These are a few of my memories of the first days of my life. There were others but these were the salient ones which I can clearly recall. Anyone who wants to understand who I am could do worse than read these episodes in my life. They would understand my rebelliousness, my hard headedness, my refusal to bend to authority and the core of my personality shaped by these events in my life. Each person in life has his or her memories and the account of the events that shaped his or her personalities. These events narrated here will give you an insight that has made me for better or for worse. Mostly for worse. My own conclusion is that they were for the worse but then only God is our judge. As I see and feel the end of my life coming rapidly to greet me, as the exit sign is flashing, I wanted to leave these small memories particularly for my children so that they can understand their father better. And that in understanding, they will be forgiving. This along with my priestly and military experience which I leave for another day.

CHAPTER 2

MARGARITA CANNITO RIGA

My mother was born on April 15, 1900 in a small mountainous village in Southern Italy called Cortale in the province of Catanzaro. She was born of poor parents, along with three other sisters, none of whom ever traveled more than ten miles from their place of birth. The family went ballistic when one sister married and moved to another town ten miles away called Maida. Families had to be close. The towns were connected by a hairpin, meandering road (unpaved) between mountains over which a rickety bus would go twice a day with passengers. I closed my eyes every time I took it. When I was there in 1956, the road was still unpaved. The locals had electricity but no indoor plumbing.

She was dedicated to farming and the gathering of firewood with a little cash crop of olives. Most of the townspeople were not sharecroppers. Most families had a small plot of land after the land reform act of Garibaldi and the Italian revolution of 1870-90. The Cannitos had such a plot about seven miles from the town on a piece of land between the hills with a stream that flowed between them ("Lo Malizoto") to which they came early in the morning by donkey and worked there all day long. There were fig and olive trees which yielded a cash crop during the productive years (olive trees give their fruit every other year.) Everything was cooked in pure olive oil which made everything taste delicious.

Life was tough for six days a week – it would take an hour and a half just to get to the fields – which required a work day of about fourteen hours, counting travel. But the people seemed to be happy if somewhat limited.

My mother never had a formal education and after a year in a local school where she learned to recognize letters and write her name, that was the end. Children were economic benefits for work in the fields. Even today, there is a higher birth rate in the Italian southern provinces than in the north because of need. But it is down quite a bit because of modernization in the mezzo giorno. The average family used to be seven or eight children; today it is less than three in the south and less than two in the north- the lowest birthrate in the world.

In the early part of this century (and, of course, for centuries before) all marriages in the town were arranged by the parents and strictly chaperoned. Pre-marital sex was unheard of. All that has radically changed with modernization (Italy today along with the U.S. has abortion on demand.) The prospects for marriage were greatly increased then if a man had a job, a home, the ability to earn. The bride's father gave a dowry for the future bride. The dowry was gifted by the bride's father to the future husband who had to keep them in trust. In case something happened to him, she would have something to live on. It was a form of widow's pension. Spending that trust was not a dishonor but could get the husband a very long jail sentence. It was not his to do with as he wished. And in Italian jails, you served your whole sentence. If you acted up, they just added more time until you died in prison. It was up to you. Marvelously effective.

In the evening the women (as well as the men) paraded up and down the plaza (piazza) separately so they could eye each other, picking out a prospective bride for the men and an acceptable man for the women. Women dressed in rich colored costumes proper to each region. You could tell where a person came from by the clothing he-she wore. Each town was distinct. Cortale was no different.

My father must have seen my mother in one of these promenades and approached my grandparents for her hand in marriage. While the marriage was arranged, the woman could negate the choice if she found him unacceptable. Marriages were arranged but the women were not slaves. Margarita must have accepted the arrangement and in 1922 they were married both at city hall (secular) and in the local parish – Santa Maria degli Angeli (religious).

My father was a good catch because he and his brother Joseph had three plots of land which they had either farmed themselves or they were "let out" to tenants who paid by sharing 1/3 of the produce with the land owner. These were tenant farmers. From 1910 my father had traveled to America working on railroads, in mines and steel mills. He would save his money and buy land in Italy which his brother and other relatives would till. Land was infinitely more important than money because land represented stability and security for the future. If you had land, you were secure for the future and in your old age. It was savings, social security and pension all rolled up in one.

My mother would till that soil along with my father's other relatives while my father would go back and forth to America. Each time he did, he would leave my mother pregnant. The first two children were Victoria and Elizabetha. Both died early in life –

three and seven years old – of childhood disease (yellow fever). The third child, Victoria, left to go to American with my mother in 1932 and today lives in Napa, California.

Margarita came to the United States to live with my father in a rented apartment at 429 Swan Street in Buffalo where I was born almost nine months later in 1933. The neighborhood was ethnic Italian and black. The two groups lived without incident for all that I can remember. Black families in those days were integral just like ours. So many things now come to mind: the Italian shops with large provolone cheeses in the windows, pepperoni sticks, Supresati, Capicole – all Italian favorites. It was almost like a scene from the streets of Naples. We would shop every Saturday morning.

I remember my mother as a hard working woman, loyal to family and husband but not very warm. This was strange for an Italian because they are usually demonstrative in their emotions. I never remember my mother or my father ever spontaneously kissing me or giving me a hug. Just the opposite – most of the hugs and kisses were formal and felt meaningless. It was a mystery for me. I could not understand why they didn't love me.

Very early in life, my mother had to find work long before it was chic for women to do so. She just had to because my father was in the hospital so often with TV (three bouts) and had to go to the sanatorium in Perrysberg, New York. We were migrant workers on the farms of Western New York from June through September (strawberries, blackberries, beans, tomatoes, and grapes) and we lived in shacks provided by the farmer. From the time I was two I can remember being in the fields with my mother. We worked so we could pay the mortgage because otherwise that would have meant the streets – a thought absolutely unthinkable to my parents. So mother and children worked all summer with my mother in the lead. She never complained but would beat the hell out of me and my brother when we didn't pick. I didn't realize it then, but in retrospect it was a matter of life and death for the family and that is why she was so tough on us. Being kids, we understood nothing of this.

But there were limits. When the first farmer who happened to be a woman, beat me up for taking a few green apples that were on the ground (I was no more than three – my brother had not been born yet.) When the farmer came around checking the fields for "clean" picking, my mother simply asked what she had done and upon receiving the farmer's arrogant reply, knocked her out with a blow to the jaw. The same for her son who came to her aid. I still remember seeing both of them laid out in the bean field as if they were both taking a nap. We walked back to the "shacks' packed and never looked back. So there were limits as to how much my mother would do for money. She took no guff from anyone much less her children. She stood five feet tall and weighed in at 220 pounds of solid muscle. You just didn't mess with my mother!

When we were not working on the farm during the summer, she was up at four in the morning to take two busses to work in the cold cellars to Niagara Food Terminal on Clinton Street on Buffalo's east side – cleaning celery. She would work from five in the morning till one or two in the afternoon when all the produce for restaurants and markets had been cleaned and delivered. She was on her feet in a damp cellar for over eight hours every day without a break. She then had to come home and cook.

One winter she got a better paying job ironing clothes at a large laundry on Seneca Street in the old Larkin Building. It was hot work but the pay was better. She worked so hard and so well that the management made her floor lady, a position which a rather large lady of German ethnicity had wanted but was beaten out by a harder working Dago. When it didn't go to her, a few days later she waited for my mother at the bus stop and confronted her there. Well, you can imagine what happened. Bam, bam, two on the jaw and she was counting sheep on a new snow bank. Of course, the woman missed her bus as she lay sleeping on the quiet quilt of Buffalo's soft snow. The next day, the woman accused my mother of starting the brawl and my mother, who knew very little English, ended up by being fired because she could not express herself well. She told me that night that it was worth it! She went back to cleaning celery because she was good at that too. Maybe it was the hardness of her life which explains why she had become so tough. Of course, being the eldest son, I was the object of her blows because as first born, I had to be toughened up to protect and defend the family. That was just the culture. But what puzzled me more than anything else was her fear of my getting involved with "American" girls. I realized later that the cultural differences between Cortale and America were so striking even in 1945 that she was scandalized. I think she thought American girls and women were whores because they were free and not chaperoned. I was bashful enough as it was with the opposite sex, but she positively could have driven me to a monastery. Even if I took a girl for a soda - there were soda fountains in those days - I'd always get my face slapped if she found out. What would she have done to me if she found out that when we went to Sunday Matinees at the local theaters, we would feel the little breasts of our girl companions? (That's as far as any of us went.) My mother would have killed me. But the only thing we ever did was "feel them up" and that was as far as we ever got. Only a few football players would "go all the way" and we considered them brutes and their women whores. Such thinking today would be considered seriously deficient in need of "counseling" and very politically incorrect. Today, I would have been given condoms!

On Saturdays my mother would do the cleaning (we all would have to help) and she baked bread for the whole week. The first three days were fine but the bread became like steel along about Thursday and maybe that accounts for the fact that I still have my own teeth. Every one of them. I used to hate it when she'd make those great big meat ball sandwiches and not use American "Wonder Bread" like the rest of the kids at lunch. But it was strange how willing everyone was to trade me two Wonder Bread peanut butter and jelly sandwiches for just half that meat ball sandwich! We should have set up a restaurant.

I loved the aroma that filled the house of freshly baked bread and pizza. Saturday and Sundays were great eats days. Not that we ever lacked for anything to eat. We were as poor as church mice but we had plenty of homemade food. Each year we grew our own garden and my mother would can everything from corn to tomatoes to fruit and homemade jelly. Canning was important because it was written into the budget. Without it, the winter would be hard and meager.

My mother was not religious in the institutional sense. She made sure we went to Mass and religious instruction and there were plenty of statues of the Sacred Heart and of the Madonna around the house. She would say the rosary but we never said prayers together, not even before or after meals, and we never went to Sunday Mass as a family except at Christmas. She thought that the clergy were hypocrites who only wanted your money. Both my mother and father were really anti-clerical in the Garibaldi sense, but not too publically. How did I ever get to be a priest? It was not from any religious example set by my parents. Later in life they became more religious but I think it was because they were getting older.

My parents were profoundly honest and honorable people. They never took a thing that was not theirs and they paid all their just debts to the last penny. When they died, they had nothing to leave us except what they gave us in life - discipline, a strong family sense, the example of hard work and an education. What better could a mother and father leave their children? I am profoundly grateful.

One of the striking characteristics of my mother was her profound wish to become an American citizen. While my mother was not stupid - she was in fact very bright - she had great difficulty speaking the English language but God knows she tried. She always spoke Italian corner grocery store style.

In those days to become an American citizen, you had to have a command of English and know about the workings of the government. We children went over the material with her time and again until she had it almost memorized. But each time she went down to the county courthouse, the judge would fail her and tell her to go home and study some more. Finally, after she had failed the third time she said with great exasperation to the judge: "I no come no more until you die." I thought the bailiff would whiz in his pants he was laughing so hard. But you know what? Two days later the judge died! The successor judge thinking that my mother had put the evil eye (mal ocuo) on his predecessor (that was the rumor) called our home, brought her down that evening, had her take the oath of allegiance - still in broken English. He was taking no chances!

When her citizenship papers came by certified mail, my mother was genuinely happy. The whole brood of Italian relatives came to celebrate. It was a great event and we danced and drank wine almost all that Friday night. The children slept where they dropped and the adults celebrated until the wee hours. My mother bought a frame for the naturalization paper and it was hung with pride right next to the picture of the Sacred Heart. She was as proud as can be of that paper because it represented for her an opportunity for her and for her family. Such opportunity was not open to her in Italy. Only in America. She would be considered quaint today.

My mother died after a long bout with pancreatic cancer in July, 1975. She had previously buried my father in August, 1968. That too, had been heart breaking for her. My father was admitted to the hospital in Ross, California in March, 1968 with terminal lung cancer. My sister with my mother and I would take turns every other day, to visit him. We did it faithfully. But one day we thought we would take off and go swim at the Boys Hot Springs in Sonoma. When we arrived home that evening, word came from the hospital that my father had hemorrhaged and died. Alone. We were devastated with grief and guilt.

I shall never forget when she first saw him laid out in his coffin. There arose from her very being the deepest groan of pain I have ever heard in my whole life. It shook her whole body. Her pain was too deep for tears, only the vibrations of her body as she held on to my father's coffin. It was really the first time in my whole life that I saw such a mark of affection, at least from her. I think she loved him very much but I doubt that he loved her as much. They had exchanged few marks of affection precisely for that reason and it must have been very painful for her to live knowing that. Those days were not days of divorce. Once you got married that is all she wrote. You were with your spouse until the day you died and that was literally fulfilled in the case of my parents.

I never really talked with my father and never got to know him well. Therefore I never understood him very much. But my mother and I fought like cats and dogs precisely because we were so much alike. She hated that I had become a priest because she knew that the institution would finally betray and hurt me. She knew I was too independent. She was right and I hated to admit she was right so often. No matter how hard we fought and argued, she was loyal to me as only blood can be. In her own intimate way she was a friend to me, perhaps the only real friend I had in my whole life. As a friend, she was always there for me no matter what I had done or not done. I miss her, terribly. To this day many years later.

She died after a lingering painful illness. It was my sister Victoria and my brother in law Frank who were the real friends and heroes for my mother. But I have nothing to feel guilty about because I was always there for her. Even during her last illness. I still remember her poignant last words to me: "Do you think we will ever see each other again?" I was sure then as I am sure now that my faith tells me that she is with God now that I can no longer see her and that someday, we shall be with each other again.

Her doctor was a fine young man who did all that he could till the very end. I shall always remember him with gratitude and prayer. He put her on chemo and as I saw her throw up, I simply asked her if a few more days of life were worth that suffering. She said no and I had the nurses take away the bottles and tubes and we both waited for death and prayed for strength. During the last hours, she looked at me and wanted me to hold her because she was afraid. So I held her for some hours - I can't quite remember how long. It was now the son who held the mother as she prepared to be born into another world. I held her until I felt her body go limp. I was filled with sorrow beyond all words and there was no consolation for me. There was only one scintilla of joy in her death - I had helped her to be born again into a new birth whose reality we know nothing except that God is love and light. Just as the child she brought into the world knew nothing of what he was being brought into, so was I honored to be there at the end for her as she had been there at the beginning for me.

We buried her on top of my father in the same grave in the cemetery in Napa under a giant oak overlooking the beautiful California Napa Valley. It was pure beauty. Like the beauty into which she was now born that ear has not heard and eye has not seen. No more fitting eulogy can be given of my mother than that which

Augustine of Hippo gave of his own mother: Remember Margarita, your *servant, at your altar and with John, her husband, who died before her, by whose bodies you brought* me *into this life, though how it was I do not know. With pious hearts let all* remember *those who were not only* my *parents in this light that fails, but were also* my *brother and sister and subject to* you, *our Father, in our Catholic mother the Church, and will be my fellow citizens in the eternal Jerusalem for which your people sigh throughout this pilgrimage, from the time when they set out until the time when they return to you.*

CHAPTER 3

HARVEST TIME: A PERSONAL TALE OF ECONOMIC SURVIVAL

A few days ago, I was intrigued in viewing a film about child labor in the fields of America called *Harvest (La Cosacha).* It followed the work of a twelve year old Zulema Lopez as she picked crops in Texas and then in Michigan according to seasons. She signed in as an adult to avoid child labor laws which would punish the farmer if apprehended. Enforcement of these laws is sporadic and the legal penalties light. All this took me back to my own childhood and the summers we spent as a family on the various farms of North Collins and Brant in western New York picking crops. We were really migrant farmers for a summer season. That was the first reminder.

The second reminder to my wonderment today is economic envy which has reared its ugly head during the presidential campaign of 2011-2012. It pits rich versus poor, the ten percent of the well to do versus the ninety percent of other Americans who earn less than the former. I personally have always thought that America was land of opportunity and that is all that is guaranteed. Nothing more. The distribution of equitable income by the government is not an American idea but a socialistic one. Some adjustments can be made in the tax code and removal of tax breaks and other economic incentives but opportunity is the real objective of American opportunity. Some would call socialistic distribution by government a form of theft to take from those who by their ability earned more than the rest. Of course, there is the graduated income tax to support the necessary functions of government. There is more today as the government takes over more of the functions that should belong to the freedom of the individual, the less freedom there is for the individual. The safety net for the poor, the sick, the aged has increased to the point where government is taking care of us from cradle to the grave. Europe is the perfect example of the socialistic state: longer vacations, generous unemployment benefits, early retirement and large pension plans, complete health care for all, less work time - all of which has led to the present disaster of large debt and economic collapse of the whole European system. America is approaching that precipice with over a fifteen trillion dollar debt and is borrowing forty one cents for every dollar spent. Clearly this is the road to economic disaster since debt must be repaid along with the interest on that debt. That is growing impossible by the day. We have spent all our money, our children's money, our grandchildren's money to benefit only ourselves.

As I said, I have difficulty understanding the constantly increasing demand on government for benefits of all kinds: elderly drug plans, Medicare, Medicaid, student loans, food stamps, universal health care, more Social Security benefits, housing, heating and other forms of benefits, income for no work (income tax credit), unemployment insurance in greater and greater amounts - all this is unsustainable under the *principle of subsidiary* (government does for the individual what the individual cannot do for himself). Government now does more and more. This principle has been jettisoned for a whole socialistic mentality of less work and more benefits. So I thought I would tell the personal story of my own upbringing and that of my parents. I do not mean to sound arrogant but it is a story of self reliance and freedom for which I am very proud and which is no longer *au currant*

From the time I was an infant, I never had a summer vacation. Even as an infant I was simply placed in the rows of fruits and vegetables as my older sister and my mother picked all day long. But I am ahead of myself. Every June 15th (the days for summer vacation in New York) the farmer from Brant called George Leon would come with a large truck to pick up our bedding, beds, tables, furniture, etc. that we would use during the summer. The farmer housed us in small "shacks" (as we called them then) with the toilets in the back ("back houses"). There was no indoor plumbing then. We never missed it. These housings were really two rooms: one for my mother and sister's bed and a very large front room which held the bed for my brother and me plus the kitchen table and stove where we ate. Bare bones with nothing fancy. Water was garnered from two fountain-wells in the middle of the shacks. We worked seven days a week during the harvest of various fruits and vegetables as they became ripe: strawberries for three weeks in June; then blackberries and raspberries for four weeks in July followed by the picking of green and wax beans for four weeks during August; from September 1st there were two weeks of tomatoes and concord grapes. School would begin for us about the middle of September so we had to return to Buffalo to attend classes at Winchester Elementary Public School in the town of West Seneca, a suburb of Buffalo. Altogether it was a period of many weeks of hard work harvesting the crops with only a few days rest between the times of the turning of one crop to the other.

We began to pick in the fields at seven in the morning after the farmer woke us up at six. We were then transported to the fields in trucks to pick the crops. There was a half hour for lunch and we continued to work until the whistle blew at Thomas Indian School at six in the evening - about ten and a half hours in the hot sun each day, seven days a week for twelve weeks. The land was mostly rented from the Indians on their reservation. The farmer would take us each Sunday morning to early Mass in Brant at Our Lady of Mount Carmel at six thirty. We had a half hour reprieve for a little breakfast and change of clothes when we went back to the fields at seven thirty. Sundays were also work days. That was the only respite during the week. Even for the few days between the next ripe vegetable or fruit picked, we had to hoe weeds in the growing fields of strawberries and other growing plants. The children, when we were near a flowing creek, would take an hour or two to go swimming but generally we had to be in the fields picking with my mother and sister. If not, we would get a good licking then or when we arrived back at the "shacks".

Commercial trucks would come in the evening to sell fresh vegetables and fruits along with the daily delight of ice cream (if we had worked diligently).

We were not indentured servants. The reason we went to the farm summer after summer was for economic survival. My father often bad long stays at Perrysburg, New York at the tubercular hospital so my mother had to work during the fall and winter at the Niagara Food Terminal in Buffalo cleaning celery and other vegetables at a very early hour. My sister prepared us for school. But the summers were a family affair when we picked to pay the mortgage on the house. By a special arrangement with the Marine Trust Company of Buffalo, my parents could pay the whole year mortgage in September after we were paid in one lump sum for the summer's work. So you see why we picked so hard and long so we would not be put out on the streets through foreclosure. Just a handshake in those days was enough because the banker knew that my parents were hard working and perfectly honest. They never missed a payment.

Looking back, I can understand why my parents were so hard on us to pick for those long hours without a real vacation because otherwise we would be out on the streets. My parents were proud and accepted no welfare or other government freebies that might have been available. They were proud and every dollar they made was from the sweat of their brows, whether from Republic Steel on Abbot Road in Buffalo or the Niagara Food Terminal on Bailey Avenue in Buffalo or George Leon's farm on Milstrip Road in North Collins. They refused to take money from welfare or from any other source they had not worked for. I am convinced that my own work ethic through the years was due to their example. They never asked for a dime that they had not earned. We were poor but terribly proud. I realize that very much today when I see so much free loading, welfare and grants that need not be repaid because they are "poor." Poor is a relative term. We never considered ourselves "poor". In reality, we were, poor as church mice but we worked and we survived. Above all, my parents insisted on education so that all three of their children became contributing citizens with PhD's. Looking back makes me proud of them. While they did the dishes after supper, we had to do homework and study the lessons for the next day. They were there for us and insisted that we study. How true is that today? They both had less than a grammar school education in Italy.

Those days on the farm were long and hard but we survived through the dint of hard work and perseverance. We made lifelong friends in those days with those who were in the same situation as we were. They too had to work for survival so we helped and encouraged each other by sharing what little we had. Welfare among us was unheard of as we helped each other as best we could. We became a small community each summer and we even looked forward to being there with them.

Once I even earned twenty five dollars for being New York State Champion Bean Picker (verified by the farmer). One day, the wax beans were so loaded that I bet the farmer twenty five dollars that I could pick over five hundred pounds of those wax beans in one day. He was on. I picked nonstop for eleven hours (I took no lunch) and came up with 612 pounds of wax beans. That record is still in the record books of New York State. Where, however, I do not know! The challenge was glorious.

Any notion that we were poor or deprived never occurred to us. My parents came from Italy not to take economic advantage of government subsidies but to work hard and put their children through school for a better life than they had. They expected only opportunity. We envied no one but we were simply given an opportunity to work, earn our keep and progress as best we could. As I have said, all three of their children are PhD's and a credit to the country. They knew that education was the way out of poverty.

Some of the days were not so pleasant as when I first had a lesson in sex and birth of babies. It was raining one afternoon and we (a group of boys) were taking shelter in a barn and speaking about the movie *Stand By For Action* with Robert Taylor we had seen the night before. It was about a destroyer in the South Pacific shown to us by health officials who came around every once in a while giving lectures on how to stay healthy. The movie was a come-on for the lectures. During the movie the destroyer picked up a life boat filled with women and children whose ship had been sunk by the Japanese. One of the women gave birth on board the destroyer. I remarked to the group on how the captain had the stork come to deliver the baby on the boat. The group laughed at me and the older ones of the group began to explain to me in gross and brutal terms the reality of sex, birth and sexual relationship. It was a total shock as my parents never spoke to me about sex or how babies came to be. I actually believed that it was a stork that brought them. To this day, I feel the shame and embarrassment of that rainy day in a barn outside of Brant, New York. I was no more than six years of age. The trauma was shocking. But I and my brother still survived because my parents gave us the key to life: hard work, ask nothing from anyone, take pride in one's work toward an ideal that we could obtain because this was America, the land of opportunity not the land of give-aways and socialism. Things have changed.

Those days prepared me for the difficult days ahead in study and perseverance to obtain my doctorates (theology, philosophy and law). I do not mean to boast but were it not for those difficult days on George Leon's farm; I don't think I would have made it as I did. That was the only freedom of opportunity I had but it was a glorious freedom. What seemed hard and difficult at the time was a perfect preparation for the difficult days ahead in other fields of endeavor. That movie, *Harvest,* reminded me of those summer days of heat, hard work and survival. I can now truly understand the plight of migrant farmers who also must struggle for survival. Even of the story of a twelve year old girl in the fields. I had experienced all her ideals, pain and hard work. I didn't know it at the time but that preparation was perfect for my future.

I know that things are more complex today than this simple story but it is an example of what this country was all about for me and my family. We didn't envy the rich because it was the rich that gave us the opportunity to work to survive, to dream. When is the last time a poor person offered you a job? That was the freedom that made us free. I wonder with all the welfare hand outs of today, are Americans preparing for freedom or for demanding more benefits that will take us into bankruptcy? The culture is radically different today but a culture that will fail us in the end. We can only hope for opportunity not for hand outs. Anything less will make us real slaves dependent on government.

CHAPTER 4

FATHERHOOD AND FATHERS - ONE MAN'S STORY

My father, John Riga, was born on April 17, 1897 in a small town in the mountains of southern Italy called Cortale in the province of Calabria. He was born to farmers as were his forefathers before him. He had one older brother Joseph whom I never met and who helped till the soil while my father sent the money he earned from America to buy the land. It was a kind of cooperative. But I anticipate.

When he was about twenty five he migrated to America like many of his countrymen and lived in ethnic communities near Pittsburgh and Scranton, Pennsylvania until he finally settled in Buffalo, New York. He was a strong man, tall for an Italian at 5'11 but not very large. He worked hard first as a section hand on the Erie Railroad laying track and ties. It must have been hard and grueling work, warm in summer and cold in winter. The work was always outdoors. More money was to be made in coal mines so he became a miner near Scranton. He was there for a number of years until he developed the beginning of black lung disease and sclerosis of the lungs which would finally kill him. The doctor recommended another occupation.

All the while he would send his money back home to Italy so that his brother could buy land and therefore secure his own future. Italians did not believe in banks or pensions. Their security in old age was their children and the land which they could feel, touch and cultivate. The abstractions of economics simply eluded them. My father never trusted the welfare state and so he voted Republican all of his life - contrary to his countrymen in the United States. He never told anyone except his family because this was considered treasonous among Italians in America. People are incredulous when I tell them this. The Democratic Party was then the only friend they had in the new world. He finally moved to Buffalo where he found a job as a steel chipper (removal of impurities from the steel) at Republic Steel on Abbot Road along the shore of Lake Erie which brought in the iron ore from the Masabi Range in Michigan. It was the last job he ever had. My father was respected among his countrymen as a hard and industrious worker who saved his money. He married my mother in 1927 in Cortale and each time he came from America to visit Italy, he got her pregnant. His family consisted of three girls (two of them died from scarlet fever in Italy) and two boys born in America after he brought my mother over here in 1932. In1932, he concluded that life in the United States would be better for his family than growing up in Italy even on land that belonged to him. So he simply gave his brother Joseph title to all the land for a nominal sum and brought his wife and daughter Victoria to America. They first lived in an Italian ethnic district on Swan Street in central Buffalo and then bought a house with some land in the country, now a suburb, of West Seneca where he could till the plot of land, grow vegetables and raise small animals (chickens, turkeys, goats) so that we would always have a source of good food all during the year. My mother canned the vegetables for the winter.

I knew little of what my father did when he settled in the United States before my mother came, whether he had a girl friend or other emotional releases. I had no reason to believe that he was anything but faithful to my mother until later. I did notice that he was never affectionate, at least in my eyes, with my mother. Nor with me for that matter. He never gave me a spontaneous kiss. He followed the Italian culture of his day by beating the living hell out of me as the *primo genito* every time I got out of line which was often. That was because I was the first born son and it was the first born who had to be taught to protect the family since the family was everything. Without the family you have no past, no future. You are simply lost waiting only for death which will obliterate your memory forever. That truly would be a fate worse than death itself. So everything had to be done to promote and protect the family. Nothing else mattered. This explained the beatings to toughen me up for the future to protect his family.

In truth, this feeling for family made sense. What do you have in life without a family? What and who will pass everything of value which you received from previous generations if you only live for yourself? What do you live for? For the moment? If everything which you have received dies with you, why then are you alive? Why were you even born? To have a good time, using up the world's resources? Why should a community respect you and why are you even alive? Certain values are more important than life itself and that is why a society will even go to war to protect its culture by and in families. You live and die for something greater than yourself. Or you, live and die; for nothing.

My father passed that family sense to me and to tell the truth, I really did not succeed in living up to his expectations. Everything in my life seems to have destroyed that hope and dream of his. He really never understood why I ever became a priest and he rejected it until the day he died (in fact, he died before I left the priesthood). I think I crushed his dreams because he thought I'd grow up to be a famous person, a doctor, a lawyer- someone really important. Not a miserable priest who would never be anyone nor become anything. I think he actually hated the fact that I had become a priest. Even on his death bed he thought I was possessed by the devil for that reason. But there was something more in our relationship.

Even before all this, my father was a cold and distant man and I never understood why the only affection he would show was when I showed him a bit of affection here and there. A kiss goodbye, a hug hello but nothing really spontaneous, nothing warm, nothing sentimental. I came to the conclusion that he hated me. It was always a mystery to me when I noticed other fathers who were warm and affectionate with their sons. Maybe that is why even today I think so little of myself since my father did not think enough about me that he would love me. He must have seen something terrible in me that made me undeserving of his love. I didn't understand what but it must have been there because I never felt his love. It must have been me I kept on telling myself only once just before I went to Europe to study and I would be gone for at least seven years did he ever show the slightest form of emotion.

My father was not without humor or talent. He played a wicked mandolin which he taught himself as well as a good guitar. He would often take me to Zwinling's saloon in Winchester, New York where he would proceed to have a few boiler makers (shot and a beer as chaser). He'd sit me down at a table and bring me a few birch beers (a favorite soda in the northeast) and some pretzels. On the way home, he would chew "sin-sins" as mouth freshener to cover the alcoholic breath and made me swear that I'd never tell my mother where we'd been. He knew he could trust me never to tell because (1) I'd lose my source of birch beer and (2) I was used to being beaten and not uttering a word. And I never did.

Please know that I do not blame him. He was in every other respect faithful to my mother, hard working and always there for his family. He would have a few too many glasses of his home made wine (which I helped make. I always thought it tasted like vinegar) in the evening once in a while, but he was not a real drunk. He never struck my mother because I think if he did, my mother would have flattened him. He was not a womanizer even thought I don't think he loved my mother very much. She loved him intensely but it was not reciprocated. That is why I think that he fell in love with someone else but that his sense of loyalty and fidelity to my mother made him honor bound to be faithful to her after she arrived in the new world. But I thought it was a loveless marriage on my father's part and that is why he had little feeling and love for me. I was the fruit of a love making which was not love for him. How could he really love the fruit of such a union? That was the only reason I could give why whenever expressed his love for me, even at the end of his life when he was dying. It was then that I discovered his dark secret and why so many of my darkest fears were really true.

He was dying of cancer of the lungs as a consequence of his black lung and silicosis. He was in the hospital in Ross, California and I went to visit him every other day. The hospital was about twenty five miles from the college where I taught philosophy and theology. We had some conversations which I have never revealed to anyone until now.

He told me of the woman he had met and loved in America while my mother was still in Italy. She had conceived a son (how he knew it was a son I do not know) and they had "gotten rid of it" (abortion). I never learned her name. It was his son who was the first born and not me and that is why he thought I was an evil person because of what he had done. God was punishing him by my becoming a priest. I think he loved that woman very much and that it killed his soul when she killed his first son. I never told anyone about that conversation with my father but at age forty two I finally understood why he did not like or love me. In fact, he hated me because he saw me as evil, as God's punishment for what he had done. I remember how little I thought of myself from my earliest childhood. Now I finally knew that I was seen by my own father not only with little or no affection, but as the devil himself incarnate in me who came to torture him by reminding him of what he had loved and lost by his own hand. Becoming a priest was the final curse for him. Twisted but it made some sense because second son would be as sterile as the one he had killed. I never got over it.

Of course I was devastated for years afterward. But at least I now knew that it wasn't really my fault that I was despised and hated but the image of the evil which my father had done which he projected onto me for reasons I do not know. This was more than a rejection by one's own father in an oedipal projection; it was far more indeed. It was an utter casting out from his life for something I had absolutely nothing to do with. How hurt that man must have been by what he had done! I think about that often in the almost forty five years since his death. I have forgiven him many times in my heart but it is a pain which one human being can hardly bear. And it was very wrong to inflict it on me. It is a wound that will not heal. It wears upon me even now and I have kept it secret in the recesses of my heart. I never told my mother so much as a word, or either of my siblings. I don't think the wound will ever heal as long as I live. That and Vietnam tore my soul to pieces for years. Even now the thought is almost unbearable and that is why I hesitate to recite so monstrous an event in my life. Now that my mother is dead, the secret need not remain any longer.

But it is better to know than to wonder always whether you had done something so terrible to merit such an unloving fate. It is good to know that why I was unloved was not really me. But neither do I think that I have ever recuperated from this disaster. Since then I have never been able to trust anyone, always fearful that I would be betrayed. And why my love relationships have always been short and fixed because I always believed I was unworthy of anyone's love. I could only wait for the ultimate betrayal and abandonment. And it would always come. It was self-fulfilling prophecy. It is a terrible way to live: an inability to really love and commit because of the dreaded thought of being betrayed and left unloved. And so far in my life, this has been a self-fulfilling prophecy with people coming into my life and passing out because I was afraid to let them into my heart for fear of rejection and abandonment. I was unable to commit to others and I just used them and called it love. It has been devastating then as now. Perhaps that is why I have such self-loathing.

Again, I do not know whether the wound will ever heal. Probably not. My example stands as living proof that the relationship of children to their fathers is not only crucial but can be mortally devastating when absent. God knows how I have tried to forgive my father from my soul but I don't think I've ever fully succeeded. The abyss between my father and me remains and will remain till the day I die. It will have to be the unutterable mystery of God's infinite mercy and love which alone shall have been able to bridge that chasm between us. Maybe that too is a dream, a longing, a desire.

Each of us on Father's Day goes back to his or her origins, to the faintest and weakest memories of our youth. There appears from that hazy mist, one who for better or for worse, has determined the example and force of what has powerfully influenced us, once again, for better or for worse. In my case, it was my father, much for the worse. No matter.

For those of us whose memory is nostalgic, of a father who is or was the closest we have known of God, that is an inestimable grace of which we can only give thanks in awe and wonder. Our gratitude is always beyond words because that fatherhood is taken up into the great mystery of the fatherhood of God. We can only repay this grace by becoming part of that mystery of fatherhood to those who have been, but only temporarily, entrusted to us. And while we have time, to love them with all our hearts and strength.

I think of my earthly father: faithful to my mother, always there for us in good times and in bad, even though without emotion and warmth. He wasn't dynamic or educated. But he was quiet and gentle. I remember now not telling him I loved him when I could in spite of my darkest secret and even before I found out. The reason why in his mind, I was not loved. Now that he is gone, we are separated by the abyss of death with only tears of regret to bridge the unbridgeable. We continue to love those who did us good as well as remembering those who did us ill. Why do children do that? Because no matter how perverted the fatherhood, there is something of God's fatherhood in him.

While we have time before our own deaths, we must try and fill the void between our children and us. Our fatherhood must be filled with the word, with communication, with the example of loving fatherhood of the origin of all fatherhood so that when we ourselves enter the great silence of death, our children will remember us not as an absence or abyss in pain and loathing but as loving memory from whose fullness they can draw courage, strength and hope for their own children. And so we fathers are all caught up in the great chain of fatherhood, from mythic origins to glorious future. "And Adam was born of God" goes all human genealogy of the Bible. And we are born of Adam's lineage that comes from God. Each of us prolongs that original act of fatherhood. Any mistakes we make, we must try and cure by the quality of our own lives and for our children before our death. We must try. And try. And try.

May my father forgive me for not trying harder to bridge that abyss while he was yet alive. I live in that hope. I, in turn, forgive him with all my heart. May my children forgive me?

CHAPTER 5

BILLY BUFFO

One of my earliest friends in Buffalo was a young man named Billy Buffo. I think his last name indicated that he was ethnic Italian (the word means, foolish, funny) but I never asked. I only knew that we were good friends and that I could depend on him. In fact, he was funny. But I think he was funny to cover the tragedy in his life. I still smile when I think of his pranks. All of them were funny but none were without meaning in his life. While he was a comi-tragic figure, he was never a bully although he was good with his fists. We once fought to a draw. We both realized that we would just beat the hell out of each other which was foolish since we had common enemies. So we joined our forces and became twice as powerful. We became inseparable and almost unbeatable.

His mother left him when he was a child. Billy told me later that she was what we would now call an abused wife because his dad was almost always drunk when he came home in the evening when he would beat her constantly. His father would also beat him mercilessly even when he had done nothing. His father was a miserable and mean human being. At night he would sit in his chair, drink, sulk and then, for no apparent reason, beat up on poor Billy. If it had been today, his father would have been arrested and Billy put into foster care. I actually saw some of the beatings he received. What cruelty had befallen that man that he should treat a child that way? He would strike with closed fists all over his son's body, including his head. My father and mother were hard on me because I was primogenitor. They thought they could toughen me up to protect the family. False as it might be by today's standards, my parents at least had a reason why they beat me so often and so hard. It was to strengthen me so that I could endure whatever happened for the sake of the family. La familia was the only thing that mattered and just like in any war, if the oldest had to be sacrificed to save the family, then so be it. Why would Americans be shocked that Italians do this when they send their sons abroad to die of fevers and shot and shell, often for reasons no one can explain to them? Or worse, for money and oil as in Saudi Arabia during the Gulf War. To give your son for oil? At least my parents beat me to save my family - not oil!

I saw Mr. Buffo beat that young man until he bled. And for no reason except that he was an evil man. It would make me cry even though I thought I was inured to pain and violence. To this day I feel shame that I did not intervene even at the risk of being beaten myself. I should have tried something instead of being the coward I was. It would have been worth it because it would have shown how much I cared for Billy. As it was, it was abuse which would end up in his final tragedy at Sing Sing Prison. He was left alone to be alone and my cowardice accuses me to this day. Billy never cried when he was beaten. He was as stoic as the day is long. Maybe because it happened so often or maybe that was his way of salvaging some personal dignity in the face of a brutal force about which he could do nothing. He was kind of an Ernest Hemingway, facing fate stoically because it was the measure of a man's internal strength that he could face his ultimate, empty destiny without a whimper or a tear. That took real courage when you had nothing else in life. You faced pain and didn't blink. The only thing I could do for him was to be there, soak his back with ointment, bandage the cuts as best I could. I truly loved Billy and in spite of his evil deeds. I love him to this day. But I had no real way to show it because I was afraid, I was a coward. I'd try to convince my mother that he should stay with us for a while. When we asked the father, the old man didn't give a damn. It would mean less bother for him and then he could get roaring drunk without having to worry about Billy. Not that he ever did much worrying about Billy. Since Billy was a little overweight, the old man would call him a fat slob, a dumb shit, a f......... no good wop, among the more gentle names.

Through the years we developed a deep friendship. There were many a fight we fought together as we passed through Irish, Polish and Black neighborhoods. Often we would literally have to fight our way to school. And back. We won most of the time but not always. Win or lose, we won or lost together. That was the important thing. The Irish were the toughest because they would never give up. You could pound on them all day long. They would run away but they would never give up. They would never say 'give'? But like in combat, we were never so close as when we fought side by side. We were each other's buddy covering each other's asses in very foreign territory.

We both caught it bad when we skipped school on a late April afternoon. All the ice had melted on the Buffalo River and the fish were as hungry as could be after a long Buffalo winter. Like kids everywhere, we never noticed the time and just fished until way after dark. On that particular day, two boys our age had drowned a mile down the river but we knew nothing about it. Home we went, with our catch of bullheads, shiners and carp. I thought that we would be received as the fishing heroes we thought we were. Instead when I arrived home the house was crowded with relatives, consoling my parents on the loss of their oldest son in the Buffalo River. The condolences were a bit premature so that when I appeared, it was like Lazarus arising from the dead. Anxious to see me and to welcome me home, first my father and then my mother took turns beating the living hell out of me right there in front of all my relatives. And in front of Billy, whom they didn't see. (It was really to show how much they cared. Imagine if they had been really angry.)

My father was particularly incensed that I hung around with Billy Buffo whom he considered to be a bad influence - he didn't want me to have anything to do with him. So he took off the large razor strap he sharpened his razor on – as did all Italian men from the old country - and began to beat me mercilessly.

"Are you going to see that damn Buffo again?" "Yes" I said defiantly. Bam, bam, bam. And on and on went that empty dialogue with consequent beating until I literally passed out. I was damned if he would make me give up the only friend I had in the world and I would never give him up even if he killed me. If I was a coward once, it wouldn't happen a second time. I kind of knew, even then, that I had to hold on for Billy. I found out later that my uncles broke down the bathroom door to rescue me from sure injury. No matter. I felt pain only of the word because I was unconscious for most of the ordeal. I wanted to show Billy that if I was a coward in not coming to his aid when he was beaten so mercilessly by his father, I could suffer for him by never denying him, even if it meant my life. It was one of the few times that I was not a coward (which I very often am) and I stood for what I believed in. We were inseparable after that. In his own way, Billy knew that I was willing to lay down my life for him. He would have done the same thing for me, I am sure.

We never learned a thing in school. Nor did we even want to. The only thing we dreamt about was playing after school – hockey and skating in winter, cops and robbers in the Shumac Forest and swamp and jumping railroad cars in the junction for the thrill of it. I knew even then that Billy respected nothing and nobody. He was afraid of neither God nor man. It was during WWII and Billy and I would break into the sealed railroad cars and take whatever was there. Or at least what we could carry. The RR detectives must have had orders to shoot to kill anyone breaking into sealed military cars. Once one of them saw us about a hundred fifty yards away coming out of one of those sealed cars. He could plainly see that we were only kids, six or seven years old. No matter - he had his orders. Seven year old Japs? He didn't care and started firing his weapon. I could actually hear the bullets whizzing by. I was running as fast as I could, hoping to dodge the bullets. Not Billy. He would stop and curse the man even as he was being shot at. I had to literally drag him out of harm's way: "You fucking son of a bitch. You can't even shoot straight at a couple of fucking kids. You lost your dick, dick. " Those were his exact words, I swear. I still remember Billy's defiant words and his obliviousness to fear. I think he actually wanted to get killed to escape the terrible pain in his life. I couldn't and didn't let that happen. So I literally dragged him through the swamp to our underground hideaway.

We found rifles and arms but they were too big to lug. But we did find a box of hand grenades which we carted off to our secret underground hiding place which no one could find except us. It took us a month to dig it out of the earth enclosed under five feet of earth and accessible by iron oil drums we stole as well. The FBI and railroad detectives looked for those hand grenades for weeks with no success. No one would snitch even if they did know because the neighborhood took care of its own. Even the local representatives of the Mob couldn't find them. And did they look! They questioned everyone. There was even a reward offered for the capture of the ones involved. No one ever reported us. Every once in a while we'd bring a grenade out, break the pin and throw it into the swamp - just like in the movies. Kapow! We ducked very low but no one was ever hurt and we caught a lot of fish that way. As far as I know those grenades are still there. Someday I'm going to call the bomb squad and tell them where Billy and I hid the damn things. It's been over fifty years and they are probably still live near that swamp. You hear of bombs dropped during WWII still going off in Germany and Japan.

Billy would drive the teachers crazy. In turn, they would give him harsh penalties. Looking back, I think he wanted to get caught and punished for all the guilt his father laid on him, about how he was good for nothing, that he was stupid, that he would go nowhere. Looking back, he had what we now call, low self esteem. Low as a snake's belly. But he had his own forms of revenge. When we attended St. William's High School for one year, Sister Claudia, the principal, was particularly hard on Billy. She meant well but she too misunderstood his whole background. So one night Billy broke into the nun's kitchen, stole all their candy and food and left a "loaf" right on the kitchen table where they ate their breakfast. Disgusting! It was particularly loathsome to me because I had to clean it up. I was paying my tuition by cleaning up after school so the job fell to me. I knew that it was Billy who had done it but nobody could prove it. It wouldn't be the last time I would clean up after Billy.

One of the few times I was disappointed and crushed by Pops Growney, the pastor, was once during the Sunday morning children's Mass at 9:00AM. Billy was talking and Pops came up and slapped him across the face as hard as he could. You could hear that thud all through the church. I have never forgiven Pops Growney for that abuse, even to now. It was so totally wrong coming from a priest. Billy had enough beatings and humiliation at home. My only excuse for Pops was that he didn't know about Billy's home life. But he should have. I only remember my own shame and cowardice in not speaking out against the injustice right there in church. I should have defended Billy, yes; right there in church and to hell what happened to me. Because <u>I knew</u>. Though you could see the hurt in his eyes, Billy didn't utter a word. But I did, at least symbolically, by crying silently, knowing that even the priest thought so little of him that he would strike this child. To this day the poignancy of that blow reverberates through my being with almost too much pain as much as the day it was delivered. It seemed to me then that we had become one. We had each other's pain.

Billy never finished high school and left for places unknown to me. I had tried to find out where he went to no avail. His father had died from drowning in his own vomit while drinking. He was found a month later when the stench of his rotting body drew notice from the neighbors. Appropriately enough! Billy had left a little before that. I never found out where but God knows I tried. I really did. A terrible void entered my life. A bigger one would follow.

After many years and after I had been ordained a Catholic priest, a phone call came for me in the middle of the night in August, 1959. It was hot and muggy as are most Buffalo summer nights. The warden from Sing Sing Prison informed me that one of his condemned prisoners, a Billy Buffo, had requested me as his spiritual guide for the week before his execution in the electric chair. It seems that Billy had led a life of petty and not so petty crime ever since he left high school. He lived by his wits from crime to crime. The warden told me that the job of spiritual guide was emotionally draining; that I did not have to take it and that it was difficult to befriend a man whom you know is going to die in a week. He felt Billy was a lost cause because he never expressed a word of regret for what he had done. As I had never done anything like that before, I simply said I would. I was not about to abandon a long lost friend for whom I had taken such a beating from my father years before. Every blow had been sweet because they were for Billy. In fact, when Billy found out I was ordained, he remembered my loyalty to him and he wanted to see whether it was still there. It was. I never found out how he knew I had been ordained. I would have gone even if my superiors had not given me permission, so intense was my loyalty. I took that oath never to abandon Billy no matter what.

It seems that Billy's life of crime came to an end on the New York State Thruway near the Dunkirk exit. He had been spotted there and in a shoot out, had killed two New York State Troopers.

I could spend three hours a day with him and we talked about what he wanted to talk about. He asked whether I knew anything about electrocution and I said I did not because I had never been electrocuted before. That got a laugh out of him. We did talk about old times and what could have been. The thing that had convinced him to seek me out for his last days was that time when I was so loyal to him that I would rather be beaten than promise my father that I would not see him again. He had not forgotten my loyalty.

We would meet in the prisoner's death row room. The noise outside was overwhelming. There were no long appeals in those days. You were tried and convicted in a matter of weeks and the governor would sign the death warrant a month after that. There was one mandatory appeal to the New York Court of Appeals and that was it. No federal courts by writ of habeus corpus were involved in those days. Prisoners did not end up for years on death row. In a sense that was a mercy. It is cruel - and more expensive – to have prisoners on death row for as long as ten to thirteen years. Electrocution was also cheaper then. In those days, death was inflicted so often that it was not considered extraordinary as it is today. Death always leaves its bloody footprints all over the place but when it is common, it becomes the banality of evil.

We spoke about God, forgiveness, Christ, our own past and what heaven would be like. Of course, neither of us had the faintest clue about what that life in heaven is like but his spirits had to be kept high, not just hoping for a reprieve, but because it was the decent thing to do.

He never expressed sorrow for what he did and he never wanted the Sacraments. The only thing he wanted was my presence and my concern - both of which he had in abundance. And what do you say to a man who is about to be killed by the state? How do you prepare a man for the greatest event in his life - his own death? We all must die but it is the mercy of God that he keeps the exact day and minute from us. Billy asked for little in his short life and he got very little. I did not then nor now ever justified or condoned the terrible acts of murder he committed. I did urge him to acknowledge his evil deeds because only then could there be hope of forgiveness and reconciliation. He did neither. The only thing he asked for was the fullness of my presence, the sound of my voice and the sincerity of my concern. I tried not to cry over life which had been so cruel to him in every way, where he had never had the love of anyone except me and that was, in itself, terribly little. I was now his bridge to eternity and he seemed to be at peace from the time I arrived.

The guards hated him because he had killed two of their own and by extension; they hated me because I still saw something good in Billy. Besides, I used to tell them, God still loved him because Billy continues in existence. If God no longer loves you, you simply cease to exist, a return to the nothingness from which we all come. But we all continue to exist; therefore God still loves us no matter what we have done in life. None of them understood- they didn't even listen. I am more and more convinced that from a human point of view, it is simply impossible for the relatives and friends of the victim to ever forgive the murderer. If it is done at all, it is only through the absolute and pure grace of God. Humanly speaking, vindictiveness is too hard to overcome in the hearts of the victims of serious crime. To my regret, I never tried to reach out to them who also were hurting.

So I accompanied Billy from his holding cell to the room of death, the chamber of death where he was strapped by the feet and arms to electrodes. They removed his shoes - I don't know why. A mask was placed over his head - he had no choice in this - and he was ready. I was with him up to the chamber and then they led me to the witness room with the reporters and the official witnesses. He never uttered a word of remorse and had no last words. The only thing he asked was that I read from Luke 24:13-34, about the strangers who went from Jerusalem to Emmaus on that first Easter morning. It gave him great consolation to hear those words. He wanted no sacraments, no confession, no funeral rituals, only my presence and loyalty to the end. I assured him I would be there to the end. He had no complaints because he expected nothing from the world and that is what he got. I think that he was ready to die. In fact, it was a relief for him because life had become such a burden. Maybe it was his own kind of inner strength facing a destiny he could not control except by facing it a la Ernest Hemingway.

At exactly 12:00AM, two officers simultaneously pulled two switches one of which sent 10,000 volts of electricity through poor Billy's body. Neither one knew who had done it. I guess so neither would feel guilty afterwards. His hands grew white gripping the arms of the chair as his head snapped backward when the charge struck his body full force. A small amount of white smoke came out of the metal helmet over his head and you could smell the nauseating scent of burnt flesh as the electricity cooked his brain and his innards. They had put a diaper under his pants so when he died and his bowels were loosed, his excrement would not go all over the floor. The officers did this three times. There was no dimming of the lights like in the James Cagney movies, only the hum of electricity as it performed its deadly task. Each time they shut off the electricity, his body slumped forward under the weight of its own dead flesh. I never heard Billy utter a sound, as Billy had never done. After the third charge, a doctor pronounced him dead and they permitted me to anoint him with the oil of the sick. What that would do spiritually for Billy was beyond me but I followed the ritual anyway. I think it was more for the living than it as for the dead - a feeble gesture that what man refused to do, God was supposed to make up for in the person of the priest. Hypocrisy! He was there to bless the murder of the state. It was all so grotesque and contradictory. God should forgive against whom every transgression was supposed to be aimed while men went forward unforgiving, to kill Billy. Religious hypocrisy all the way. All these people went to church on Sunday and listened to the same gentle man from Nazareth: "love your enemies, do good to those who hate you ... " Rather, here, these Christians were really saying, "Fry your enemies, deliver death to those who hate you ... " From that day forward, I don't think I much believed in people's faith anymore. While Billy had done evil things, those calling for his death could not avoid their own evil. Deep down, they were all or mostly all, vengeful creatures who could think of nothing more to do for a man than to kill him. They hadn't learned a damn thing from the New Testament they carried around with them every day.

I do not make excuses for Billy nor for the terrible things he did in life. The only thing I do know was that from the beginning he had no one to love him unconditionally.

Neither mother nor father nor family. I was his only friend and clearly that had not been enough. Alone in a world, terrified of life itself and what it brought him, he had lived by his own wits, the only way he knew how to live. He had remembered only one act of loyalty as a child and that was enough for him to trust me even as he made his adieu to this cruel world which had found no place for him in all his twenty eight years. I knew that he had to take responsibility for what he did and I think he did. I do not know. But I have wondered ever since what I could have done that I did not do. Maybe nothing. Maybe Billy was one of those tragedies of evil which simply escapes everyone's ability to help. And so he died alone, seemingly unrepentant, sent forth by force to meet his Maker by a group of people who could not understand or forgive so they kill. It was a terrible message from earth to the Creator: "Take him. We can't." Killing is no solution because it begets only further killing - something which morally obtuse Americans have never learned in their whole history. Every other group of people in the western world seems to have learned that very simple lesson except Americans. What made it so difficult for them to understand? Was it because, believing themselves and their system the "best" in the world, God was punishing them for their moral blindness and arrogance? That the whole world can plainly see just how barbaric, vengeful and hateful Americans really are deep down in spite of all their arrogant words that they are the greatest, most innovative people on earth? How ignorant and hateful they look before the people of the whole world. Foolishness is always the price of arrogance.

I do not know. I only know that from that August day until now, I never again trusted religious people in spite of all their religion and religious words. Perhaps my own ministry had been dealt a mortal wound that day and it would only take time before it would all crumble. Did the beginning of my own despair appear that evening or morning or whatever? I do not know. I felt no real guilt; after all, it was Billy who had killed two innocent human beings doing their job and inflicting a terrible and everlasting wound on their families.

But I do feel a terrible sense of betrayal because Billy was always a part of me, of my common humanity with him and I could not help him when he needed me most. "For whom the bell tolls ..." More. A part, a true part of me died that night with many of my stupid religious rituals. I came up against the Mystery of the Cross with all of its horror and stupidity. I did not understand. I could not fully understand. I do not yet understand. The only thing I understood was this open and bleeding wound in my soul which has never healed since and will never heal till the day I die.

It was really my last temptation, a dark secret in my soul which I have never told anyone in over thirty five years. It was and remains mystery, the mystery of evil and of the Cross to which I remain affixed and transfixed even to this day.

I remain affixed and transfixed even to this day.

CHAPTER 6

EARLIEST CHURCH EXPERIENCE

I was baptized in Buffalo on February 23, 1934, or that was what the record shows. Of course, I was much too young to remember the date but my godparents so reminded me. The Church of St. Columba now sits in the middle of a large black ghetto where once stood a thriving Italian community. I was born on Swan Street which was then Buffalo's Little Italy. I remember my crib and that I drank so much milk that my mother used to fill up an empty beer quart jar bottle with a nipple on it so I wouldn't cry so much. I remember once in frustration I took the bottle and threw it through a large frame window in the front of the house. I was not yet two. I don't remember what happened to me as punishment but it was the first sign that (1) I had a temper (2) I knew what I wanted and (3) I wanted it when I wanted it. That would have to be disciplined in the years ahead but those instincts are with me yet. I feel it all the time.

Our family was not particularly religious. There were a lot of pictures and statues of the Sacred Heart and of the Blessed Virgin all around the house. It was more cultural than religious. We said our prayers before bedtime but that was about it, around the house at least. My father came from the Italian anti-clericals of the Garibaldi variety so he never went to church except, of course, Midnight Mass at Christmas and on Easter Sunday which were cultural events. There were Italian cultural holidays as well as religious holy days. I never knew which was which. We always had a crib under the tree at Christmas but other than that I never knew what Christmas was and certainly not Easter. Those days were associated with presents so that was just fine with me. Let the good times roll, to use a phrase from New Orleans.

My first introduction to religion was when I was five. We had moved and bought a house on what seemed to me a real farm but it was in a suburb of Buffalo, West Seneca. We raised chickens, turkeys and a goat. We also had two acres which seems like a lot of land now but back then land was quite inexpensive. My brother and sister and I would help my father turn over the soil each spring - we always did this by hand. We also each had a chore to do after school; clean and feed the animals, shovel the coal to the bin, take out the garbage, clean the snow (in Buffalo it seemed like it snowed almost every day from

November to April), mow the grass and in the spring water or how the garden. We had to do our chores before any play. If we didn't, there was a beating to be had and it was always on me. I do not mean to bear the martyr's crown but as the oldest son in an Italian culture, it was only me who was beaten. It was called the law of the primogenito, of the first born.

And I mean beaten - not with a few slaps but with straps and sticks. Once I was chained in the cellar (all Buffalo homes had cellars) for some offense. You see, I had a stubborn streak. I simply would never give in, no matter what punishment was given. I'd shut my mouth but I'd never give in. Even as a child it was a contest of wills and I would rather have died than give in to what I thought was wrong or simply for what I wanted to do. It wasn't pride or my spleen but simply me who always said no. I wouldn't have lasted very long in the Roman Empire. Even today I have lost every job I've ever had in my life for saying what I thought, not caring about, or thinking about, the consequences. And they were jobs I really liked.

Once when I was five, my brother Frank and I went over the fence to National Fuel on Mineral Spring Road. In those days they stored natural gas from Texas in this giant, round cylinder that went up and down on its own moorings, depending on the level and need of natural gas. I wanted to go to the top but my brother was afraid. So I went alone up layer after layer of steps to the very top. It was very high - about five hundred feet - and I still remember that sense of wonder as I looked about when I got to the top. It was like a first airplane flight - awesome and wondrous. The land below me was in even strips, the people and cars seemed tiny, the sense of freedom from all the small concerns of daily life so trivial in comparison. I was free but frightened all at the same time. I was afraid to move and afraid not to. I stood there for what seemed hours, breathless with each turn of my head to see the great newness of what was before me. It was like what the astronauts saw in space for the first time. One could only be filled with awe. In the meanwhile, it seems, Frank had become frightened. He didn't think I could get down by myself so he went for help. I could see the fire trucks and police cars converging below me. There was no TV then, but I would have made first story on the evening news! I remember two police officers approaching ever so gingerly, candy in hand. I told them that I was afraid of a beating when I got home but they promised me that that would not happen, that my mother who was waiting below told them so. Like a fool, I believed adults and of course was later introduced to adult duplicity for the first time in my life. I have never trusted them since. I went down with them and they gave me over to my mother who, once we arrived home, proceeded to beat me within an inch of my life. The same with my father when he arrived home from work and was told what I had done. That's when I got tied in the cellar because I would not promise not to do that again. Even in the darkness of a cellar, the memory of that vision from above remained with me. There are peek moments in life which you do not forget. That was one of them.

Still another time, Billy Buffo and I skipped school and went fishing in the Buffalo River which was particularly treacherous because it was very deep in order to accommodate lake steamers. In addition, its fast flow was assured by the fact that it was a connecting link from Lake Erie to the Niagara River above Niagara Falls. Small children who fell in drown as a matter of course, year after year. So when Billy and I skipped school to go fishing, and two young boys downstream from us drowned that very afternoon, the authorities concluded that it was us and actually went to tell my parents. Well, you can imagine the grief and the pain of losing the first born son of an Italian family. Relatives and friends from all over the city came to console my parents as word got out about my "death." Oblivious to all this, Billy and I came home after dark with two suckers, a carp and one bullhead fish which I had proudly caught. I was certain that I would be forgiven once my parents saw that I had actually caught four fish which, mistakenly, I thought we could eat. In Italian families, men are separated from the women during mourning periods with the men in the front room and the women in the kitchen. As I came in the front door, I must have been seen as Lazarus from the grave. In our family, relief was expressed not by hugs and kisses but by a rain of blows from my uncles and as I rolled into the kitchen my mother and aunts had at me with another thunder of smacks all over my body. Then my father took me into the bathroom where he took the razor strap and struck me.

"Are you ever going to do that again? Are you going to see Billy Buffo again?"

"Yes," I responded defiantly.

Then more blows and the same line of questioning to the point where my uncles had to break down the bathroom door to rescue me. I passed out from the pain but yelling defiantly "yes, yes, yes." I woke up during the night, still unwilling to apologize and I remember that wracked with pain, I didn't give a damn. I cried 'yes' in the darkness of that empty room.

All this may seem strange, not to say grotesque, in today's never-beat-a-child world. And it was cruel, so much so that if it were done today to a child, the parents would be arrested for child abuse. But in those days, especially among Italian, Greek and Polish families, you had to toughen the first born by frequent and hard beatings because he had to defend and fight for the family's survival. Everything depended upon him, even the safety and well being of all the rest. So the more you were beaten the better prepared you were for the hard life ahead where there was no quarter asked or given. Kind of like a fighter who gets beaten by his trainer so he can fight better later on. Everything depended upon you, your strength and your courage in the face of all the odds. You had to be willing to die for your family – it was that important. All this seems rather ludicrous in an age when fathers abandon wives and children in seemingly very easy fashion. Where any kind of physical discipline is seen as abuse; and where children are in charge, not the parents. Not so in those days. If you married and later fell out of love, tough shit. You were married forever, you swallowed your self- pity because the family is more important than you, greater than you. Looked at from that perspective, which custom was/is better? I am not certain.

It was also part of the Italian family to go through the rituals of Catholicism. That was as much a cultural part of what we did as spaghetti on Thursday and Sunday. My first real religion was at Pops Growney at St. William's parish in Winchester – about three miles from our home. We never called him 'Pops' to his face but it was an endearing nickname for one whom we both feared and respected. At 230 ponds and 6'1", he was worthy of respect. I can still remember those biting, cold Buffalo winds off of Lake Erie in January, February and March. I can remember how cold we got when we went to Monday night novenas to Our Lady of the Miraculous Medal and every Friday night to the Stations of the Cross during Lent. We went or else. I became an altar boy when I was five – quite young even for those days. I bluffed most of my Latin, just enough to fool the Pastor. "Ad Deum qui laetificat juventutem meam", "to God who gives joy to my youth." I'd mumble the whole thing but just enough of the Latin to convince the pastor that I knew. I didn't know. There was much joy in going to church with Pops Growney. This priest actually read books and in my opinion was the greatest preacher since Cotton Mather. He was head of the Catholic Actors Guild of the diocese and played Shakespearean parts as well as other drama roles. He was an actor when he spoke, but with a sense of humor and delivery second to none of all the preachers I ever heard in my whole life. And I have heard a lot. He taught me everything I ever learned about preaching and public speaking – as well as the beginning of my love of reading. When he spoke, he engaged you personally and if he were speaking about Hell, you'd enjoy the trip! He was a loyal pastor who was there for his people at all times. His mother was his housekeeper and made the greatest apple pie I have ever tasted. Every once in a while he would invite the altar boys in for breakfast and to this day I remember how Pops ate. He enjoyed his food immensely and smacked his food as he ate it in such a way that even if you were not hungry, you got hungry just listening to him. And he would tell us stories by the hour. He loved to talk and he loved to tell stories - that's what made him so interesting. Story telling is the heart of keeping people's attention as well as teaching them. You teach through stories. He mesmerized me when he spoke and taught me everything I know about public speaking and dramatics as well as fidelity to books and study. He would discuss books he had read - later in life - with me. He simply took it for granted that priests read and kept informed, theologically and philosophically. I was also impressed by his fidelity to worship and his parishioners. When we would not be there for Sunday Mass - he had a fabulous memory - he would go to visit us at home. His visits to the sick whether at home or in the hospital were on a weekly basis. And he was strong as an ox at 230 pounds with not an ounce of fat or flab anywhere. He was the typical self willed, strong and charming Irishman. And never, never so much as a whiff of scandal. Never.

I once asked him what made him so courageous in speaking on matters of social justice and on other controversial topics (in those days social justice was very controversial). I was expecting some deep religious reason or explanation. Instead I got a very earthy answer: one thousand shares in the Nicoplate Railroad which later became the New York Central which still later became Penn Central. Those were the heydays of the railroads and his father had been vice president for years. The elder Growney set up a trust of a thousand shares of the Nicoplate for each child. By today's standards, he received about a thousand dollars a month from the trust which was a lot of money then. He was no poverty priest (he enjoyed good cigars, good food and a new Cadillac each year) but neither was he stingy with his money. He helped many parishioners who were laid off. In any case, the trust gave him an independence from the local bishop. "Go ahead and fire me" he seemed to say, "I don't care. I've got my own stash and I can live on my own anytime. " Money", said Marx , "was the foundation of all human desire." In Pop Growney's case, it meant independence and freedom and the local bishop damn well knew it. And outspoken he was.

Pops didn't like to get up early in the morning. He would be up reading books and magazines until the wee hours. So eight o'clock Mass saw him as mean as a bear when someone came between her and her cubs and you didn't disturb him in the least at that hour of the morning. Once when the Easter liturgy was celebrated early on Holy Saturday, a scene occurred that left a lasting memory. I shall never forget it - I was six at the time. There was a part of the liturgy where the new Baptismal water was blessed. The priest was supposed to breathe gently on the water as in Genesis when the Spirit of God was above the Tahom-Bahom of creation (i.e. confusion) and come to bring creation out of that confusion. But dramatic as he was, he let out such a guttural sound that I laughed out loud. "Peter" he cried with his eyes literally bugging out of his head. He picked me up - he was an incredibly strong man – and put me on a hook by the top of my cassock and I observed the rest of the ceremony from high up. It was actually kind of exciting since at the time I was short and had a hard time seeing anything. I mean, how tall can you be at six? Another altar boy had to remind Pops to let me down or I would have stayed there all day. Still another time at the "stations" on Friday night during Lent, I was chewing gum while carrying the candle alongside the crucifix carried by yet another altar boy. The whole ceremony stopped while I was ordered to the sacristy to discard the gum. My parents were humiliated before the whole congregation because everyone knew everyone in the parish. "Riga falls for the first time" Pops intoned when I got back. The congregation got a hearty laugh at my expense (Pops had a fantastic sense of humor and timing. He laughed all the time except in the morning!) and I never forgot the lesson: never chew gum when an altar boy! Not much of a lesson but it became one of my precious memories of my youth and believe it or not, those precious memories were very influential in choosing the priesthood later on. I admired everything he did: speaking, fidelity, learning, enjoying the good things of life. But he was surprised later when I chose to become a priest.

Religious instructions were on Monday afternoon on the release time program for Winchester public schools. Catholics were released an hour early so we could walk up to the parish and sit for an hour so the local Mercy nuns could drill us in the Catechism. We memorized a lot of formulas and the nuns answered a lot of stupid religion questions (Will you go to Hell if you eat something and then go to Communion?) One nun in particular, Sister Peter, got on my case. She thought I was destined for great things in life in spite of the fact that I was the most undisciplined kid in the class, maybe, in the school. I got many a slap in my knuckles and back for the shenanigans both at religious instruction and at school in the principal's office (Mr. Ferrand). But Pops Growney never hit me - he hated violence of all kinds even when he hung me on the hook. Only twice do I remember him striking real troublemakers, Norman La Bounty and Billy Buffo. These acts still stick in my memory both as a jolting reality of violence (I never considered what my parents did to me as 'violence' but as the natural course of things in preparation for the future) and as a complete contradiction in Pops Growney. Only later could I accept the evident fact that he too was only human, with horrible human faults. But it was shocking, just as the first time I saw him urinate when I was in the bathroom. I just never dreamed that priests took a leak just like me. I thought ordination brought priests an angelic nature! I never even thought of what happened and where all that good food he ate with such relish actually went! It never dawned on me in the least. I accepted it as just another mystery along with the Trinity and the Incarnation.

In any case, Sister Peter kept on telling me that she dreamt I would be a priest, a bishop and then Pope. The first American Pope who was half and half -Italian-American Pope. In those days, it was 450 years since there was a non Italian elected Pope (Adrian II in 1523) who, incidentally was probably imprisoned because he was a non-Italian. That thought of becoming a non-Italian Pope therefore did not sit well with me in the least. Besides, what, no sex? Even in grammar school days, the girls started to look good. In third grade they had to be tortured; in eighth, laid. Of course, we never did. I liked "feeling them up" at the cinema on Saturday afternoons and Doris Shelhammer' s small breasts were delicious to feel and to stroke on Saturday afternoon matinees at Shea Seneca movie theatre. But that's as far as we went. So the thought of no girls was simply off the radar screen and anyone who suggested differently was simply nuts, nun or no nun. Sister Peter was half right and half wrong as my life finally unfolded.

I shall never forget another shocking event when Pops sent me over to a neighboring parish to borrow what was called an aspergillum, that is, a holy water sprinkler used during liturgical ceremonies. When I approached the pastor and asked him for the aspergillum for Pops Growney, he looked at me in utter amazement. "What the hell is that?" "I think it's what you use for sprinkling holy water," I said. "Oh, OK. I thought it was something you shoved up your ass." I was genuinely shocked that a priest would use such vulgar language particularly in reference to a sacred utensil.

None of this made much religious sense to me then, even though I loved old Pops Growney. The one thing which did impress me religiously (besides Pops) was the example of a friend of mine when we worked on the farm during those summers as migrant farm workers. Tom Pera wanted to be a priest and he went to Mass almost every morning at 6:00AM on his bike. It was three miles each way so he had to hustle to get back on time to get to the fields by seven. He never swore like the other boys, never told dirty jokes and didn't masturbate en masse with the other boys. I admired him for his courage amidst a pretty morally obtuse bunch of farm boys. He would be disgusted when four or five of them would line up and begin to masturbate to see who would (1) ejaculate first and (2) to determine which one could ejaculate the furthest. The winner would take the bets. No time limit. Pretty raunchy stuff but that's what they would do when they went to swim at a creek or water hole. Tom never participated and made every effort to swim downstream away from what he considered dirty play. He made a fine impression on me. He did go on to the seminary but left and got married before he was ordained. I married him and his wife later on. Maybe I should have done the same since he had the courage even then to know that a life of celibacy was not going to be his role in life. Neither was it to be mine but that realization would come only after ordination. And I think I hurt a lot of people when I came to my decision. We are still good friends because I still admire him after all these years.

So it was the example of these people in my life which drew me to study for the priesthood. The example of my pastor, a nun in Catechism class and a friend on the farm during those long summer days. Two are now dead - I think I broke their hearts when I left. Even to this day, I do not know why I went to the seminary since my parents were so strongly against it. They thought it would be a waste of my talents. In fact, they threw me out of the house when I announced the news that I wanted to be a priest. But that is another story for another day. Three people, all of whom I must have deeply disappointed when I left the priesthood. But three people who taught me what the word 'Christian' meant and to whom I shall always be deeply grateful even in my disappointment to them. It is unusual to encounter one Christian these days; but to encounter three, this I shall consider an extraordinary grace in my life.

CHAPTER 7

THE EDUCATION YEARS

I actually do remember fairly far back in my education years. I was such a terror at home that my mother lied about my age to get me into the first grade at Winchester Public in West Seneca. She claimed that I was four to be five in October. In fact, I was only three. The principal kept on asking my mother for my birth certificate and when it finally came, I was held back for a year in the second grade. Even then I hated school and searched for excitement. I remember ringing the fire bell at the school just for ·the heck of it and the whole school went wild. Mr. Ferrand, the principal, searched for days for who had done the deed but he never found out because there were no witnesses to my evil deed. I was so scared but I wouldn't have done different even if I had known I would be caught.

My first grade teacher, Ms. Colley, was as sweet as could be. I got hurt playing on the playground with skinned knees and elbows. She patched me up and held me tight for a while. I still remember those large warm breasts and her tender kisses on each of my wounds. She was the first woman I fell in love with but that was short lived. I came upon her and Mr. Ferrand kissing in the classroom after school had let out and I was depressed for weeks afterwards. It didn't help much when I found out that they were to be married that summer but in retrospect~ it wasn't all that bad. At least he wasn't kissing one of the students who were my rivals. I could have at least beaten the crap out of them.

There were other teachers I had that were just plain mean. In fifth grade we got a male teacher - I have since forgotten his name - who just loved to slap the boys around. He thought it was macho and it would help build character. During a fire drill I was simply talking to the guy ahead of me. He took me out of line and slapped me five or six times right across the face as hard as he could. I actually saw stars and thought I was going to pass out. My ears rang for days after that and I think that he damaged my left ear. But I'd be damned if I would show him that I was afraid so I just stood there and took it without complaint as he slammed away. When I wouldn't cry as he hit me, the next blow would be harder. He finally stopped out of frustration (or maybe he just got tired) but I shall always remember the utter humiliation - it was that which really hurt - as I stood there before the whole school beaten and my nose bloodied but unmoved and unbended. I was no hero but I had received worse from my Mom and Dad. It was the way of discipline in those days and I never told my parents. They probably would have beaten me more had I said anything. Clearly, I wasn't the teacher's pet; I was his terror. We hated each other with mutual disdain and he knew it. He beat me every time I gave him the occasion. Today he'd be arrested.

One thing I remember about those early years was the consistently poor grades I received. I had no incentive to study or read- I don't think I even knew how to read until I was in the fifth or sixth grade. At least I do not remember reading anything serious until the sixth grade. In those years, they simply pushed you on to the next grade "on condition" no matter how poorly you did. The only grade I made on my own was the eighth grade. But I was literally illiterate until Sister Claudia got hold of me.

One year the public school nurse came around to test our hearing. She gave all the kids earphones in which a voice would come on. It got progressively lower and you were supposed to mark on the sheet if you heard anything. My right ear was normal but when I started on the left ear - I heard nothing. I knew I couldn't hear out of that ear but I thought everyone could hear out of only one ear. Funny thing about a disability. You only know about it when others tell you about it. Unless it hampers your work or your mobility, others must tell your about you disability. I thought everyone was deaf in the left ear and no one was supposed to hear out of two ears. To my surprise, they told me that that was not normal so it was only then that I realized I was "handicapped." I was given no special assistance and was fully expected to keep up with the rest of the kids. I was diagnosed as border line retarded because I was not supposed to hear as well as the others.

Neither did I realize that in school you were supposed to learn something. I thought it was a necessary interval before play and raiding the railroads. Learning was not fun. God knows they tried to teach me but I neither learned nor did I want to learn. Above all, I didn't want to learn. In those days, grades were given by letters and my father would laugh when he would see all those "Ps" (poor) neatly lined up in that Palmer handwriting. But he would sign it every time and not make much of a deal about it. My father would call those "Ps" soldiers all in straight lines and always at attention and marching in a row. It was only in eighth grade that I began to realize that I was supposed to be learning something and that I was missing something big. I actually started to study then and got an 85 average all on my own. But my real education was yet to come and from another source.

The pastor of St. William Catholic Church in Winchester wanted to start a high school and progressively go through the grades until it reached twelve. He actually hounded my parents to send me there. Since I had no money to pay for the tuition, Pops Growney arranged for me to clean the school every day after school let out so that I could attend. I really didn't want to go to a Catholic high school because I had heard that they actually made you work. I didn't realize the pressure they put on you. Public high school would be a continuation of the Big Easy. But a combination of the pastor's insistence and my parent's encouragement finally made me attend. Even my illiterate parents knew that I was going nowhere in the public schools. It was really the turning point of my education. Without that first year of Catholic high school taught by two nuns, I would have quite simply been lost in every way. I owe them a lot.

The date was early 1946 and the school opened with two nuns in charge of about fifty boys and girls. The principal was tough as nails and a stickler for details. She actually insisted we learn. She was a no nonsense nun. Sister Mary Claudia ("Clawed Balls") euphemistically called by the boys) meant business. The very first day she told me to go to the blackboard and parse a sentence. I didn't have the slightest idea of what she was saying. She proceeded to humiliate me utterly and completely. "What's a verb?" I didn't know. "A noun?" "A pronoun?" "A subordinate clause? " A conjunction?" The direct and indirect object?" I didn't know a thing. It could all have been Chinese for all I knew. "Heaven help us and save us" was her favorite expression and with me, she meant it. I needed radical surgery.

"Didn't they teach you anything, you boob?" More humiliation but richly deserved. "They did but I never learned anything." "What did you do all day long?" "Just thought about sports and what I would do when school was over." "You boob" (that was also one of her favorite expressions) "you wasted your whole life and how do you expect to pass? What am I going to do with you?" "I'll study hard." "You darn well better, you boob or I'll rip your lips." God, think about that. Getting your lips ripped off would mean that you would never talk again!

She struck utter fear in my heart from the very first day. She was absolutely unlovable. Just the opposite of Ms. Cooley. But then Ms. Cooley never taught me anything. If you ever saw "Song of Bernadette" Sister Claudia was the spitting image of the Superior in Saint Bernadette's school and later her novice mistress. She had the demeanor only a mother could love but she was dedicated to giving us an education come hell or high water. But she was not popular, to put it charitably. She did not want to be popular. Just successful. Two episodes would show it perfectly.

Terry McNamara was one big guy. He stood 6'4" and weighed in conservatively at 250 pounds. For a high school freshman, that was a big boy and he had arrogance. He could beat up anybody in the school. Except me. Highly independent, tough and rebellious, he was a bomb waiting to go off. His parents sent him for discipline and discipline he got. Early in the semester he was called on to go to the bulletin board and get or write something or other. "Get it yourself," he said to a shocked teacher. The students froze because the great confrontation had come.

"What did you say?" asked Sister Claudia in feigned surprise as she approached him. He stood up to his full stature and was not about to take anything from a woman, let alone a mousy nun. As she approached, much to our horror, he said "You do it. I don't feel like it."

At that moment he actually let go with a right round house which she easily deflected with her left hand as she dropped her book as if on cue and with her right fist came up with an upper cut right to his jaw. He went down like a ton of bricks right there in the classroom. I mean like out cold.

"Pick him up and take him to my office," she said calmly which, of course, we did. It took six of us to carry him to the nurse's room. When he came back about ten minutes later, he was quiet and reserved - for the rest of the year. He had met more than his match. To her credit, Claudia never told it to anyone and swore she would do the same to anyone of us if we ratted to anyone. I admired the way she kept the problems of the school at the school and did not tattle on anyone to anyone. She solved her own problems. But boy, did she resolve the issues.

Billy Buffo had been one of my best friends in grammar school. How he got to come to St. William is beyond me. While I knew what a beating from your father was all about, what he got was downright criminal. His father was a violent drunk and his mother had abandoned the family for that reason. He was the only child so his father took everything out on him. In those days, it took a whole lot for a mother to abandon her family. But Billy would often come to our house and I had to lend him a T-shirt because his would be bloody from the beating he got from his father. I washed the wounds and bandaged them as best I could, only to send him back to a drunken bastard who would someday kill him. Yes, his father had a great responsibility about what would happen to Billy's life.

Claudia was hard on Billy because that was her way of showing concern. Billy was not impressed and above all, could not really understand. One day - or night - he broke into the school, broke into the nun's kitchen, stole all the candy which was offered for sale to the students and then he defecated on the nun's eating table. It was disgusting but Claudia never mentioned a word. She never found out who had done it in spite of interrogating every male in the school. She suspected Billy but could never prove it. She drilled me for about thirty minutes but I really didn't know who had done the terrible deed. Billy only admitted it to me years later when he was in Sing Sing awaiting death. I suppose confession was good for the soul. He admitted that he was the one who left the loaf for

Sister Claudia. Now he could die in peace! What I didn't tell him was that it was me who had to clean it up.

While we did not like the woman, there were two things we did not doubt. First, she scared the hell out of us (I studied four to five hours every night) and second, she gave us one hell of an education. All I know today about English and Latin I learned from her. Whether it was fear or respect, I learned more English, Latin and social studies from her - enough to give me an intellectual discipline and love of study to last the rest of my life. I still feel a sense of tremendous gratitude for that nun coming into my life.

The school closed after a year because of finances but it left an indelible memory and a discipline in study and work which would never leave me. I was forced to go to West Seneca Central for two years. I had learned so well and so much at St. Williams that I never had to study an hour later and I was always at the top of my class. Such was the poverty of education at the public school. The teachers would call on me all the time at the Catholic high school had instilled confidence in me as well as-solid learning. I was the star pupil and outshone everyone. I simply basked in the classroom.

But the one thing I had no time for at St. Williams (I was too busy studying to avoid Claudia's wrath) was girls. All of a sudden they became mysteriously important and very attractive. But I was painfully shy. God, I couldn't even look at a girl without almost crying. And I longed for them sexually like my testicles were going to explode. I was afraid that stuff would back up and maybe kill me. I particularly longed for Edna Mae Whittit who sat in front of me in Mr. Quinlan's world history and social studies classes. She had great legs and I wanted to ask her to all the school dances but I was just too shy to even think about it. Besides she had a brother big enough to kick my ass all the way to Niagara

Falls. I also feared she would tell me to get lost. So I played practical jokes - as if that could ingratiate me to the girls. I began the rumor that Edna Mae wore no panties. I mean, under her dress she was buck naked. Every young man in that school waited for her to come down the stairs so they could look up her dress to see the heavenly kingdom stripped of all cover. Just imagine what two hundred boys looked like, hanging under flights of stairs, moaning like cows in pain and fainting as Edna Mae passed. And Edna Mae didn't have the slightest clue of what was happening. I don't think she ever found out which was just as well. Her brother - a big, hefty guy - would have beaten the crap out of me had she found out. But I never got close to her.

To impress the girls about whom I was so shy, I joined the football team. I no more wanted to play football than make sausage. Burst, the coach, was also the geometry teacher. Now math had never been my forte. I had to take the New York Regents three times to even pass the math section. I was so poor at the blackboard that old man Burst used to tell me, "You know, Riga, you got to know how to count to have a banana stand." This guy who hated Italians - he thought they were either retards or gangsters - except the quarterback, Charlie Vastola. Charlie was good and fast. He was also the only quarterback the team had. I played defensive end and on scrimmage and I would get to the quarterback two out of four times. I wasn't bad. What I didn't have in weight I'd make up for in tricks. I was fast so I could easily fake out 225 pound linemen. I'd go around and sometimes even over them. Once I even went under a line man's legs. Unfortunately for him, I went up too fast and my helmet must have crushed his <u>cologni</u> and he screamed in pain. They carried him off the field stiff as a board with the coach telling him not to touch certain parts of his body because someone might be looking. The poor guy just lost his manhood and Burst was worried about his grabbing his nuts.

So I was pretty good but Mr. Burst would not put me in any game so I could shine for the girls. But I stayed, hoping again hope that I could be a hero and win Guinevere. One of the last games we played was against Blasedale, a Buffalo suburb and we were ahead 48-6 with two minutes to go in the game. So Burst put me in the game, to get my uniform dirty, I guess. I caught three passes and we were well on our way to score again when I was suddenly taken out of the game - with 1:08 to go. I mean, I was in there for a total of about fifty seconds and the bastard took me out of the game! I went up to him, "We're ahead 48-6 and you couldn't leave me in the game for two fucking minutes?" I took my helmet and threw it at him and told him in no uncertain terms "shove this up your big fat ass" and never played football again. It was juvenile but after all, I was only a juvenile. I mean, did he have to cut off the only inlet I had with girls? It was my way of dealing with the terrible time of adolescence and he ruined it. So ended my quest for girls.

In any case, the two years spent there were mostly a waste of time - no girls, no learning, no football. What's left for a teenager? Greasy hamburgers?

Until I got it in my heart that I should be a priest. Don't ask me how, when or why. I heard no voices, no aspirations, no revelation. To this day I do not know why it all happened. I spoke with the pastor, Pops Growney, and that was it. I had never before dreamed of becoming a priest, not ever. It never even dawned on me, so help me. My calling to the ministry was no more mysterious than that. I mean where does a guy get a thought like that, a guy with boiling hormones in his veins and too shy to ask the object of his desires? When I told my parents, they couldn't believe it. Mostly because it wouldn't make me any money. Besides what would become of the family and primogeniture? Who would pass on the family name? It was the duty of the eldest to do so and no one else. If I had been a bit younger, they would have beaten that simple thought out of my head. And when they were convinced that I was serious, they just took my things and threw me out of the house. Just like that. You would think that they would have given me a valise to put the stuff in! I had to go to the grocery store to get some paper bags. I guess my parents thought that the shock of throwing me out of the house would put an end to all this priesthood nonsense, I'd come to my senses and then I could again be welcomed home and take my place like the primogenito that I was. It was not to be. They just didn't know how stubborn I could be. Besides they had trained me with mighty blows not to give in to superior physical power so they had really defeated themselves. So I walked the two miles to Pops Growney, explained the situation to him and he made a few phone calls.

The all night vigils around the casket of a dead nun scared me terribly. It gave me second thoughts about wanting to be a priest. I too would die without family and if I lived long enough, without friends as well. These thoughts often went through my mind as I kept vigil with those dead nuns at 2:00 AM. It was stark and dreary. And in all the long, cold Buffalo evenings, it became depressing. Would I end up like them, old, friendless, waiting to die and alone?

The studies at the minor seminary were very good. Msgr. Leo Hoen was the rector and each Monday morning, He'd give a thundering talk about how guy's dicks would fall off if they became priests, then left the priesthood and got married. Let me assure you that was and is not now the case. All those things happened to me and my own dick is still very much alive and kicking - so to speak. In fact, not having used it for so long, it has conserved its youth and vigor! But the talks were hair-raising at the time - the fear of the Lord. To tell the truth, though, I thought he was full of crap then as I do now. You become a priest because you love enough to want to serve and help others. Even at the terrible price of celibacy. Not because otherwise you were destined for hell. That was nonsense.

The studies at the seminary were arduous and demanding. Latin, Greek, Hebrew, Apologetics, calculus, German, psychology, Church history, biology. I would stay awake into the early morning hours studying and getting my assignments done. Being young, I could do it then. Now I fall asleep at 9:30. But the teachers – all diocesan priests - were good priests, the best in the whole diocese specially chosen for their learning and good reputation. And you had to produce or out you went. I studied hard and came out with the highest average of the whole class. And from a public school! The faculty could hardly believe it. Msgr. Hoen was shocked because I had come from one of those stupid public schools - how could I beat the best he had? - and many were very bright. So he made up a new rule so as not to award me the honors at the end of the high school year: you had to be a four year graduate and not just an added year end like me, to win first prize upon graduation. I was shocked at the patent injustice, because the man could not accept that a relative stranger could beat his favorites. And beat them handily. Even then I began to realize the injustice of the Ecclesiastical system. But the Church was and is a human and sinful institution and I had to accept that from the very beginning. Since I came at the end of high school I made no lasting friends there. Even then I felt ostracized from the ecclesiastical organization.

My greatest sorrow was the premature death of a young priest, Father Ray Liska, who had befriended me from the time I arrived at the seminary. He was a genuinely holy man - maybe because he realized that with his heart problems, he did not have much time to live. He was also very learned - he read theology until the wee hours of the morning. He heard my confessions and was my spiritual director. He genuinely cared for me - and that was a genuine novelty in my life. Up till then I had been beaten, rejected, thrown out and considered a retard. Along comes a man who trusted, respected and actually cared about me. He was the first and to this day, I still experience the poignancy and pain of that day when the authorities announced that they had found him dead in bed from a heart attack. I must have cried for a week. Maybe it was him. I also think it was that I was crying for myself because I had lost the first real friend I had in my life, one to whom I could really reveal myself, to myself, not afraid of who and what I was. That has always been important in my life. This was something I could not admit, even to myself. I was profoundly afraid because I was profoundly lonely. I was afraid to open myself to anyone for fear of being hurt. Deep down, I was afraid no one would love me if they really came to know me. Even to this day I have a perfectly low esteem of whom and what I am. Not so Father Ray Liska, dead at thirty five. Even today when I am now twenty five years older than he was when he died, I miss him terribly. It just takes some of us a lot more time to become wiser and holier. He was all that when he died. Death came to perfect who he was and he was truly great and in his youth, he now belonged exclusively to God. While men and women are alive, they belong partially to us. Once dead, they are freed of all bounds and they belong totally to us and totally to God. They can truly be themselves only in death. I am honored beyond all words to have known him, met him and to have him as one of my few friends in life.

Maybe because it was the realization that he was always so close to death that made him so genuinely good. That can come, of course, at any age but for those who are young; it comes both as a shock and as a blessing. They do not have the luxury of magnana (none of us really do) but we think we do. That is why death catches most of us unaware and unprepared. Roy had to be prepared - he had no choice. He therefore lived his life fully, perfectly, because he lived it in service and love. You could tell because every time you went to him, he was there for you - no matter his own pain or the press of other duties. He was there for you. There are few people I've met and who have died whom I think are absolutely with God. Roy is one of them.

I graduated from that loved institution in 1951. I call it loved because it taught me much more by who those men were as much as by their learning. I acquired the discipline of rigor of thought, the beauty of languages, the meaning of literature, modern and ancient, a sense of history that goes back thousands of years, a love of the Church which is both saint and deep sinner, mother and whore and a sense of priesthood beyond all the evil stereotypes enlisted so often in our world. They were truly dedicated, good men who gave of themselves without counting the cost for no other reason than they truly loved God. They created in me my first sense of love of learning, of study, which was not in contradiction with my love of God. In every respect they were mentors and years later, I am grateful.

During that summer the local bishop informed me that I had been chosen to go to the American College at Louvain, Belgium. I had never even heard of the place. Belgium? Wasn't that the place where it rained all the time? I was to find out that it indeed was, but a whole lot more. I was disappointed because I wanted to study in Rome both because of my heritage and because if you were from Rome you had a shot at a higher ecclesiastical route. Yes, I admit it; high ambition was a natural with me. I should have suspected, however, that with my big mouth I would never go anywhere. And how could Louvain ever fit into that scheme of things? It couldn't and I hated the thought of spending the next seven years there. We were required to spend the whole time there, not returning home at all. They called it a matter of discipline, but I think it was more economics than anything else. We tried to cover up a lot by calling it the will of God while it really was the iron law of wages! But off I went on a Dutch passenger ship called the Ryndam across the North Atlantic.

I had never been on a steam ship. The food was scrumptious and all you wanted to eat. One day into the trip, one of the ballasts malfunctioned so the ship rocked abnormally. Everyone at my table got sick except me. I just ate my way across the Atlantic for nine days. Even the waiters got sick seeing me eat!

On that ship I saw for the first time a woman in a bikini. More, I think it was a thong. God, I couldn't keep my eyes off those women by the swimming pool. I pretended I was reading Jacques Maritain' s Introduction to Philosophy but all the way across the Atlantic, I managed to read four pages. The rest of the time was spent watching those great big breasts and those luscious rear ends on the most beautiful women I had seen in my life. I took more cold showers and played more shuffle board and jumped more times playing volley ball - even when the ball wasn't near me - Just to keep my mind off those women. I must have seemed nuts to those around me but I was desperately trying to burn off excess sexual excitement from seeing all those scantily clad women. When they would bend over, I'd moan. To myself, of course. I don't know how I made it without diving off the ship to kill myself so that the throbbing would stop! I knew then and there that celibacy was going to be one hell of a battle if European women were like this. Luckily, in Belgium they were not! In fact, in Belgium the women were so unattractive and large, that I never had a dirty thought in the five years I was there. I now think that is the reason they sent me to Louvain to study. That throbbing came back in spades when I studied for two years in Rome where the women under twenty five were absolutely gorgeous.

My first months at Louvain were tied up trying to speak the French so that I could understand the professors at the Institute Superieur de Philosophie which specialized in Thomistic philosophical studies. The professors were all the very best in their fields. It was marvelous that a country of less than ten million people could produce so many high class philosophers and theologians. Americans were practical people. One of my Hebrew professors actually suggested that we had substituted basketball for Greek which was not far from the truth. Can you imagine teaching Latin and Greek in a public school in 2013 or whenever? Hardly!

Three years of philosophy. When I finally did learn French it was a lot of fun. We had small groups of students who studied together to learn philosophy. We would each be assigned a particular philosopher and report on him to the rest of the class. It was a marvelous way of learning and philosophy was a fine start for theology. It trained the mind in the discipline of thought and respect for research which are both vital for learning. This was in stark contrast to the flabby thinking I recognized when I got back to the States. It is not to be arrogant or prideful, but a philosophical mind goes a long way to think things through in a society dedicated to bottom line and sensuality-sexuality as the epitome of human existence. It was a shock to return to a society taken over by sensuality, consumerism and a distinct inability to reason from basic principles. I am still amazed at this foundational lack in American society.

In any case, what struck me about those men even beyond their vast learning were two things: a fine sense of humor and a deep sense of humility. Now that was terribly unusual as I associated great learning with great arrogance. Maybe the two do go together. They were always kind and approachable and long suffering of the thousand practical questions of the Americans (there were over a hundred nations represented at the University and in the faculty of theology.) As I grew older these men grew wiser. I had always thought that their humility was a false one because they clearly were the finest Catholic thinkers in the whole world. But they were not faking it. The more I learn and know each day - and I know a lot more today than I did forty years ago - the more the vista of my ignorance grows and grows to the point of utter discouragement. My final conclusion is that knowledge alone can never satisfy the human heart. Never. Because there is and can be no end to it. There had to be more and that "more" was transcendent belief or faith which is "belief plus love." If they taught me anything at Louvain it was that very profound lesson. A lesson however which can come only from great learning and not from superficial learning which produces arrogance. And I shall forever be grateful for that most invaluable of all lessons of what learning really means. It has stood by me all during my life, to avoid the arrogance that I really know something, that I'm really intelligent! The more ignorant I am and become, the more intelligent I become. It is a supreme paradox but unless you learn that small lesson, you will understand nothing at all. You will certainly never attain to wisdom which is to accept that you know nothing in comparison to the ignorance of what you do not know which is vast and even infinite indeed. Life is spent in the exponential growth not of knowledge but of ignorance because that is what true knowledge will ever bestow upon you. And yet you can measure your intelligence by just how great your ignorance is. So the next time someone calls you dumb and stupid, accept it more as a compliment even if it comes from a malicious tongue. I have grown into my own ignorance and stupidity. What the ancients called docta ignorantia.

I have spoken in another place of the depth of holiness of the Rector Magnificus of the University, Honore' Van Wayenberg. The great example of such men who had suffered for their faith combined with their great learning and humility, was the greatest lesson for me during those five years at the University of Louvain – the oldest on-going University in the whole world (1425-2013.) Today when it is not politically correct to remember, learn and be grateful to white European males for their great contribution, past and present, I hold the contrary view. They were paradigms of virtue and learning, of discipline, hard working, thoughtful and always charitable and kind beyond all expectations of such learned people. I shall always remember them and I shall always be grateful now that they are mostly dead. My greatest regret in life was not to have been able to have followed in their footsteps and make my own contribution to their legacy. God knows I had the opportunity and the talent - I just wasted it, as any reader can garner from these pages. But at least I have enough brains to recognize how grievously I failed them - and myself only because I did not and perhaps could not measure up to their example and their learning .

I think it was my arrogance that was the beginning of my downfall even from those earliest days when I was headlong in love with myself, when I thought I was so brilliant and that I actually knew something. I had won every medal and competition there was at Louvain. For the first time in the history of the American College (1857-1996), I beat out all the competition from a hundred and fifty nations and brought all trophies back to the College. My professors could not believe that a son of basketball had overtaken their own and beat them at their own intellectual game. An American intellectual? It was almost an oxymoron. They were not jealous – in fact they were universally supportive and applauding - but shall we say, surprised? An American and scholarship was an oxymoron in their minds. Much water has since flowed over the darn but at the time it was a shock to the Belgian intellectual community. I can say that before God that I did it to bring pride to America since I was then so damned proud to be an American I cannot say that today.

Perhaps I exaggerate but it seemed that way to me. In any case, I'm glad today that I finally learned the great lesson of those days: ignorance and humility and kindness. If I live to be a hundred, I shall always remember them and be profoundly grateful to those who taught them to me much more by example than by words.

Just when I was in the flow of things, I was transferred to Rome to get a Master in Theology in the Eternal City. Rome was breathtaking and its description will have to wait for another day. The land was beautiful; the history right there to grab you and all the women had large, beautiful breasts which heaved as they spoke. And since Italians spoke vivaciously. There was a lot of heaving. The thing that amazed me was the huge rotunda at the Gregorian University that held 1000 students all looking down into a well from which the professor taught. The acoustics were perfect. If the professor dropped a pencil, you could hear it all over the hall. You might know that it was built by Michelangelo in 1585 or thereabouts so it had to be perfect. Each nation had its own seating as well as a distinct robe color. The Germans had red cassocks so that they could easily be spotted in the beer halls of Rome where they loved to congregate, drink beer and sing for hours. The Roman authorities were not pleased at their example to the town folks. But what the hell! Italians are the most unreligious people on earth. I didn't know people could memorize so many verses to so many songs and sing for so long. We Americans wore black with blue sashes so we were sort of "blah."

One of the professors of New Testament, an Italian of some note, used to try out his multi lingual repertoire by calling on students from all over the world (there were 160 nations represented- even more than at Louvain - all speaking Latin.) His English was fair but not perfect. He called on me one day to exegi te (explain) a passage from Romans. In Italian the word "exegite" (se esponga) is an intransitive word which is funny when translated into English: "Riga, get up and expose yourself." Without missing a beat I answered, "I really can't because I didn't bring my rain coat." The Americans and British laughed but the professor didn't quite understand. When after class he found out what I had said, he personally threw me out of the class even though I had recited perfectly. He would tolerate no smart ass in his class. I had to go to the Cardinal Prefect of Rome (second to the Pope) to get re-admitted into his class. But first I had to give and compose an apology in Latin for my grossness or at least for my impertinence. I did it in the best Ciceronian Latin I could find and he seemed quite pleased. To this day I do not know whether it was my apology or my Ciceronian Latin that he liked. Maybe both. In any case, I didn't pull another stunt again. The next time he might have sent me packing.

My thesis was the Ecclesiology of J.A. Moeler, a 19th century ecclesiologist (one who writes about what the Church is). It was published in a few learned theological journals but mostly it was one of those theses that simply adds to the library gathering dust. But I enjoyed defending it in Latin before all the professors of the Gregorian University. They gave me highest honors but I knew that the bishop back home was not much interested in learning or scholarship or ecclesiology. He wanted priests to fill vacancies in parishes in the bureaucracy of the ecclesiastical kingdom, hearing confessions, giving monstrous and long winded sermons and carrying on the day to day pastoral ministry. He could care less whether Matthew wrote the first Gospel or Julius Caesar. It was inspired, wasn't it? It was all the same to him.

I tried to keep up scholarship but when I entered the ministry I slowly lost touch. I hated to lose it but that's the way things were. After being arrested and imprisoned (and creating a scandal) for civil rights on Washington, D.C. and Birmingham, Alabama, my superiors didn't know what to do with me to keep me quiet. In those days it was unheard of for a priest to simply get up and leave the whole ministry so they did the next best thing outside of defrocking me. They exiled me just as they used to do in Roman days to other troublemakers. Exile was not to come near the city of Rome for a distance of 500 miles. If anyone caught you there, they could kill you on the spot. They might well have killed me there. I was sent to Catholic University (after first trying a chaplaincy in the Army which also didn't last long) to study -get this - library science for a large seminary they were building in East Aurora. It was God-awful since I loved books but hated libraries. So I signed up for two graduate schools, one in theology (day) and the other science (night). I clearly had no desire for the later so I used the hell out of a librarian from Omaha who had a crush on me and who was studying for her Masters in Library Science. I had her make two copies of everything (e.g. cataloging), I'd come in a few minutes early, look over the material and since I had a gift of B.S. I could put it over on the teachers who were nerds in any case. I mean, people making a science out of a library? When I got A in my courses while the librarian got mostly Bs, she cried that there was no justice in this world. She was right, of course. The only question I had was why it took her so long to find out what was never a secret. If you ever want to kill yourself without sin, study library science where you will die of boredom and where you will pray that a stack of books will fall on you and crush you to death!

Unfortunately for me, justice did catch up with me. The authorities of the University found out about my double dealing and kicked me out of the theology program and permitted me to finish what I had been sent to Catholic University for in the first place; earn a Master's degree in Library Science which I did. The University stripped me of all my credits and my dissertation in theology. I hated it then and I hate it now. Later I did manage to get my PhD in Theology from Graduate Theological Union in Berkeley while teaching theology at St. Mary's of Moraga.

Looking back on all those years, I agree with one of my clients who saw all my degrees on the wall and remarked that all of them and thirty five cents will get you a cup of coffee. The only practical value was once in 1980 when I won $250 from <u>The National Enquirer</u> for entering a contest to see who had the most degrees in the U.S. (I have that honor) . Other than that, they have no practical value in the least. Yet, all was not lost during all the years of "perpetual studentship." I finally came to realize that knowledge itself and by itself can never fully satisfy the human heart. Education is good if it leads you to ignorance, that is, to true wisdom that the more you know, the less in fact you do not know. It is a wisdom born of knowledge but it becomes wisdom only when you realize its insufficiency and final emptiness. That's what all those degrees taught me and a most valuable lesson it was.

For that, I am profoundly grateful to all my teachers from the lowliest grammar school teachers to the great minds of philosophy, law and theology in the greatest universities of Europe.

CHAPTER 8

PRIESTHOOD: THE CHOICE

To this day I am not entirely sure why I wanted to become a priest. I knew that it was a free choice going in and a free choice going out. We are defined by freedom and it was my choice from beginning to end. It is much easier to explain why I left the ministry (it wasn't sex) but much more difficult to explain why I entered it in the first place.

Clearly it was not because of the pious example and urging of my parents. They opposed it all the way as good Italians would. Italians never wanted their sons to become priests, particularly their first born. The eldest son had to take charge of the family and make sure that the lineage of blood would continue. He it was who had to protect the family. That is why they were so very hard on the eldest son to toughen him up to protect the family. The harder parents were on him from early life, the better he would be prepared to protect and endure for the family. It was he who had to be ready to give his life for the family, if need be. There was nothing more important than the family, not even God himself. It was better to curse God than to abandon one's family. Else there would be nothing left to live for.

That gives you an idea and a little background of my family's opposition to my choosing to become a priest. In fact, when I finally told them of my decision - it was back in 1948 – they literally threw me out of the house, clothes and all. It was one of the most terrible days of my life. I didn't know where to go or what to do. I only had one friend - Pops Growney - and I landed on his doorstep, clothes and all I owned in a few paper bags (I didn't own a suitcase). I shall never forget Old Pop's kindness during those terrible days. He put me up in an-extra room in the rectory until he could work something out. He contacted the Mother Superior of a Franciscan Order in Williamsville, New York. Her name was Mother Aquila. She was also very kind to me until sometime later when there was a dispute over a "special relationship" with one of her nuns (Sister Elise). I was reported to my superiors who condemned me without a hearing or due process. But that was years later when I was an assistant pastor in the city.

In any case, I spent the next three years at that Motherhouse in a room next to the boiler room. It was a small room and always warm (if you have ever been to Buffalo, it is cold and/or damp for eight months of the year) and joined by a tunnel to the Motherhouse. The Baptists at the time would have been ecstatic to find out that little bit of <u>Catholica</u> to prove up the fact that nunneries were places that served the sexual needs of priests. And some of those nuns were beautiful.

In any case, as a seminarian I had three chores: serve the 6:00 a.m. Mass; serve the adoration of the Blessed Sacrament each day at 6:30PM and dig graves for the nuns who died there. As the place was the Motherhouse, it served as a retirement home for the old nuns as well as an infirmary hospital for those who were sick. I performed all the duties well except for those damn graves. In winter I would cheat by digging only five feet down because the ground was so hard. I mean, who would know whether a dead nun was buried five or six feet? No one of those nuns would ever come back to snitch on me! I lied so sue me!

I also helped with the funerals. Some of the nuns were over a hundred years old and by that time all their friends and relatives had long since died. I mean, they made George Burns look like a teenager. There was only the grounds keeper, the undertaker, his assistant and me to carry the casket into the requiem Mass and

then to the cemetery which was about a half mile away on the grounds. Luckily, the undertaker had a hearse.

I shall never forget one particular nun. Every nun who died. She was laid out in the chapel and there were always two nuns praying at the casket throughout the night. Except when one died of a communicable disease (TB), they were prepared, washed and clothed by the nuns themselves and there was no embalming. No one seems to know that there is no law mandating embalming. One nun had died from a particularly painful cancer of the spinal cord. Her only comfort was to sit up in an "L" shape and that is how she died. After rigor mortis had passed, the nuns washed her and laid her out in the chapel dressed in a clean habit. Well low and behold, in the middle of the night with only four candles for light and two young novices praying, the nun resumed her upright position, right there in the chapel. Jesus Christ be praised, for the two young nuns it was the biggest miracle since Lazarus and they went screaming down the halls to wake up the others. It was one hell of a commotion when one of the nuns came to my room, pounding on my door. It scared the living crap out of me. So the grounds keeper and I got some rope and tied her down so she wouldn't bounce up again. What had happened was that the rigor mortis had not completely subsided so that nature took its natural development along the lines that she had assumed when she had died. I had a hell of a time getting back to sleep.

But the memories of "why the priesthood" go back even further. I was greatly influenced by the example of Pops Growney. I admired him so. He was strong and virile, he spoke with learning and authority, he loved life and good food, he related to people marvelously, he was vigilant as to the sick and dying in his parish, he prepared his sermons well by study and reflection, he was rough and gruff in the morning - a clear sign of his basic humanity and he was kind (except in the morning.). He was independently minded but always faithful to the teachings of the Catholic Church. He was never obsequious or boot licking. When the bishop was wrong, Pops told him so in no uncertain terms. He must have been the only priest from whom the bishop ever heard the truth. In fact, when one was installed as bishop of Buffalo, Pops gave the talk and told him that this was going to be the last time he would ever hear the truth again. That is like making fun of President Clinton's infidelity in a public ceremony. The bishop could not have been too happy. Pops didn't give a rat's ass, so to speak.

I think his example was profound on me. Sister Peter, who taught catechesis when I was at Winchester Grammar, was also an influence. Who says words of encouragement don't work? She was a good and holy person (but she scared the hell out of me because if what she told me was true, no more feeling the little titties of girls like Doris Shelhammer! And I loved feeling their small titties.) I really liked girls a bunch but I was bashful beyond words. Maybe it was this bashfulness with the opposite sex that was a powerful incentive to become a priest - a reason I would have to go through a lot of therapy to find out. I have neither the patience nor the money to discover whether this is true or not. Besides, why bother? What has been chosen has been chosen and there is no way to uneat the apple.

What clearly influenced me was the priests at the minor seminary in Buffalo (last year of high school and two years of college - junior college as it is called today) and the seven years I spent in Europe in the finest Catholic universities in the world.

The professors of Europe were of course all priests. They were experts in their respective fields - Old and New Testament, dogmatics, church history, patristics, Greek-Hebrew-Babylonian and other ancient languages, archaeology, the spiritual and mystical life and ancient Jewish and Christian literature (QumRan.) The thing that struck me was not only their great learning but also just as great, their great humility. I realize today after what little learning I have been able to accumulate during all these years, that true learning leads to wisdom and wisdom clearly sees how little we really do know. Therefore humility is based on truth and the truth of the matter was that the more we know, the infinity of what we do not now opens itself to us - to the point of maturity, it can easily degenerate into domination since our fallen nature loves to dominate and control others - control of race, sex, economics - everything. You can see this among individuals, groups and nations. The same is very true in the Church as well. Ecclesiastics love to control people and their biggest enemy is freedom, afraid of people who are truly free. They love to dominate so as to control. In the Church that is easier to do than in a democratic society. People in charge in the Church tend to identify their own self will with that of God and that is the very worst form of domination. One can see this in the history of the Church with its long tale of violence, witch-heretic hunts, trials,

Crusades and individual desire for self aggrandizement and career advancement. That is why Christ warned his disciples and apostles that their authority must not be exercised like that of kings and judges but would stern from love, that the one who wanted to be the greatest had to be the servant of all. I will tell right from the beginning that I did not see such an exercise of authority in all my years as a Catholic priest in the U.S. What I saw was the very same type of secular domination and desire for power over people's lives in the name of God as I saw in political life. That is what made it all so scandalous. This desire for power was not measured by the Gospel or by the example of Christ, but by the power as exercised in society, the society of the Church. That is why that for centuries the Church got along very well with tyrants and autocrats. They both understood each other very well because they

were blood brothers. Having forgotten the lesson of Christ's discouragement. In other words I have come to know that their humility was not fake or put on but real, born of wisdom and hard work.

Those professors were faithful to their religious calling and to the scientific study of their faith. Their influence permeated Vatican II and their thoughts made Vatican II. Mostly they were approachable, kind and never put down any person or any idea. They also had a great sense of humor which is always the sign of self assurance and not taking oneself too seriously. Above all, there was always a sense of joy which permeated their teaching and everything they did. I wanted to be like them - humble, kind, approachable by anyone and everyone, learned and faithful to what I had wanted to be and to what I aspired to be. Not a counterfeit or a hypocrite.

All this was to be severely tested later in life and all during my ministry. The arrogance and put down of so many who purported to be learned and PhD's and the pride and the love of the first places at table by so many ecclesiastics really turned me off and finally killed my desire to be a priest any longer.

So if I had to attribute my calling to the priesthood it was what through some internal attraction or movement of the Spirit. It came from the outside, above all from the example of others, mostly priests and mostly professors. It was their humility above all that drew me to want to be like them. It was as if God's calling was from their example, calling me to become like them, to imitate them, to become a priest so that I could be as Christ-like as they were. The Christ of the Gospels came alive in their persons who influenced me in ways they did not even know and who unknown to them, solidified what had only been a limp desire up till then. It was all so strange: I entered the beginnings of a professional vocation for which I had but a lukewarm calling and then in the midst of its preparation, that calling became more solidified as the years in Europe rolled on. Most men and women are called by or through an interior drive, some sort of internal inspiration which they attribute to God. I never had any such feeling. In fact, my feelings in this respect were nil. My calling was progressive, growing and became real only when I was ready to receive Holy Orders (towards the end of the third year of theology when we were ordained Deacon.) By the time of my last year at Rome, my heart had said "yes" and I was prepared to assume the burden of celibacy to which I always had difficulty keeping later on. In any case, when I was ordained, I did it freely and lovingly because I was convinced that it was what I had to do, maybe not for the rest of my life but for that time and for the foreseeable future, the priesthood was what I had wanted to do.

Ironically, the end was already contained in the beginning of my vocation. It is ironic because that was always part of the struggle in becoming a priest in the first place. Let me explain.

What can be garnered from all these pages is that I have always been rebellious of all authority even though I was finally respectful of that authority. But authority is a strange thing. Without the necessary components of humility and spiritual contained in the Gospels, the exercisers of authority in the Church became like kings and emperors, in whose hands authority was exercised exactly like their secular counterparts by domination covered often by a call to obedience not to the Gospel but to their own human traditions and desires. In light of this, one can readily understand the Protestant revolt because the Church in her "highest" members had deviated so from the Gospels and the example of Christ. There must be a freedom of faith responding to a loving authority of example.

But I anticipate myself. I do want my readers to know that the unraveling of my vocation was not due principally to women or sex or even rebellion. Those were only the results of that unravelling until I finally left the whole thing in 1974 when I entered law school. Neither do I blame the authority in the Church, at least not wholly. It's what they had become through the centuries. My leaving was free and for reasons that were honest with me.

The beginning of that mortal struggle in my life was with the rector of the College in Louvain, Belgium, Thomas Maloney. He had been an assistant pastor for twenty five years in Providence, R.I. before he was appointed rector of the College. He was a stern man, terribly distrustful of learning but essentially one who was personally good and faithful to his vocation and his person. He would not have really survived Vatican II with its new ideas and attitude of freedom. In 1962 he was appointed auxiliary bishop of Providence and he died a few years later - just in time to avoid the winds of change from Vatican II. Thank God for him and for the Church that he died when he did.

Maloney and I had an ongoing battle from the beginning of the opening of the college year in 1951 when I arrived there. He belonged to the old school exercise of authority and his highest virtue was obedience, sheer blind obedience to the orders of superiors which I thought contrary to the Gospel. I must have been a Protestant at heart because I was in a continuing act of protest to his rigid direction and view of what it meant to be a Catholic and a priest. His authority was to be accepted without question and any defiance or rejection of that authority was viewed as a rebellion against God. He and God were one because his authority came from bishops who came from the Apostles who came from God. To this day I do not know why he didn't throw me out because we were constantly at loggerheads.

For example, when I won the theology competition over some 600 applicants from 125 nations with a Summa Cum Laude (the first time any American had ever won such an honor in the 100 year history of the College), his only reference to me was not one of congratulation that I had brought honor to the College and to America, but that I was filled with pride and arrogance and that the award would increase those terrible qualities that I had. I was crushed beyond words because I had secretly thought that maybe such an honor would break the terrible logjam of distrust and dislike between us. It didn't, of course. What it had done was only to increase it. All because I would not and could not confuse his stupid (in my mind) and small directions as the will of God. I obeyed them as best I could but I could not resist telling others that they were mostly bullshit. For example, why must all the lights be turned off by 9:30 in the evening? Some people like me were night people and liked to work till midnight and even later, while others were early retirees. I obeyed but always in protest. That was taken to be rebellion against God because it was rebellion against lawful authority which came from God. That I could not and would not accept.

One final example of this beginning of the mortal struggle. The College had a custom after the ordination of deacons to assist various priests in the chapel who came in for that ceremony. Over the years, I had developed a deep and loving relationship with the Mother Superior of the Carmelite nuns next door to the College. Her name was Mere Marie Claire (after whom I named my daughter) and
we were very close. Since I was off to Rome after my ordination, she asked whether I could assist their chaplain and give her communion during the Mass. I did so in spite of the tradition of the American College. In fact, I had to jump out a window to do so because the large entrance door to the College was locked. Upon my return, I was told by the rector that I was no longer welcome at the College and that I was to get out in twenty four hours. I couldn't get a train that quickly so I had to spend twelve hours at the train station because I was literally thrown out of the College. I had disobeyed a tradition of man to make an old nun happy. I couldn't believe or accept that God did not want me to do that. That rector had substituted human tradition for what I thought was a divine commandment (charity) which was the final battle between us. His hate was so great that when I tried to send some money in thanks for my training there, he not only did not answer my letters but he must have torn up my checks (they were never returned for presentation). Even then I

began to have deep reservations about the way authority was exercised in the Church and those doubts were only to grow over the years. While I never broke with the Catholic Church. I still observe and practice my faith. I have always been distrusted by Church authorities even to this day.

After ordination and my return to the U.S. that profound difficulty only grew. I have already touched on this when I spoke earlier about my stint in Vietnam both in battle and in protest with Cardinal Spellman. He was the most politically oriented ecclesiastic I ever knew. It finally dawned on me that almost single handedly, he created the disaster which was to become the Vietnam War. It was he who suggested to then President Eisenhower that Diem, a Catholic and fervent anti-Communist, should establish the political machine for the Republic of South Vietnam which was always supposed to be part of one whole Vietnam after the French gave power to the "North" Vietnamese at the Geneva Peace Conference in 1955. Eisenhower was the first to send arms to Diem along with thousands of U.S. "advisors" who were not advisors at all but actually fighters in the field. All this came about by the machinations of Cardinal Spellman in the name of anti-Communism and God - because his authority came from God. We now know what nonsense, bloody nonsense all of this was. It is one thing to be wrong politically - nations are all the time - but it is quite another to say and do all this in the name of God. What scandal that created and continues to create even today. When I protested the war, softly in 1960 and vociferously after 1964, I was a marked man by the Cardinal and he made sure that there were many places where I could not enter or preach or teach.

If I could tell you of all the confrontations I had with superiors from New York, Buffalo, Oakland, San Francisco, Los Angeles, Notre Dame, St. Mary's in Moraga, etc., etc., it would take more than any one book. It was all over the nature of freedom and authority.

From New York to Buffalo to Vietnam to Notre Dame to Oakland to San Francisco has shown you a little more of why I no longer desired to be a priest. What it all amounted to was a slow death where I was more and more ostracized from the Catholic community and distrusted by all authority. I was lonely as well as alone.

I could see it in a loving assignment I had teaching theology and philosophy at St. John Vianney Seminary in East Aurora, New York in 1963 after the Vietnam fiasco. I was there for two years and I taught courses in dogmatics, scripture and Church history. In my courses I interspersed the works from Protestant theologians in a spirit of ecumenism. I thought that they had powerful things to say which should be heard by future Catholic priests. I even published several books to this effect. Unfortunately a very conservative bishop was appointed to the diocese (McNulty) and when he found out what I was teaching, that was the end of a very dear assignment. From there I was shipped out to the far reaches of New York State - Whitesville. No explanation was ever given me, no hearing, no nothing. Off you went by the grace of God and by the will of God. All these things preyed on my mind to such a degree that six months later I had a complete breakdown after I almost killed the pastor in Olean. I knew I had to confront this basic problem but I simply could not. And not being able to deal with this internal conflict, I had a complete breakdown. I wanted to give it one more shot in spite of the pleadings of my parents. I should have listened to them then (I wish I had) but I wanted to go it one more time. Like an alcoholic, I could not leave what I had come to love in spite of the fact that it was killing me. It wasn't sex, it wasn't a desire for a family- although I longed for both - but that conflict between the Gospel and the example of Jesus Christ and the wary authority.

So after a year of recuperation I accepted a teaching position at Notre Dame when the same development occurred. By that time I had become a well known, up and coming theologian and I was invited around the country for talks, conferences and other important positions. All the while the super patriot Father Hesberg was becoming more and more nervous about Notre Dame's squeaky clean reputation. So when I and the head of the English Department organized the first public protest against the Vietnam War that was the end of my teaching career there. I got sick again but still refused to give it up. My personal life was rapidly disintegrating and that too weighed heavily on my conscience and yet I still was not prepared to give it all up. In retrospect, it was simply stupid to believe that anything serious was going to change in my lifetime but like a gambler who had lost a lot, I still was willing to put more into the pot to see if I could win. In fact, I put in the whole shebang and I lost it all. But when I come to die, I shall always be able to say that I tried and tried again.

So off I went to California, home of the fruits and nuts. More receptive to my ideas in a climate of greater tolerance, the Church in the form of the Christian Brothers and my superior in the Church were just as unbending as anything I had to deal with in the East and Midwest. I managed to get tenure in 1970 but the next year the Brothers came in with a very conservative president who wanted me to get lost or at least jump in the Bay. I told him I was not prepared to do either but the walls were closing in on me. Robert McAfee Brown and I established "Clergy and Laity Concerned about Vietnam" and other forms of racial protest. I became more and more a persona non grata at the College. I mean, how could you blame them? Conservative parents from all over California sent their children to be protected from the infections of the Babylon by the Bay and on the news each evening; this radical priest was giving fiery speeches. They had to get rid of me just as soon as possible.

By 1974 I was exhausted with fighting with the Brothers about the local Church authorities. I was forbidden to speak in about three quarters of the dioceses in the U.S. and when a federal grand jury in San Francisco indicted me for conspiracy and other crimes, the religious authorities in Oakland and at the College were beside themselves. They wanted me out just as soon as humanly possible. I knew there was nothing for me in the ministry as I had become totally disillusioned by the attitudes and examples of Church authority. I would never be at peace with them no matter how long I stayed. I would always be a marked man, a rebel with a cause, a radical and a troublemaker. There was little if any possibility of doing any more good by staying in the priesthood. My personal life had completely disintegrated and it was time for my life to become honest and whole again.

So I made a deal with the College to give me some mustering out pay so I could go to law school in San Francisco where I thought I could again be able to do some good. I was always the dreamer, the visionary. That would ultimately destroy me. But do you know, if I had to do the whole thing over again, I wouldn't change a thing in that life. Perhaps a little - my personal, sexual life. But I wouldn't change an iota of what I fought for to be who I was and what I was to become. At least when I come to die, I won't have any regrets that I should have done this or that rather than that. I know who I am and I know what I stood for.

Good, bad or indifferent, I shall never have to look back and say, I regret what I did and who I was.

Chapter 9

THE AMERICAN COLLEGE OF LOUV AIN: 1857-2011

The death of the American College of Louvain came as all death comes, suddenly after 157 years of faithful service to the church in the United States. It started as a missionary preparatory seminary filled with European seminarians destined for the missions in America. The tide turned after WWI when the American bishops started to send seminarians to the American College to experience the great scholarship tradition of one of the oldest Catholic universities in the world (1425) filled with great learning. By the 1920's the American College was almost fully staffed with seminarians from all over the United States. It was closed during WWII for fear of the Germans but was reopened in 1952 with some 150 seminarians from many dioceses of the United States. In full disclosure, I personally did my three years of philosophy and four years of theology at the University which were the most rewarding years of my religious and intellectual life. As Fulton Sheen, a famous alumnus of the College once put it, "All that I am I owe to Louvain".

The University for the Americans was divided into the *schola minor* (theology classes for seminarians) held at the College and the major school located at the University proper which awarded superior degrees of theology (STB, LLD, PhD, Mag.). Philosophy was taught at the Institute Philosophique separate from the College. All the professors were priests and lecturers of theology were given at the College for us Americans. They were of the highest quality in each of their fields as evidenced by the fact that many of them became *periti* at Vatican n (1962-1965) and made great contributions to the documents which came forth from that Council. Such scholarship from Msg. Phillips wrote in great part the decree on the church *De Ecclesia* while other professors such as G. Thils had a hand on the documents on ecumenism and the spirituality of the laity as the People of God.

These professors were all renowned in their fields; L. Jansens (ethics); E. Massaux (New Testament); J. Coppens (Old Testament); R Van Roy (ecclesiastical history); Van Riet and Van Steenberg (philosophy and metaphysics); Donahue modern philosophy); G. Thils (spirituality and ecumenism). They are all dead now but their development, learning and humility had a profound effect on the students of the College. Their theology was so avant guard that when I returned to the United States, many priests and bishops thought I was a heretic with some of the things I had learned at Louvain. It was only Vatican II that finally came to the rescue for me. I remember them all as if it were just yesterday. I owe those men so much. It was they who challenged me theologically, intellectually, historically. Everything I ever learned in theology and philosophy I learned from them and it was they who set me off to a whole lifetime of learning and love of learning.

The one and perhaps the most important thing I learned from those scholars were their profound humility and approachability. Among the most prestigious personages in their fields of theological work, there were no airs of pomposity or arrogance about them. You could approach them at any time, with any question no matter how stupid. They never humiliated anyone. When in fact a stupid question was asked, they would always turn it as a brilliant insight by the questioner.

The regimen of the College was austere and disciplined. Early to rise at 5:15 with chapel and Mass at 6:00AM, breakfast at 7:00 with a half hour of recreation. Eight o'clock was for chores and cleaning followed by classes from 9:00 to 12:00. Chapel and prayer at

12:05 followed by lunch at 12:30 five days a week. Study from 1:00 to 4:00 except on Tuesdays, Thursdays and Sundays when we could walk around the city and the area to drink in the culture of art, architecture and other masterpieces of the Middle Ages perfectly preserved. On Sundays we biked to Malmedy and Bastogne where, when they found out we were Americans, no charge for lunch: "Votre argent n'est pas bon ici" (your money is not worth anything here) because of the memory of liberation by American troops in 1944. They never forgot and we were the beneficiaries of the toil and blood of other Americans. We were proud as peacocks with all the praise with which we were received. I wonder whether that would be true today.

All this followed the High Mass in the chapel on Sunday after which we were free to study, sleep, travel around the city or play games. The College owned a farm outside the city which we quickly turned into a baseball- football field in imitation of American sports time back home. The Belgians often gathered to watch these strange games of which they knew nothing. Their thing was soccer which had not yet become an American sport back home. I don't remember attending any of the Belgium soccer games in Louvain which at the time was of little interest to us.

The studies went from the opening of the University on October 1 to December 10 when the oral exams would be given. There were no written exams but orally before the professor who listened for hours on end. The professor would sit there, ask an open ended question and you took it up from there. He would blow cigar smoke in your face as you talked in Latin (they permitted some French). That's where I developed a love of cigars which I smoke to this day. I think it was an act of imitation. The exams were preceded by a whole week of study called "le block." This took place before the winter and the spring semester. The end of the year was celebrated at a great colloquial gathering of the whole University where the grades were publicly announced (summa cum laude, magna cum laude, cum laude and cum fructu). Yours truly (if I may brag a bit) was the only American to receive the *summa cum laude four years* in a row which the Europeans found surprising. They thought we Americans majored mostly in basketball and not in Greek and Hebrew. In any case, I for one am terribly grateful for the level of education we received at Louvain.

Having a knack for languages, I edited "notes" for the classes and sold them to all the students for a price. I made enough money each year to pay for my motorcycle (a BMW with auto shift- top of the line). I traveled all over Europe and the near east in that wonderful machine. I hated to part with it when I was ordained.

The really important times for me were vacation days which were long, fruitful and plentiful. There were two weeks at Christmas (which we mostly spent in Switzerland, Engleburg); two weeks at Easter when we biked to Holland, Luxemburg and northern France to see all the medieval cathedrals and three consecutive months during the summer. We were obliged to spend six weeks of that summertime in monasteries or parishes to learn the language and absorb the culture. My choices were Spain, France, Germany, the Holy Land and Italy. I learned some six languages and had one heck of a good time. I even worked at Qumran (Dead Sea scrolls) in Cave IV. We sifted through piles of bat excrement to find little pieces left over after they removed the large jars containing the major scrolls (I never found anything). The people at that time were very friendly and inquisitive. When I got to Qebec, France at the local parish (Normandy), I asked the pastor where was the "petit quin" (bathroom). He opened the door and said half seriously, "Voila, tute Ia France" ("behold all of France").

I spent four weeks at Lourdes as a Brancartier (stretcher bearer of the sick from the railroad station to the hospital Sant-Lazor). I arrived with great skepticism and left a true believer. What turned me around was the faith of the sick who came for a cure and ended up praying for others, "the other guy." I was placed in charge of an old, retired bishop from the Ukraine whom I would help get into the baths each day. He was a true saint and our conversations lasted into the night. One day as I helped him into the bath at Lourdes (there are about thirty such baths from the miraculous spring discovered by Bernadette at the direction of the Blessed Virgin Mary), he simply said, "Pierre, Je meur'' (Peter, I die. Thank you.) He died right there as I held him and closed his eyes in death. It was really a premonition of later days of the many soldiers in the 101st Airborne in Vietnam where as a chaplain I closed the eyes of many soldiers in the field. The difference was that the old bishop's death confirmed my faith whereas the death of all those soldiers whom I could not help, helped me lose my faith. But I still remember those vacation days with youthful joy as I grew in knowledge and in faith, the faith of others that strengthened my own faith. We really are mutually dependent in the faith. It was then that I understood the communion of saints.

I must tell you of the saintly bishop rector of the University of Louvain, Honore' Van Wayenberg who was one of the holiest and the most humble man I ever met. When we walked along the narrow streets of Louvain it was he who always walked in the street to let us pass. His background and history were just as impressive. In 1943 when he was made rector of the University, all the young men had departed the University. Honore' destroyed all their records so the Nazis would not find them. When imprisoned for not providing the names of the young Belgium students, they tortured him for days until he almost died but he never revealed a name. Frustrated, the Nazis sent him to the death camp at Maria Straat to work and die. A few days before his scheduled incineration, the camp was freed by American soldiers who began to feed and give medical care to the prisoners. Honore' was one of them. He often told us about this big black American sergeant who cried when he saw all those emaciated bodies. He carried Honore' to the medical facility, fed him like a baby and stayed with him for a week to make sure that he was well taken care of. Honore' loved Americans as God sends and he said his Mass each morning in the chapel of the American College. At each of our celebrations - Christmas, Easter, Fourth of July, graduation, there he was at the head table precisely because he loved Americans so much. He spoke perfect English. He never forgot the sergeant who was responsible for his loving America and Americans more than anyone I have ever met in life. I remember him always at prayer and with the greatest affection. He never mentioned the filet that Belgium awarded him its highest honor after the war.

Life at the College was strict and yet the College produced men of sterling loyalty to the church, with intelligence and dedication and with great learning and culture. It is difficult for me to understand why the American bishops closed the College in 2011. The quality of the priests produced by Louvain was of the greatest loyalty to the American church, most of whom remained in the priesthood all during the priest crisis of the 1960's and 1970's. Nor do I recall one Louvain priest who was caught up in the priest sexual scandal that almost ruined the Catholic Church in America. I do not recall so much as one Louvain priest who was ever caught up in that sexual scandal. This is a testament to the strength of faith and loyalty to the church of the priest graduates of the American College in Louvain. Even the few (myself included) who finally did leave the priesthood, most (I think) remained loyal Catholics who served the church as married laymen. Why they are not accepted back into the priesthood as a married priesthood when the Catholic church in America so desperately needs good, solid and intelligent priests is a question for which even today I have no answer. After my family was grown, I asked many times for re-installation to no avail. It seems that all can be forgiven in the church except sexual infidelity of former priests who marry and have raised solid families. I leave that mystery to God who must have a plan to draw from such inexplicable ways of men in the church called bishops.

This memorial was written as a testament to the greatness of the American College at Louvain in its 157 years of glorious history. It is a deep shame that the American bishops have seen it just to close the doors of such a loyal and sterling place that has done so much for the Catholic Church in the United States. It is a shame that some way could not be found to continue its existence. But like every death in the family, we mourn for the disappearance of the loved one and consign all the good the person or institution has done and it is a lot to the mercy of God and go on from there. RIP The American College Louvain April 22, 2011.

CHAPTER 10

THE YEARS OF SUMMER

Perhaps the most pleasant times I had in Europe were the summers and vacations. Europeans really believe in vacations and most countries have over six weeks of paid vacation time for their workers. In that they are far ahead of their American counterparts who think vacations are a luxury. On the contrary, they are vital to a well balanced life. European lives flow much more at ease and eating and vacations are part of the rhythm of life. It is no wonder that Europeans have about half the number of heart attacks and strokes that Americans have. They also believe in siestas from noon to four each afternoon so that helps a lot.

The American Colleges in Louvain and in Rome thoroughly believed in their European traditions. We got two weeks at Christmas, a week at Easter, a week at Pentecost and three full months during the summer. The vacation at Christmas was always taken in Switzerland at Grendewald, Engleberg or maybe Innsbruck in Austria. The winter there in the mountains was unbelievably cold and breathtakingly beautiful. But that in a moment.

When I arrived at Louvain in the fall of 1951 the American College there had just been reopened after WWII and conditions were stark. We were each given a room and some blankets. That was it. We brought our own linens and blankets. Up at 5;15, meditation and Mass at 5:45, breakfast at 6:30, study at 8:00-9:00, classes from 9 to noon, prayer noon to 12:30, lunch 12:30-1:00, recreation from 1:00 to 2:00, study 2;00-4:00, snack and walk at 4;00-5;00, study 5;00-7:00, supper 7;00-7:30, recreation 7;30-8:00, evening prayer 8;00-8:30, grand silence and lights out at 9:30. Pretty full day except that on Tuesdays and Thursdays and Sundays we could walk around the city from 1:00-4:00 pm and visit the ancient buildings, walls, churches by the hundreds. It took a year in Louvain to visit all the sites; two years in Rome hardly covered the superficial.

We were immediately sent to study philosophy at Institute Superieur de Philosophy with some of the great names in Thomastic philosophy who taught us. Everything was in French and I didn't understand a thing for months while I kept studying and studying French until it came out of my ears. But everyday it was the same thing; study, go to class where I understood only a word here and there. It was lonely, discouraging and depressing: no relatives, new friends understanding little and a land in which I was a stranger and where language was incomprehensible. Then all of a sudden in the middle of Ferdinand Van Steenbergen' s Ontology class, it dawned on me that I understood everything the professor was saying. I stood up in the middle of the great hall (there were about six hundred students composed of lay and cleric) and I yelled at the top of my voice: "Je comprends." "I understand." Everyone simply stopped including the professor and looked at me as if I were a complete fool who had just flipped his lid which of course, I was. The professor was gracious and said, "Congratulations. It's not often that a student understands the intricacies of ontology." Thereafter I was referred to as "Le Americain qui comprends"... the American who understood. Kind of like the Indians who named their children after the first thing they see in nature.

We all wore clerical garb - the long Sutan - but Americans always wore black pants underneath and the Europeans wore - well we never quite found out what they had underneath. Maybe their underwear but we Americans were not going to take any chances. If we had to run hard, we were ready. What if the wind blew it up, the whole world would know of our big, round, hairy ones. To hell with that noise.

For the first year we had no hot water or showers. During the war the College was used as a dorm for medical students - with no showers or baths. We couldn't figure out how they kept from stinking. Then it was clear. At the drug stores around the city, they had those huge dispensers of perfume which the Belgians liberally used as a substitute for showers and baths. Of course, that had been a tradition for thousands of years before indoor plumbing and baths proper in each home ever come to be (the indoor toilet was invented by Sir Thomas Crapper, an Englishman who invented the indoor toilet. Of course his name never survived his invention except in a slang sense.) But we did have indoor plumbing. Except that the toilet paper was not your soft Charmin but a very rough paper called "papier crepier" which we called crap paper. It felt more like sand paper to get into all the nooks and crannies or so it seemed. But a year later, the rector of the College put in real honest to goodness showers but with only cold water. And you have not felt cold water until you've been in Belgium where the sun comes out once a year on Bastille Day. A slight exaggeration but not much. If it's any day, it's raining. They were also fresh air fiends. They left their windows open no matter how cold or rainy it was outside. I think Belgians slept with their clothes on. In any case, they were a hardy lot. The College had heat from eight in the morning until four in the afternoon and that was it. For the rest of the time you wore a lot of sweaters, coats and blankets. Never bothered the Belgians even when it rained every day. It seldom snowed but it was cold and damp ten months a year and that cold wind went right to the bone. It was great for study and maybe that's why Belgium produced so many scholars. When it did warm up a bit in the summer, we were not there but scattered to the four winds. But the icy showers at the College were the worst of all and I never got used to them. I think my dick disappeared into my body every time I took one and I prayed that it would come out when I got warm enough. We weren't supposed to think of these things but a disappearing dick is a horrendous thought. My prayers must have been successful because I still have it to this day. Didn't use it then but I conserved it for future use.

I'd like all future priests to know that no matter how unused, it don't go away. "Use it or lose it" is a bunch of baloney. In any case, we lived for the vacations. We were free to go anywhere we wished in Europe, the Holy Land and the Near East, even Africa if we had the money. In those days the American dollar was supreme and for about four hundred dollars you could live for the entire summer. Not luxuriously, but you could have enough to go where you wished. My mother would send me two dollars each week in her letter to me written by my sister Victoria. News came from home once a week and like a dutiful son, I'd write my sister once a week as well. Technically, my mother still did not approve of my vocation but the money came anyway. But I had to have another source of income for my vacation. It came to me when I first started theology in 1954. I knew Latin very well and since all the classes were in Latin, I had an advantage. It took me a few weeks to get the hang of it from the professors but it wasn't new to me as was French. I caught on very well. The other Americans did not catch on so well. Some would borrow my notes and it finally came to me that I could copy the "notes de lecture" or "notandae in re theologica" (theological notes) and sell them to the rest of the classes. Why not? Americans are capitalists, right? There were nine courses (Old Testament, New Testament, Dogmatics, Patrology, Spiritual Theology, Architecture, Moral Theology, etc.). I would prepare the notes by comparing my notes with a few of the other students whom I knew to be intelligent and awake (ever try to stay awake in Latin?). I would take them to the professor for revision, have them typed on stenograph and print them off a steno machine. There were no computers in those days so each student was assigned a number of pages to be typed on a stencil master sheet from which I reprinted 100, 200 or 800 copies, etc. I sold about 450 sets ($1.00 a set or $8.00 for the whole nine... a discount.) I'd make about a thousand dollars net after I paid for the labor, typing and paper. They profited and I'd have enough money to travel.

First thing I bought was a 750cc DKW (succeeded later by BMW) - first motorcycle drive shaft in the whole world. Since there were no speed limits on the autobahns I once got it up to 195 mph which was fast even for Germany. As long as it was on the autobahn, cops never stopped you. I had a race with a Ferrari who tried to pass me going to Kohn. I simply let it all out. If he was going to beat me, it would simply be because he had a better machine than I. He didn't. I did. The speedometer only went to 200 kilometers and I went beyond it. To this day while I can't afford a Ferrari, I know I once beat a Ferrari's speed on the open road.

So I had one of the finest motorcycles in Europe bought by selling notes to fellow students because I had a knack for Latin and other languages. I also sucked up to the professors a lot because I genuinely admired them. In fact, I began to smoke cigars because I wanted to be exactly like them. They were the most brilliant theological minds in Europe and most of them were to become the thinking cartel of Vatican II in 1962-65. The thing that struck me above all was just how humble they were. Brilliant, most spoke and wrote anywhere from five to ten languages. In addition, they had a great sense of humor. They could even laugh at themselves. It has always struck me that truly great minds are humble not because they put on airs but because in knowing so much, they have only realized the great expanse of their ignorance. Now that is true learning contrary to what goes on elsewhere. Realizing this, they truly knew just how little they knew. Their humility, therefore, came from their great knowledge because it made them realize how ignorant they really were. I was in awe of them. When I contrast this with the arrogance and lack of proportion in American ecclesiastics and judges I have known, I simply marvel at the difference. My professors never asked for a thing except that we become as excited as they in the process of learning and growing into holiness. This was the dyptic at Louvain: seat of wisdom which came from great learning. They gave unstintingly of their time and effort at all times and they were never too busy to answer our questions and give us the value of their knowledge and insights. We even went to their homes and apartments with our questions. Everything I have ever become or can hope to be, I owe to my professors at Louvain and Rome. I shall never forget them as long as I live... men of honor, learning, humility, humor, perseverance and holiness. They were a gift from God.

All our examinations were oral and were given once a year in May. There was a week before exams - dead week - where we called le blocque - the block week or cram week. It sounded like block head. You kept what you didn't like and studied it last. We studied 8-10 hours each day.

All the professors smoked cigars, Dutch cigars (that's where I first learned to smoke cigars. Right to this day I associate smoking cigars with intelligence but not moral growth.) They would blow smoke in your face, give you the text in the original Greek or Hebrew, pick a passage and have you exegite or explain the passage - all in Latin. It was a harrowing experience. One Italian Franciscan friar from Naples would be before me (we went alphabetically) and I used to tell him that I was happy that he was in front of me because he made me look good. It was perfectly cruel and I was glad his robe was brown because I swear he crapped his pants. He hated me but was afraid to curse me because I knew Italian and I would report him. Not really because Americans weren't snitches - but he didn't know that. He would then have to beg for his supper, that is, eat his supper kneeling down until supper was over. I only had to do it once and I regret it to this day. But the meal was delicious, just that once.

Now that I have dated or seen much of the opposite sex, I have to tell you that Belgian women are exceedingly ugly. While Italian women grow bigger after age twenty five, Belgian women grow uglier. God forgive me, but it was absolutely true. In the whole five years I was there I never had a dirty thought about a Belgian woman. Never. I swear. Belgium is God's answer to concupiscence and it was the perfect place to have a seminary. No trouble with celibacy.

Many of us were terribly immature about anything and everything. We even had water fights with bags of water thrown strategically against and through the French windows which were part of all rooms of the College. One of my missiles missed and hit the Archbishop Rector some thirty feet below. Suffice it to say that he loved Americans because of his background and there wasn't a mean bone in his body. He laughed at what happened to the rector and I was called on the carpet immediately. Msgr. Thomas Maloney was stern but fair even if he didn't much like me. We never understood each other because he thought I was arrogant and prideful. Maybe he was right. When I graduated Summa Cum Laude in each year of theology, he never came to the awards banquet to hear my exquisite Ciceronian Latin acceptance speech (it always had to be in Latin.) Here I thought he would be proud but praise from my professors was enough.

Belgium is nominally Catholic only because most people there are baptized Catholic but fewer than five percent ever practice their faith. But they still celebrate the big religious feasts but mostly as secular feasts, much as we celebrate Christmas as mostly an orgy of splendor and luxury. The churches stand as great monuments to a former faith which today lies in ruins. Le Grand Guerre 14-18, for example, is celebrated every November 11. In that First World War the Belgians lost some 250,000 of their young men -

not a small number for so small a country of only eight million. Many of the older women were still wearing black shawls when I was there in the fifties. In France it was worse. They lost millions of their youth. Every November 11th, the Belgians honored their fathers, brothers, cousins and friends who died in that war. "In Flanders fields the poppies grow between the graves, row on row. .. " Those cemeteries are large and full. During the High Mass celebrated by the Rector Magnificus of the University, about 25 soldiers would come into the church and fire their weapons (blanks) during the Consecration of the Mass. The shots were so loud in the church that it always startled me as we knelt there amidst all the dignitaries of church and state. There was no separation of church and state in Belgium. It was very strange. Hardly any practiced the faith but all observed it. I Never met the mayor of Louvain or Rome. The only time I ever saw them was at that memorial Mass - even if they were mentally Communists or atheists. They would always be there to celebrate the commemoration of La Grande Guerre because the religious ceremony had become a secular one. Then we would solemnly progress to the cemetery, lay a wreath at the tomb of the unknown soldiers (there were many of them since so many were simply blown up beyond recognition by giant artillery shells) and then we would visit the tombs of former rectors, pupils and professors in a special section of the place. Somehow it was never morbid since we celebrated them as part of a larger family some of whom were alive while others were dead waiting the great day of the resurrection of the dead. Quite beautiful really. We would then break out the champagne and with real crystal glasses toast and salute those who had lived and preceded us in faith. We would have a few glasses of that champagne so that even if it was cold when we entered the cemetery we were quite warm when we left. Some of the professors were observed to be extra jovial after a few rounds.

But the practice raised my faith more than I can say. Its memory has never left me and even now I spend some time at a cemetery on Memorial and Armistice Day. I feel at home there because someday they will bring me there to rest among my relatives and friends and even with those I had never known while we all await the voice of the Son of Man who will summon us from the grave. And then we shall be one as God intended it from the beginning. So my theological training was not just from books but from the living faith of others, from the ancient faith of the Belgians which was there but still dormant.

As I said, Christmas Day was celebrated at the College but the next day, off we went to Switzerland and Austria for winter sports and recreation. It was glorious. I loved the evenings in the Gasthouse where we would drink beer, sing German songs, watch the beautiful women we could never have and go home to quilts made of down feathers which were so toasty warm that you needed no other heat. And with the thoughts of those beautiful maidens asleep on your mind. I longed to take one of those Jungfrau or frauleins home with me and just lay there with her. I cannot tell you how I longed for that. I would often go to sleep weeping that I had no woman to love and hold me, to tell me that I was the most important thing in her life. I think that was quite normal at age 17-24.

But the next day was always glorious. The sun always shone in the morning. The German nuns would prepare great breakfasts. Zwester Aguila took a shine to me from the start and always brought me the best prepared eggs and bacon no matter what time I'd come down to breakfast. She was always proper but I do remember the gleam in her eyes whenever she saw me. I never had a dirty thought about a nun before (but not after) and I never dreamt of making love to one until much later in life. It just didn't dawn on me that nuns were sexual beings who could long for a man as much as any man could long for a woman. How stupid and immature I was. Even though I was always kind and polite, looking back I should have shown greater gratitude and expressions of affection for her. She was human as I was human. But the spirituality of the day taught me not to go near "temptation" of the flesh and to avoid all forms of sensual and (God forbid) sexual expression to and for the other sex. What it really was fear of the other sex and nothing less? It was always risk but that is what freedom is all about. We were afraid to show the slightest sign of affection for fear that it would destroy our "vocation" to be celibate which we all hated in any case. Or at least did not want to become. It was not that I wanted to go to bed with Sister Aquila - not in the least. But I did want an exchange of authentic affection while recognizing its limits and dangers. We were not allowed to be honest, neither with ourselves nor with others. We should have been allowed to risk the whole emotional scene. If we survived, we survived but we would be forever true and authentic human beings with feelings and emotions and not the shriveled emotional creatures we were becoming. How could we become authentic and loving priests if we did not run the risk of emotional failure or success? The Church seemed to prefer emotionally dried up men and women more than authentic, true and emotionally whole men who confronted their humanity, struggled with it and finally could feel in their own depths what all other men and women did and could also feel. We would then be prepared for love, for relationship and for humanity.

I took some ski lessons in 1953 and thought I was hot stuff in only a week's time. That was my first mistake. I was to learn my lesson very soon. I arrived late one afternoon at the top of a rather difficult course overlooking Engleberg. Alone - and that was my second mistake. It was breathtakingly beautiful at dusk when the sun began to disappear over the tall mountain leaving a shadow of the great mountain Titless (not its English connotation) covering the whole village. Down I went - there was no one on the trail - weaving and bobbing just like in the movies. That was my third mistake. I was doing quite well until I hit one of the trail markers which had been previously broken and was now covered with snow. I went flying through the air and landed on my left leg. It was broken in two places along with my ankle which was also broken. The pain was excruciating as I laid there helpless, literally helpless. I crawled over to a ledge overlooking the town but still covering my back. Just below me was an expanse of downhill slope and with the full moon I could see for miles. I covered my leg with snow to quell the pain but I knew that unless help came fairly soon I would freeze to death. Literally. Or be attacked by wild wolves. In those mountains on a clear night, the temperature would drop down to thirty degrees below zero so I had to be found soon. I also knew that there were wild wolves in those mountains known to attack humans. With my back covered, I tried to stay awake. But it was very difficult. I kept on passing out because of the pain but I fought it for fear of the wolves. Maybe the sweat and heart from the pain actually saved my life. Then I saw three of what appeared to be wolves coming straight at me about two kilometers down. I prepared as best I could with a broken ski but I knew that if they were wolves, I was a dead man lying. But I wasn't going to go without a fight. As they came closer I could see that they were St. Bernard dogs coming to my rescue. They still had them in 1953. I was so glad to see them that I cried. They were a friendly lot licking me all over. And sure enough, under their neck, strapped to their bodies, was a packet filled with small bottles of the liqueur Kirsch and small ampoules of morphine which could be applied immediately to the wounds. I drank all the kirsch (three packets) and by the time the rescuers who were following the tracks of the dogs found us, we were all singing to the moon: the dogs with their howls (to attract the rescuers) and me in gladness that I had been found. It seems that when I did not show up for supper, Sister Aquila became worried (she knew that I wouldn't miss a meal!) and pulled the alarm which any adult Swiss could pull to summon immediately the rescue party from the volunteers in the town. The dogs were given a whiff of my clothing and off they went to find to whom it belonged. It was uncanny because they never ever lost a man or woman once the dogs were released.

My leg was set in the clinic and I was sent back to the inn to start recuperation right away. They didn't believe in long hospital stays. Sister Aquina took care of me like a small child, fed me, bathed me and washed my clothes. We became very close. It was the closest thing I had ever experienced of womanly love – even if I didn't know it at the time. I actually liked it and missed it terribly after I left. I called the rector and told him that I would be a week late. He didn't like it but I had the pleasure of being the honored guest of Engleberg for a whole week. No charge and the kindness of Sister Aquila was an addition to my life that while it did not change it, it finally began to make it grow in depth and yes, love. When I left we were both in tears. I held her tenderly and she kissed me gently on both cheeks and on my forehead as is the European custom. I wanted to speak but I could not. I think back now and it was then that I first loved a woman and here she was - a nun! Maybe that is why I could never admit this to myself after all these years until now. I was afraid to be honest with myself because I really was afraid of love. The next vacation was at

Easter when we would get a full week off at Easter Week. Since it was so short we would usually bike to Holland to see the beginning of the tulip season or we would go to the Rhineland and travel through the German wine country on a royal barge. The Germans were never as friendly as the French and Dutch. The first choice of Easter vacation was the cathedrals of Northern France: Amien, Lille, Notre Dame of Paris, Rouen and finally Chartres which has the most beautiful stained glass windows in the world. It took days to appreciate the beauty of those buildings as they were buildings of faith which were built 800-900 years ago and were still standing strong as the day they were made. They were made by generations of true believers - taking sometimes as long as two hundred years. A cathedral was built by the faith of whole generations. The thing that impressed me was that a statue on the porteil was as exquisitely made as a statue at the very pinnacle of the cathedral where no one would ever see it. Why? Because the cathedral was made by men of faith who made their artifacts for the glory of God and not for the glory of man. Since only God could see them, it was important to make what could not be seen by man but would be seen by God just as well as what would be seen by man below the doors and in the nave of the cathedral. That truly was an act of faith. "To those who have not seen but have believed."

In the evening we would choose a rectory or a monastery at which to spend the night. Invariably they would give us a bed for the evening and breakfast for the next morning - an unusual bed and breakfast site. They were intrigued that American seminarians would be traveling throughout Europe, on bicycles yet, and they would engage us in lively conversation. We sometimes had to prolong our stop by a day or so because they just wouldn't let us go. And when we did leave, the cures, nuns or monks would be there to load us down with food. The whole monastery at Orbec in Normandy providence of Calvados, turned out to see us off after we had stayed there a whole week. They were Trappists so there was no talking during the day. Only between 7:00 and 8:00 at night would they talk - and they would get in, in one hour, what it would take the rest of us a whole day to say. While we were there, we worked for our room and board along with the rest of the monks. The food was plain but delicious. It is hard work mixed with hunger that makes any bread delicious. I'll never forget the taste of their freshly baked bread and their wonderful lentil soup. After working in the fields you would eat a whole loaf and you didn't mind not talking - you were too busy eating. All you wanted. The one thing I always noticed in these monasteries was the joy, the laughter, the peace and holiness of the place. You could feel it when you entered the monastery. No long faces they or morose cadavers. The monks were there not only because they wanted to be there; but also because they were doing the work of the Lord by praying and working. Nothing else could justify their existence. Their joy was always contagious.

They would always ask us to give the guest homily at Mass. I always repeated the story of the prodigal son who went afar off to spend and dissipate his fortune only to repent of what he had done before returning to his father's house. The monks made me feel how much I was loved when I traveled abroad and I could return to my Father's house after vacation renewed in spirit to continue my studies toward the priesthood, sinful as I was. I was received as gift by these monks. I really meant it and the monks were always terribly glad that they had some small part in my formation. I often think these days how much I must have disappointed them when I had so much promise for the Church in my future. They all thought that by the way I preached that I was destined to do great things in the Church. I'm glad that they are all gone to God now. Little did they know that in the end I would amount to nothing. I'm glad that today most of them are dead so as not to grieve. I do not regret my leaving the ministry - it was something that had to be. But it is quite another thing to hurt all those who had so much confidence in you and helped you along the way. It has always been and it will always be a thorn in my side with which I shall always have to live.

The real exciting part of vacation was the three months of July, August, and September when we could go wherever our fancy dictated. The only thing required of us was that we go to one country; learn the language, customs and practices after which we could travel wherever we pleased for the second six weeks just as at Easter and Christmas. The first summer I spent in France, the second in Spain, the third in Germany, the fourth in the Holy Land, the fifth in Italy and the sixth was spent all over. Each of those summers were memorable and it would take another book to narrate it all. St. Augustine used to say that one who has not traveled is like one who has opened only the first page of a book.

My trip to the Holy Land was the greatest of all. By motorcycle I passed through Trieste through what was then Yugoslavia, over the Bosphurus, through Turkey down through Lebanon and into Israel proper. There was a relative peace then and there were no Islamic fundamentalists. At the time I simply did not realize how dangerous it was for an American to travel alone but it was great fun for me. The Dalmatian Coast was so beautiful for such a long distance that it was actually difficult to get through the country. The only thing you wanted to do was lay on the beach. You wanted to stop frequently so that you could take in the utter beauty of it all. The people were something else. They were not friendly and you had to make sure exactly where you were before you could tell them of your religious affiliation. The best was to stick to national identity and skip religion. A wrong answer could get you into a lot of trouble. Even then I knew that in the future there would be great difficulties ahead for that country. The people had been divided religiously for hundreds of years and it would not heal soon. Catholics, Orthodox and Muslims lived in comparative peace because Tito would not permit otherwise. He imposed peace: "live in peace or die" should have been his motto. I spent most of my evenings under the open sky because law and order was still good and it saved me a lot of money in lodging. The trip took me all of seven days of hard riding. The great difficulty was finding enough fuel along the way. Although I got 60 mpg, the cycle only held five gallons with an extra five gallons in my emergency can strapped on the back. You were a self contained unit or you were fast out of luck. If anything happened to the cycle you were simply dead, stuck in the middle of technological nowhere. In places like Turkey you could go some 250 miles without encountering a gas station. I had about 500 miles contained in my unit so I felt fairly safe. But every time I came upon a station I would make sure that I loaded up again. I never had to worry about money exchange because in those days they all took American dollars. The dollar was universal and instantly recognizable and acceptable even by the lowliest peasant at any restaurant or gas station. So that was a great help. You had to be careful not to show just how much money you had for fear of thieves. That is why you had to keep on going.

The only time I felt threatened was once outside of Ankara when I stopped for gas. For some reason, a cross I wore around my neck became exposed. Some Muslims saw it and immediately reported me to the local constable who proceeded to warn me about exposing Christian symbols. I protested that Turkey was supposed to be a tolerant state but I rapidly found out that such was not the case, at least not in the backwoods. The constable warned me to get on my way or he would not be responsible for my health and welfare. I took off like a bat out of hell and from that day, I kept my cross to myself. I never dared tell anyone who I was or where I was going. "I'm a philosophy student" was close enough to be truth. Or I was only a "tourist" sightseeing. I did have my first lesson in Muslim intolerance which I would never forget. There wasn't much of it in stark contrast to the rest of Europe.

After eight days I arrived in Jerusalem which in 1956 was still a divided city between Jordan and Israel. This would cause me difficulty since you could not go back and forth as you could in any normal border crossing. You could enter Israel from Lebanon but not elsewhere. You could exit Israel into Jordan but not vice versa. Most of the holy places were in Jordan and after a few days in Israel I crossed over in to East Jerusalem and Jordan under watchful eyes of Israeli and Jordanian police. I stayed at the Dominican Friary known as the Ecole Biblique - a biblical school which was then in charge of the excavation of Qum Ran or the caves at the Dead Sea which gave us the Dead Sea Scrolls. They had a huge, air conditioned room where they piled small bits and pieces of scrolls they found in the various caves (there were four). Their task was to try and put them together like a giant jig saw puzzle. The place was supported by the Dominican Order, private funds and university grants which were very interested in reconstructing the scrolls. Jewish scholars were not allowed by the Jordanian authorities to cross over to work on the texts. What many of them would do (because many had dual citizenship) is travel to New York, have their U.S. passport stamped and come into Amman as American tourists. Everyone winked and nodded but it was a known secret. Then they proceeded onto East Jerusalem where they would work alongside of a whole international equipe of scholars from all over the world. When it was time to go home, they would do so via New York. It was exciting. To even qualify you had to know Hebrew, Aramaic, Babylonian and preferably some knowledge of Arabic, Sanskrit, Cuneiform and other ancient, non spoken languages. We simply do not know how any of the ancient languages sound because no one speaks them any longer. But you had to have some knowledge of them because they are all related to the ancient languages used formerly at Qum Ran (Dead Sea). Father Pierre Benoit, the head of the excavation team as well as Superior of the Dominican monks at the Ecole Biblique took a shine to me right away. He let me do a little work at the caves. He liked Americans because of their refreshing attitude toward mostly everything. We were bubbling and anxious to learn with no airs of pretentiousness. He liked our simplicity, openness and anxiety to know and to learn. So he put me on an excavation team working on Cave IV. There was a very long ladder to climb to get into the cave. The temperature exceeded 120 degrees and it was stifling. You could not work in the caves for more than an hour at a time. You had to be careful to take salt pills every two hours and drink a quart of water each hour. That may sound like a lot but you would evaporate that much water from the body. The humidity around the Dead Sea is very low - less than one percent so that water intake was crucial. You wouldn't even know it when all of a sudden you would keel over dehydrated and unless you received medical treatment quickly, you could be seriously and permanently injured. So they would blow a whistle every two hours to remind us to take our pills and drink two quarts of water. That was an absolute rule which was neglected at your own peril.

The work was not very exciting. I mean, how would you like to sift a pile of bat shit from morning to dusk to see if you could find tiny fragments of manuscripts which would then be put into that big room in East Jerusalem and find a place for it in the big jig saw puzzle? That's because for almost 2000 years the only visitors to the caves were bats who came in through a hole which ultimately led to their discovery by a Bedouin shepherd boy. In over six weeks of sifting I never found so much as a morsel. Every once in a while a yell of joy would go up signaling that a piece had been found and we would all look at it through glasses and simply be amazed that in such a climate texts could be conserved for centuries and centuries. The texts of Scripture found at Qum Ran predated by some 1000 years earlier than our conserved texts from the 9th century AD. Both sets of texts were identical so that textual criticism was the same even if you could jump back over 1000 years in textual history. Amazing and faithful were the scribes who reproduced them century after century. The reason is that when a text is old, it is not conserved by Jewish rabbis but burned.

Visits to other holy places were frequent on days off. Christians through the centuries had killed each other as well as Muslims to take control of these places. It was a continuing scandal. So much so that when I was there all the holy places were controlled and administered by the Muslims to keep the Christians from killing each other. But I must say that their administration of the holy places was fair for all groups - except Jews, of course. It seemed strange to visit Bethlehem in August and hear the Mormon Tabernacle Choir singing Christmas carols in the Church of the Nativity around the great star on the marble floor in an edifice which went back to the Emperor Constantine and his mother Helena about 330-340. On the silver star was written the motto: Hic de virgine Maria

Verbum Dei nacitur et homo factus est" ("here from the Virgin Mary was born the word of God who became man.") It was thrilling then as it is today to recall it. The place may not have been exact - we do not know exactly where Christ was born - only that he was born and that is enough.

While all these places mean nothing to the real Christian - all places have now been created sacred by and through the resurrection of Jesus Christ from among the dead still, it was thrilling to visit and see them as they were at the time of Christ. Nothing much has changed. Of course we do not know whether these were the exact places but it was certainly around there that those sacred events occurred. There are a few memories in our lives which never really fade and they simply grow richer as your life goes on: sacred events in your life such as marriage, the birth of your children, grievous deaths, professional success, the making of good friends. The visit to the Holy Land was one of those memories which have never faded from my memory and which I ruminate on from time to time. It is unique and there is nothing quite like it. I must admit that it has strengthened my faith in every respect. I miss the simplicity of great men like Father Benoit, O.P. whose humility and learning is now in such contrast to the little men who think so much of themselves because they occupy positions of authority: "You know how the powerful of this world lord it over others. Not so you. The greatest among you will be he who serves the rest." That passage of Scripture is so profoundly true and the longer I live the truer I see that in my life. And I am so thankful that God has given me the inestimable grace to meet such men in my life so that I would never again be fooled by the pomposity and arrogance of those who exercise power – whether in the Church or the state makes no difference since the arrogance is the same and the human drive to power is also the same. To keep oneself servant while one is in power is a very difficult task indeed. A few have managed it. Not many. I have been free once and for all from the absurd notion that "making it" is to lord it over others by power. Rather, the truly great person is one who exercises humility and who really loves and is loving, who serves others as proof of his love. Words without action is, well, bullshit. Or in the case of the Holy Land, camel shit.

Another of my favorite summers was 1955 when I spent almost the whole time in Lourdes, France. I had always been skeptical about miracles and the extraordinary because I considered too many people caught up in the marvelous and the extraordinary without paying too much attention to the essentials of faith and to the ordinary miracles of life itself.

I came to Lourdes in July, 1955 highly skeptical of what went on there as befits a highly intelligent theological student who thought he knew so much but who in reality knew so very little. I was to find out just how very little I really knew. I stayed a few miles out of town on the side of a mountain overlooking the valley where I slept in a sleeping bag even when it rained. It was extraordinarily beautiful. The Pyrenees came down as if to cradle the town of Lourdes and each morning the mist would rise from the Gave de Pau River which skirted the northern part of the town. The Masabielle (the old garbage dump where the Virgin Mary appeared to Bernadette Subirou in February, 1858) was situated just above the river in one of those non-descript niches along the eastern side of the river. There in February, 1858, a simple peasant girl claimed she had seen a beautiful lady in the rocks of the Masabielle with roses on her feet wearing a blue girdle and who smiled at her. She was so simple that when she asked the Lady what her name was she did not understand when the Lady told her: "I am the Immaculate Conception" - a title not even the local pastor even understood. Bernadette came there some dozen times and recited the rosary. The religious message of the lady as given to Bernadette was orthodox but plain: pray for sinners, do penance for the world, return to the teachings of Jesus, pray for each other. Nothing terribly unusual or revolutionary.

The same message can be read by opening any passage of the New Testament and yet, pilgrims came there each year in the millions with the most diverse illnesses and sicknesses. No where on earth, neither Jerusalem or Rome or Mecca, do more pilgrims come than to Lourdes, France. Some eight million a year. No color changing rosaries, no dancing suns, no extraordinary events. Only a simple Gospel message which goes to its authenticity.

I came highly skeptical, full of hard theology and theory and while I did not exclude the possibility of divine intervention - who are we to question the Creator of the universe - I- was skeptical because pilgrims are like consumers, I thought: they expected good things at a cheap price, thinking of no one but themselves. Or as Karl Barth put it, we all seek cheap faith without the cross. That was surely unauthentic faith. I had enough faith to know that Christian faith was nothing of the sort. And it most assuredly was not cheap. Faith is surrender to God in his divine and unique Son come to earth to teach, to suffer, to die, to rise for our love and salvation. Everything was Christocentric, everything was Jesus, the Son of God who is the visible revelation of God among us who conquered death and gave us new life in his glorious resurrection. I held that tightly in my heart in spite of the arrogance and pride with which I came to Lourdes. I thought myself superior to those simple pilgrims who came only for magical cures. The vast majority of them would go home, disappointed and further broken in their faith. At least, that is what I thought when

I first came. Which, I thought, they richly deserved. How could I have been so judgmental and obtuse is beyond me even fifty years after those fateful events in my life. I still remember that attitude with sorrow and shame. And I was to learn a very simple lesson of my faith.

The journey from the railroad station to the hospital Saint Lazare (one of three hospitals) was a direct route. Each brancardier (stretcher bearer) was assigned by pairs to a stretcher which we carried or a wheel chair which we pushed to the hospital. The more seriously ill pilgrims were taken by ambulance. We checked to see whether each patient had his medical charts in case of re-examination by an equip (small group) of doctors at the hospital. Each patient was examined de novo by the doctors at the hospital, X-rays taken and finger prints clearly marked so there would be no doubt if ever a patient claimed a miracle at the pools. No one was obligated to go through this vigorous procedure but no miracle could be authenticated without it. We simply do not know the extent of the miracles at Lourdes.

The doctors at the hospital were truly ecumenical. Any doctor could qualify for staff privilege if he or she could produce proof of a medical degree and licensure from a recognized jurisdiction or medical profession. There were Catholics, Protestants, Buddhists, Islamics, Jews, atheists, agnostics - you name the country or religion and there were representative doctors. The hospital made no distinctions of race, color, creed, religion or national origins and all were freely welcomed.

If a patient claimed a miracle, the same doctors re-examined him/her de novo and made a preliminary medical report by comparing the before and after. Their only report was this "cure" could or could not be explained by any known medical procedure, operation or drug. That was all they could conclude to because that was the limit of their proper expertise. Any further investigation had to be done by Church officials who examined the evidence. Only then could an authentic miracle be proclaimed by the Church because that was her proper expertise. As of 1955, only 66 miracles were so proclaimed. This does not mean that there were no others; only that the others were never authenticated by the Church. There are today at Lourdes archives meticulously kept by Church authority containing all the documents of these miracles which can be examined by anyone during the day at reasonable hours. Notes could be taken but nothing removed. I suppose that today they have Xerox and computers.

I made my own informal study of these miracles and I found a few which were truly astounding. In 1926 an eleven year old girl was brought to Lourdes by her parents. The girl had no eyes, that is, her sockets were empty from her birth. It was an abnormality of birth. She had X-rays, finger prints, previous medical history and a re-confirmation of the whole condition by a medical equip from the hospital. She entered the "bains" (baths from the spring dug originally by Bernadette Subirou at the direction of her lady vision,) bathed and came out with two perfectly 20/20 vision eyes. She was then re-examined by the same equip of medical doctors who then signed the medical report: simply put, there was no known medical procedure in 1926 which could explain this phenomenon: same girl, no eyes before and one hour later, two healthy eyes with 20/20 vision. The Church authorities accepted this as an authentic miracle from God. There were other miracles as well catalogued in the archives of Lourdes. I was in a state of deep wonder and amazement.

This was impressive. But, to me, not as impressive as the faith of all those sick pilgrims who came by the tens of thousands. Each, seemingly, came for a cure (who could blame them?) and bathed in the baths. But they experienced no visible cure - just an internal one. After a few days they were no longer praying for themselves but for each other, pour les autres. Almost overnight they had learned to accept their pain and suffering with a quiet and serene calm and they had found peace. This was an amazing turn around: from wimps to faith and prayer for each other! Even though they had the same disease, paralysis or suffering they came to Lourdes with, they left with great faith and peace, knowing that their lives had meaning in Christ and they were changed forever. They had become people of faith. The Gospel had been fulfilled for and in them. In their own way, they became witnesses of faith. I was humbled.

This then was the true miracle of Lourdes. Millions who come to Lourdes depart with the same ailments. But they depart different people from the ones they were when they arrived. They departed as people of faith whose love was manifested in their lives and prayers, shared with their fellow sufferers. I never heard a complaint and I know just how much some of them suffered. They were grateful beyond words for the small efforts I put out for them. They made me weep with the deepest emotion at their goodness. They asked me to pray for them when I felt I was in the presence of men and women of true faith and sanctity. They still inspire me in memory of all those blessed days.

You guessed it I became no longer a skeptic and arrogant theologian but a humble believer in Our Lady of Lourdes who has conquered my pride and arrogance by means of these simple sufferers of faith. The experience changed my life forever because the miracle of Lourdes had managed to work its wonder on me as well, unworthy as I was when I came, skeptically and arrogantly to Lourdes. I am grateful for this experience beyond words. It was clearly the hand of God working on me through his courageous and faithful sick servants whom I had come to help but who, in the end, helped me.

In reality, it was I who was sick from a lack of faith and it was the sick by their faith and love who helped heal my ailing and starving soul. I shall always be grateful to them by the grace of Jesus through Our Lady of Lourdes. I am full of thanks.

To more secular concerns, one Easter in 1957 an upperclassman and I wanted to go south to the Riviera just to get warm for a few days away from the Belgian winter and cold. It took us two days to get there and two days to return but as events would have it really was worth it. As I have already said, there was only a week at Easter. But when we stopped at Monaco and as luck would have it, we were greeted by an American priest who invited us to stay in the guest quarters of the Palace. He was the Prince's private chaplain and the world wide marriage of Prince Rainier with actress Grace Kelly was about to take place in a few days. He invited us to stay for the ceremony and to help him as acolytes at the marriage. It was phenomenal: royalty from all over the world, dignitaries, the Archbishop of Marseilles and the Cardinal from Paris were all at the wedding. I thought Grace Kelly was extraordinarily beautiful but then I wasn't supposed to notice such things. Word of all this got back to my parents via my letters and postcards and it made headlines in the Buffalo Evening News. My superiors did not much appreciate the publicity but it created a little excitement in an otherwise dull year. In fact, the Chaplain gave us each five hundred dollars in gambling chips which we proceeded to lose in the casinos of Monaco in a matter of hours. I loved the one arm bandits. Of course, this was nothing next to the loss of hundreds of millions by Arab sheiks who would come each week without fail in their private jets to the airport at Monaco especially built for them. Later while the rest of Europe shivered from lack of oil in 1973, Monaco always had more than adequate supplies of oil and gasoline. No one could figure out where they got the gas from but you would know if you knew about the millions which Monaco earned from these sheiks. Money talks and that is exactly what were going on in Monaco during those shortage years.

In any case it was an exciting Easter and the food and accommodations were terrific. I'll never forget a great pool under the balcony of my room (this was really high class stuff.) I came out that first morning, looked down and saw one of the most beautiful red heads I had ever seen in my whole life. She had on a bikini which I had seen only on the ship coming over to Europe and - get this - she was topless like many of the French women who bathed on the beaches of the Riviera. Her breasts were virginal, not large but with very large nipples which, well, just stuck out. My eyes must have bulged out of my head. It seems I must have stared for a long time, to the point of embarrassment when she finally saw me looking at her. Instead of becoming indignant, she smiled the most beautiful smile I had ever seen in my life. She wore a blue bathing bottom- what little there was of it - and those beautiful breasts! I saw her later at the wedding, the daughter of a famous surgeon from Paris. After the wedding Mass at the open reception I hoped against hope she would come over to me, take me in her arms and tell me that she loved me so I could become properly indignant. She did single me out and we talked for hours. Her eyes were almost as green as the Riviera itself. She was disappointed when I told her that I was a candidate for the priesthood. Hell, what I should have done is simply take her and damn the torpedoes. My virginity would have gone but at least I would know what I was giving up. To this day I wonder whatever happened to her and whether I made the right choice in not following up on what she clearly invited me to have. I didn't because I was afraid of women, beautiful women in particular, for fear of not becoming a priest. But if it was fear that led me to such a vocation, was it really a vocation; was it anything at all if I did not want to risk my freedom for it? I shall never know the answer and I regret it greatly. I wish now I had succumbed to temptation that night. Not just because she was breathtakingly beautiful and serious before any dream that I had; but because I was unwilling to risk in freedom what I so jealously guarded with my life. I should have put it to the test or in the end it would amount to nothing. I found this out only much later in life.

In every respect - except for my relationship with women which I was afraid to risk and to test - the vacations were one of the most determining factors of my early life. I was free and on my own. This required discipline and determination to persevere- no matter how I longed to do otherwise. I had to really manage my money and even find my own way to live on my own for three months every year. I had to meet new people, make new friends, learn new languages and customs. The people I met from all sectors of different societies taught me differences, goodness, humility, brilliance in endeavor and self gift. Those were invaluable lessons in my life which I could never learn from books but only from life. They all made me a better and disciplined person and a more human person. I only wish now later in life, there was some way I could thank each and every one of them: the cures, the monks, the professors, the beautiful women, common ordinary people exercising gratuitous acts of kindness - all taught me something unique but very valuable in my life. All these insights and virtues would stand me in good stead later in life. I shall never forget them nor cease being grateful to them all.

CHAPTER 11

Honore Van Weyenberg

After Schindler's List, a hundred stories, truthful stories, are being told about other singular heroes during the Nazi occupation of Europe. These heroes are not well known except to a precious few close friends and colleagues. Heroes seldom tell their own stories (if they are alive) but it is good to re-tell them for the encouragement and edification of those of us who are overwhelmed by the preoccupations of daily life and who seem to experience everything except edification and heroism. Our heroes are mostly vacuous and superficial: sports figures, movie stars, once in a while a statesman. Heroes are few but we should know who they are.

History is replete with the heroic stories of ordinary men and women from all walks of life. Great evil silences the many out of fear and retribution if not for themselves, then for their family and those whom they love. But great evil also gives rise to a species of human beings who forget themselves and dedicate themselves to the protection of others at great cost to themselves. Few of us understand why they appear in history but when they do, we ought to know their stories in order to hand them on to our children as the patrimony of good to strengthen them and give them moral guidance. Stories of good men and women must be told and retold. The Roman poet Virgil used to say that the human race is saved by a few and those few are testimony and witnesses that good is finally stronger than evil and that the last word is not given to the monstrous people of history but to the chosen few who edify and strengthen us by their courage in the face of great evil. They are not necessarily those who have killed other men as states celebrate the fallen in their cause. Most of them have refused to kill. Even their oppressors.

Honore' Van Weyenberg was a Belgian cleric who was ordained just after the great war of 1914-18. It was a great war for the French and Belgians because they lost almost a quarter of their young men in battle. He was ordained a cleric in 1920 and served in various posts and positions before his appointment as rector of the oldest on- going Catholic University in the world (1425). He could speak ten languages fluently. His organizational talents did not go unrecognized by the Cardinal Archbishop of Malines and so Honore' rose quickly in the ranks of ecclesiastical positions.

The ancient Catholic University of Louvain is the oldest university going back uninterrupted to 1425 by Pope Martin V. Some of the greatest scholars of the medieval period taught there: Erasmus of Rotterdam, theologians such as Bellermine and Dionetus, philosophers as Justus Lipse and Mercier and a host of others. Louvain is unexcelled in Catholic scholarship. Its student body represents practically every nation in the world but mostly from Belgium and Holland (Flemish and Wallons as they are called today).

The University was a thriving university during the great war and its former library, one of the largest in Europe, was maliciously put to the torch during the first German occupation in 1917. It was an event filled with great bitterness for the Belgians. At the Treaty of Versailles in 1919, reparations were extracted from the Germans for its rebuilding and a toll of 25,000 books each year was to be delivered to the university for the next 50 years. In addition, large donations for reconstruction come from America since Cardinal Mercier, Archbishop of Malines, had become an international hero for his resistance to the Germans during occupation. The Cardinal had been imprisoned and tortured for his non-cooperation which placed him among the authentic heroes of that war. Mercier was honored by Americans in 1922, being the only Catholic Cardinal in history to address a joint session of Congress. When the library was rebuilt in 1931, the Belgian government tried to put an inscription over the library entrance: Fuore Tutonica Destituta: Generositate Americana restituta (destroyed by Teutonic ferocity but rebuilt by American generosity). The Cardinal adamantly refused the inscription because he believed the time for reconciliation had come even for hated enemies. The crisis did not last long, so great was the stature of Mercier.

Honore' was himself appointed Rector Magnificus of the University in 1936 in recognition of his scholarship and organizational abilities and held the post until 1962 when he died. Up to the point of his appointment, he had been an able cleric who ran a tight ship and ruled with aplomb. In fact, he recognized very soon in his tenure that the Germans would attack the Netherlands and Belgium soon after the invasion of Russia in 1939. Knowing the vengeance of the Germans who had been humiliated at Versailles, he ordered most of the books from the library transferred to the American college which had no prospect of war with Germany at the time. He knew that placing the books there would protect them from any German retribution because the American immunity. Sure enough, when the Germans invaded the low countries in 1940, the first German attack on Belgium was Stuka dive bombers which reduced the library to rubble. It was their way of retribution for the humiliation of forced reparations after WWI. They could not touch the books during the early occupation because they were on American property. It was a time saving measure since after the declaration of war by the U.S. on Japan and Germany on December 8, 1941, the Germans came and took the books anyway. There was nothing Honore' could do to talk the Germans out of removing books which they were going to burn.

But the real problem lay with the Nazi SS who came to see him in March, 1940. The University had not opened that semester because of the real danger of war. After Germany invaded Poland and then Russia (1939), it was only a matter of time before war would come to the low lands. This happened in early 1940. Because the young men were not attending classes at the University, it was difficult for the German authorities to know where they were and what intellectual qualifications they had. Even in 1940, the Germans knew that the war would be long and difficult - particularly on the Eastern front. As it turned out, the Germans suspected more than they knew because some *50* divisions were thrown into the war with Russia. There was therefore a great need for men to work in German defense industries and other public works for which Germany was short of cheap manpower. The easiest, most economical way for the Germans to keep up with the great demand of defense and public works would be to indenture workers from the countries they came to occupy. It was in Hitler's master plan from the beginning to impose on each occupied country a quota of men to fill for shipment back to Germany for such work. In addition, there was the "traditional" Nazi roundup of Jews for "repatriation" to what amounted to concentration camps. All the Belgians knew the whereabouts of their young men as well as the Jews in their midst. Along with Denmark and the Netherlands, Belgium hid the most Jews during World War II and so the Nazis were particularly brutal in their discovery methods in Belgium.

Their favorite targets of course were universities, colleges, gymnasiums and other private places of learning for young men 15 and above (who were all subject to deportation). The Nazis fanned out over the whole country to fill their quotas. They came to the Rector in March, 1940 and asked him for a list of all the students of the University with addresses and academic qualifications. These were the days of before computers so the names had to be meticulously typed and reproduced from master copies kept under direct supervision of the Rector. Knowing full well what was coming after the invasion of Belgium and its defeat and surrender by King Leopold, Honore' simply burned all the records so there would be no chance of discovery by the Nazi authorities. But having almost a photographic mind, Honore' could reconstruct those names from a multitude of other files which he had at his disposal. But it could not be done by one unfamiliar with University rules and references. So it was imperative that Honore' do it himself personally. The result was that without him, the Nazis could never find these young men.

The Rector's refusal was polite but absolute. He had no authority to release the names and their academic history to people who would use that information to harm them. He would not be an instrument of deportation to slave labor for Hitler's Wehrmacht. To do otherwise would be to betray the students, the University, the Church and his own conscience - something he was unwilling to do. The Nazis gave his 24 hours to consult with other officials, particularly the Cardinal Archbishop of Malines. When he would not even do that ("There is nothing over which to consult. It is against God's law and my conscience. I have consulted with a higher power and all other votes do not count.") He had a dry sense of humor which of course passed the Nazis by. They never smiled or laughed because they took their work very seriously. How else would a universal Third Reich be established except by very serious men with no sense of humor.

He was arrested on March 18, 1940 and taken to Central Nazi headquarters in Brussels some 25 miles away. There again he was interrogated but this time with more persuasive "methods."

These methods were the usual: electric currents to genitalia, beatings, shock therapy, lack of sleep, purch ties, etc. They also tried Sodium Penatole but this was essentially useless even under the serum since Honore' would only give them the contributing documents but it was Honore himself who had to creatively put them together to produce the results. So without a free Honore' to combine the documents creatively, the Penatole was useless. The torture and interrogation went on for six months. He was kept without proper food, medication and toilet facilities. He was not allowed to wash or bathe. His cell was 10 x 5 with a cot and a bucket as a toilet. He was fed once a day with thin soup, a few potatoes and two slices of bread. No sheets for a urinated mattress and he was allowed a bucket of foul smelling water with which to drink and bath as best he could. He lost over 35 pounds and some of the open wounds from the beatings had become infected and full of puss. In short, he was humiliated beyond description.

Even the Nazis had to have some form of public trial since the Cardinal of Malines and the Papal Nuncio to Belgium had loudly protested the treatment of this distinguished clergyman. The Nazis could put Honore' on trial very easily since he would admit his guilt without hesitation. He would be a hero to the Belgians but a criminal under occupational law. The Nazis meticulously recorded everything and that is the reason why we have excellent records about the torture and imprisonment of Honore' while in Bruxelles.

It was common knowledge among the prisoners in the same cell clock with Honore' that he never complained about anything. He asked for nothing but he did try and intercede for food and some decent medical treatment for his fellow prisoners. The cruelty of the Nazis was such that when he asked for others, it would be granted but never for him. Honore' never uttered a word of complaint but was cheerful for the other men in the cell block. He even performed as many religious rituals as possible to console the other prisoners. He heard their confessions and consoled them. He was considered a holy person even amidst, or more properly, because of the filth and stench of a Nazi prison.

A month before trial, he was transferred to a low security prison where the food was plentiful, clothes were clean and he received medical attention for his festering wounds. No evidence of maltreatment would be allowed to be seen by the outside world since the Nazis wanted to make a showcase example of the Monsignor (while in prison, the Pope had elevated him to the rank of Protonotary Apostolic -- a rank just below that of Bishop as a sign of his disapproval of Honore's treatment -- a kind of promotion in absentia).

In October, 1940, Honore' was brought up on charges of not cooperating with the occupational authorities. To everyone's surprise and against the advice of counsel, he was allowed to plead guilty on condition that he make no statement for public consumption. He had written a statement and managed to give it to his lawyer. But before he did so, he made his counsel promise that the message would be given only to the Archbishop of Malines because otherwise his lawyer and his family would be arrested by the Nazis. He even thought of his counsel who was willing to risk arrest and perhaps even death. Honore' would have none of it and so the statement was never made known until after the war. It was however delivered to the Archbishop and is conserved for us in the archives of the Archdiocese:

Monsignor,

> I am fine. God has granted me the grace thus far to be loyal to my students and to Holy Church. You know how weak I am. What God holds in store for me is within is mystery. I only ask mercy and grace to do his most holy will and that I am faithful until the end. I ask you not to intervene for me again as this may endanger the person of his Eminence whose people need him in this hour time of need. All who know you will marvel at your strength and holiness. I ask only a

small remembrance before the holy altar when you offer the Holy Sacrifice. May the Holy Spirit of Christ guide us in his way to do truth and holiness. May he grant us both the strength to persevere in his holy grace to the end. I remain your most obedient servant.

Honore' Van Weyenberg

The trial was public and short. Honore was asked only a few questions before the three German military judges found him guilty of refusal to cooperate with the German authorities of occupation. He was sentenced to 10 years at hard labor at Bergen Belsen. He was allowed no public statement. He was personally driven to the camp by the Gestapo.

Honore' arrived in Bergen Belsen on January 1, 1942. He was there for two years before being transferred to the death camp at Auschwitz. Bergen Belsen was also a death camp but only for Jews. The camp was close to factories which used slave labor. Honore' was assigned to the heaviest work since he was considered an admitted enemy of the Third Reich who refused to share valuable information with Nazi authorities. To show their utter disdain for him, they placed him in this camp with mostly Jews which, after Auschwitz, was the cruelest of them all. They had hoped that time in the camp would loosen his tongue. His work was laying railroad tracts in nearby towns after the allied bombing. It was also dangerous work because many of the bombs dropped by the Allies did not detonate and he was assigned the task of overseer of this operation. Since the bombs were live and delicate and could go off, the Germans assigned squads of Jews to drag them off to safe areas where they could be set off by other explosives without any danger of loss of German life. Even though Honore' was exempt from the most dangerous tasks (he was like the foreman because he was a non Jew) he took his place along with the rest in removing the unexploded bombs which could go off at any time. A few times the bombs detonated, killing some prisoners. Honore' tended to the wounded as best he could but for the most part, the wounded were left to die where they lay. The work always came first with the Nazis - particularly from Jews whose fate it was to die anyway after they had been literally exhausted to death.

At Bergen Belsen, German scientists practiced particularly horrible experiments to see how long people would last when they were thrown into ice cold water. This was to measure the time it took to freeze to death so that the Germans would know how long they had to rescue their pilots who had been shot down in the North Sea and in other frigid oceans. This was a particularly horrible and painful way to die, shivering to death, because the Nazis always tried to revive the prisoners thrown into the ice water. This was part of the experiment. One froze to death with almost no pain but the revival by blankets and hot water was very painful because when the blood began to circulate again, the pain would begin with uncontrollable shivers.

The Nazi scientists always asked for volunteers- the ones who survived were promised extra rations and lighter work. Some actually did survive (about 1 in 15) so that the chances were not good. In fact they were terrible. But some prisoners simply didn't care anymore because their reason for living had long ago vanished from their souls. As philosophers say, if you have a why, you can endure any what. So they volunteered because most had given up on life. But the majority did not.

One particular Monday there were not enough "volunteers" so the Nazis simply chose at random. One of the men chosen begged the Commandant not to be thrown into the ice water because he was a father of five children who needed him. But pity and mercy were not the virtues of the SS. So Honore' stepped forward and asked the Nazi officer to have him take the man's place because he was a father of a family whose children needed him. He explained to the Commandant that he was only a priest, of need to no one and so it would be better if he were taken rather than the other prisoner. The Commandant refused under superior orders because the authorities still believed that Honore' would relent and give them the information they sought. His request was denied and he was told not to make such a request again. "What will you do? Put me in prison?" Honore' had a sense of humor that never failed him, even in the terrible darkness of a death camp. The Gestapo was not amused.

Since Honore' spoke and read Hebrew, and since there were no rabbis in that section of the camp, he was often asked to recite the Skema Israel and read from the Torah for the Jewish prisoners who were almost everyone. In a death camp, everyone knew that Honore' was a Christian and so they made him an honorary Jew, a righteous gentile, one who sought to help and save Jews, one of the upright honored by Jews. His encouragement and help did not go unnoticed by all those condemned men. When he left for Auschwitz, to the biggest death camp of them all, they gave him a Menorah which had been fashioned from tin cans from food rations (donated by the Red Cross). Neither did they overlook the heroic deed of sharing part of his two ounces of daily ration of bread with those who were worse than himself. It was hard to imagine such a person but the witness swore that it was so. The word actually got around that these Jews had finally met a righteous and holy gentile in the person of this distinguished cleric. It was marvelous what a death camp could produce: the best and the worst in men. Men would actually kill for a slice of bread and others would betray their companions for a few more crumbs. Honore' never judged because he knew well what hunger and starvation could do to a human being. When someone even stole what little he had, he uttered not a word of vituperation or curses: "The Lord gives and the Lord takes away."

From time to time the Nazis would still interrogate him. In the beginning they would try the usual methods but hunger and exhaustion softened the hardest blows. Since the human body can feel just so much pain and then shuts it off, these methods were useless with him. Having nothing much else to threaten him with, the Nazis were convinced that he was of no value. Therefore he had to die in a camp destined for both Jews and non Jews: Auschwitz in Southern Poland. Toward the end of 1943, he was shipped to what was supposed to have been his place of death. He remained there until the end of the war.

Over the death Camp I (there was another camp just for Jews a few miles down the road which contained the crematoria) was a motto: Arbeit macht Frei (work will make you free). In the camp the gallows humor was that the Nazis worked you to death which was the only freedom possible from the death house. If anyone tried to escape or actually did escape, ten prisoners were hanged and the whole camp was assembled to witness the hanging. This gave everyone pause because in escaping you were in reality putting ten of your friends and countrymen to death. There were few attempts. Fewer escapes.

Once again Honore' was made a foreman of a work detail which started at 6:00 a.m. and finished 6:00 p.m. with a few minutes for a ration of bread and thin soup at noon. If you were lucky, there was a potato in the soup. Since the cooks knew who Honore' was and respected him, they would almost always try to dig deep into the soup and put a carrot or a potato in his helping. Invariably he gave it away. Bets were placed each time to see whether he would or would not. Those who bet against him always lost. Always. The others hoped he would break down. Honore' never did. He was strong for others without complaint or curse.

It was difficult for Honore' to try and give one or another prisoner in the detail lesser work because the very lives of the crew depended on their completing specific amounts of work each day. If not, they were either shot on the spot and buried right where they lay or they were sent to the crematoria. The Nazis thought this method would give added incentive to the prisoners to complete their quota of the work detail. There were no executions. So Honore' worked hard alongside the other prisoners so they could all survive another day.

There was no war news since the prisoners had no contact with the outside world. From time to time they could hear the rumble of hundreds of allied planes overhead but since there were no strategic targets near the camp (it was strictly a death camp), they heard little of the bombing - contrary to the camp of Bergen Belsen which was located near strategic areas. Honore' was down to 80 lbs. and his ribs began to show, his hair fell out and all of his teeth had become infected. He found it terribly painful to even eat his ration of bread. The work details became fewer and fewer as more men died from starvation or they were executed for not being able to fulfill the work detail which was demanded at even a greater rate. There was a noticeable increase in the number of deaths beginning in January, 1945. No one knew why.

Then toward the beginning of March, 1945, a strange and eerie silence fell over the whole camp. The prisoners who were still able to walk went out into the courtyards to discover something they had never seen before. The guards were gone along with the soldiers. Even the smoke stakes were now free from the constant belching of think black smoke. Everyone knew that this smoke was from the bodies of thousands of human beings which burned day and night. The grey silt covered everything - a constant reminder that death was ever present - in the air, on the ground, in the clothes and beds - everything was covered with it. It was like being covered with a thin layer of snow. That too had ceased.

About 12:00 p.m. a load of armed soldiers pulled up at the gate and entered cautiously. After securing the camp and convinced that all the German soldiers had abandoned the camp, a very tall, black sergeant came into the barracks where Honore' was housed. He looked around at the living dead, gaunt eyes and emaciated bodies too weak to give their liberators a joyous shout. That big black sergeant sat down and for ten minutes sobbed in the presence of the prisoners and of his own men. He then collected his emotions and ordered that all the rations his own men had, be given immediately to the prisoners. He then ordered one of his men to go back to the American depot some 10 miles away and steal, confiscate or grab any food and clothing he could find. Within an hour, fresh water and rations were being distributed to the prisoners.

It was a marvel to behold. These big strapping men gently feeding, bandaging and bathing this poor mass of humanity. The gentleness and compassion of these men made Honore' weep. The only gratitude of the prisoners had to give was their tears and to kiss the helping hands of these strange men. From that day ever after, Honore' held a very special place in his heart for Americans. He never forgot, whether at Christmas or the 4th of July - he would spend it with his beloved Americans at the American College in Louvain. He said his daily mass there until his death in 1962.

Within a few weeks, Honore' had regained five pounds and was beginning to help the soldiers around the camp. He spoke English, German and Polish so we was invaluable.

He importuned the chaplain from the American 3rd army for some wine, vestments and a wooden chalice. It was appropriate, he thought, that the chalice be made of humble wood since only the poorest of the poor would be present at the celebration and the only thing the prisoners had to offer was their suffering, their despair and their joy at liberation. It was a dream come true which not one of them had dared to dream. Such things did not happen to the poorest of the poor, only to the rich and powerful. But by the grace of God, it happened. They were free of the tyranny that had choked their lives for five years, a cruelty so great and so thorough that many could not believe it had happened. It was a suffering so great, so deep that Honore' did not think possible. It was truly the Cross which all his life he had been taught to honor and worship, which had become utter reality in his life. And God had given him another day with which to worship him and to help his fellow human beings. In fact, God was to give him another seventeen fruitful years in the vineyard of the Lord.

These thoughts must have gone through his mind as he said Mass openly for his fellow prisoners in the midst of the largest and greatest death camp which a human monster had created for his unspeakable evil deeds. It was life amidst death. Even in the midst of horror and death, a ray of hope had been born. There were still good men on the earth who do good and who showed the prisoners that there was yet hope. These American soldiers thought that they had seen much of man's cruelty during these days – and they did. But they also taught the prisoners hope by their action of compassion and gentleness.

So Mass was celebrated in the midst of death. That was not strange to Honore'. Mass is a celebration of life and death, life through death since there can be no human hope without passing· through the crucible of pain and death. That is the message each time a Mass is celebrated, each time Honore' signed himself with the sign of the cross. Evil and death and hope meet there in a camp of death. It was mystery. But a mystery of life which would ultimately conquer death.

Honore' returned to receive the greatest honors from his countrymen and to his position as rector of the Catholic University of Louvain. He was awarded his country's highest medal of honor while the Pope later made him an Archbishop. But those honors meant really nothing to him because he had seen too many men and women die horrible deaths who, he thought, were infinitely more worthy than he of all these honors. He was that humble and gentle. But he never spoke of his experiences again. What little we know of this man's courage, humility, and self giving in the midst of the most trying times and places, are known to us from others who had seen his witness in the camps. He did not consider himself worthy of telling their stories. Not even his own.

But people knew who he was and who he had become for them. His life at the University was the same and yet entirely different. The intensity of his humility and charity were legendary. He would even go into the street and let others pass on the narrow sidewalks - that was a standing laughter among the Americans at Louvain told not as a mockery but as profound respect. Honore' would not be outdone in humility!

The only expression from the past which he allowed himself were his celebration of feast days with the American students from the American college home he held in most special regard. The one thing he could never understand among Americans was the longstanding prejudice against Blacks. To him, they were the incarnation of God's mercy and gentleness at a time when he had utterly nothing to give to his saviors except undying gratitude. It was total grace and it came in the face of a black man. It is true, he thought, God is black! To him, God's salvation came in the face of a big, gentle black American sergeant. He never forgot.

The Americans loved him as much in return because they recognized in him the incarnation of goodness but above all of hope. Hope that in the darkest of darkness, a man was faithful to responsibility at great cost to himself; who loved his fellow humans so much that he would not betray them in any way no matter what the cost; who forgave his enemies and harbored no ill will for anyone; and who now spent the rest of his life as the visible reminder that the only thing which matters in life are the three great theological virtues: Faith, hope, charity. And the greatest of these is charity and forgiveness. Honore' was charity incarnate. He had become a true Christian.

Every once in a while in the history of mankind, there appear visible manifestations of self giving, of truth, of love of others, that so go beyond the common measure of even good men and women, that words are inadequate to describe them; and one's instinct is to simply wonder in worship at the mystery who deigns to raise up such men and women in our midst. Honore' Van Weyenberg was just such a grace in the darkness of an undeserving world which treated him so painfully and so cruelly. And low and behold: he gives back only thanks and goodness, love and forgiveness, absorbing into his own person the hatred and the violence of men. One can only worship the loving mystery who raised him up for our courage and edification.

Honore' Van Weyenberg went to his God on October 28, 1962 in peace and forgiveness.

Deo Gratias.

CHAPTER 12

A SUPREME PASTORAL MEMORY

I was ordained in St. Peter's in Rome by Pius XII on June 29, 1958. The brilliance of that day was astounding as I gazed up from Bernini's columns upon the Papal altar. A shaft of light shown down upon the altar as if guided by the Holy Spirit. I thought I had learned so much, that I was prepared for a ministry that would enrich me and those with whom I would come in contact. I was filled with religiosity because I was prepared. It just so happened that God was not prepared and it was more with myself that I was filled rather than any spirituality with which the Holy Spirit had taught me. I really thought that I knew a lot after all those years of philosophy, theology and pastoral guidance. I was shown how wrong I was not much later.

Upon returning to Buffalo, New York, I had many short assignments. They were always short because I kept on getting fired or removed from them all. They finally settled on a place with a pastor who was ruff and gruff, a Msgr. Donato Valenti at St. Francis of Assissi Parish on Buffalo's east side.

The parish was a mixture of Italians and Polish, but mostly Italian. Most of the Poles went to the Polish church next door so for all practical purposes it was an ethnic Italian parish. The pastor knew that I had been a "troublemaker" so he started me off on the most difficult jobs, i.e. the ones he did not want to do. He was a gentle man but one constantly consumed with money. His really good quality was that he was always there for the sick and the dying. He didn't have much of a personality but he was always there for them, visiting them in their homes and in the hospitals almost every day. That impressed me more than all the other drawbacks he had. He was not very learned, his preaching was not dynamic (he was the Bob Dole of the clergy), he was abrupt in all relationships, afraid of being seen alone with a woman, any woman and who used to tell me that he had never broken his vow of celibacy (it would have been more fun if he had told me that he did, where, when, how and for what reason!). In any case, be taught me that simple pastoral guide which I have never forgotten: tend to the sick and the dying as well as their families. He was gentle with them all even though his personality forbade him to have that gentleness shine through.

That trait alone has always endeared him to me in my memories of those days. I do not recall much about those days of ministry but I do recall that.

There was one woman in particular who fascinated me from the day I arrived at St. Francis. It had been my "function" to take Holy Communion each First Friday of the month to all the sick of the parish, at least to those who had requested it. Mrs. Olivadati lived right across from the church at North Ogden Street so it wasn't far to go. And each First Friday, there she would be immaculately clean in her bed (she had been bedridden for several years), terribly respectful and pious in a genuine sense. I would hear her confession full of sins only a holy person would notice. As people become more holy, the slightest uncharitable act becomes a genuinely big thing - to the rest of us it would be trivial. That's because none of us are very holy so we consider these acts trivial. But this holy woman who knew in humility what she really was as she entered more deeply into the inner sanctum of God, uncharitableness, lack of patience and understanding in the least degree, became huge as the greatness and holiness of God was revealed to her.

She fascinated me over the weeks and months. I used to stop by frequently and she greeted me with genuine joy and openness. It was Leon Bloy who once said that the true mark of the Christian was joy and indeed, that was her constant mark. Once I happened to run into her doctor and asked what paralysis Mrs. Olivadati had. He smiled and told me there was no paralysis. Why, then, I asked, was she bedridden? He smiled again and said: "Father, why is it that the priests understand so little?" "I don't understand." He smiled and continued to my dismay.

"That woman, Father, has terminal bone cancer throughout her body. She's filled with it and the agony must be horrible. She refuses everything but some aspirin for her headaches. I have never heard her complain - not once - or be irritable or unkind to me or to the nurse who comes to see her daily. And that's the God's honest truth."

I was astounded. Terminal cancer? Of the bones? Agony? Refuses medicine? Cheerful and joyful? Something was wrong here and I was to find out the truth: I understood nothing about being a Christian even though I had studied its theology at the greatest Catholic universities in the world in Rome, Munich and Louvain. It was a sick, bedridden woman in cold Buffalo who would teach me.

Armed with that knowledge, I was determined to get to the bottom of things. So on one of my visits, I broached the topic as gently as I could. I asked her permission to speak of her illness and she readily granted it. We spoke of what the doctor had told me and she confirmed it all. But, why, I asked, did she never reveal any of this to me. She just simply said that it wasn't important. Finally, frustrated that I couldn't understand (what was finally not understandable) I blurted out: "But a woman like you. Kind to all the poor, who clothes the naked, never turns away anyone in trouble. You who raised such a fine family whose reputation for goodness and charity goes far beyond the confines of this parish, why you with such an agonizing death? Why you and why not me?" I remember her answer vividly some thirty five years later. I shall never forget it.

"I spoke to God about that once. Like you, I did not understand and told him that straight out. You know what he told me? "Olivia!" he said, "'you have tried to follow my commandments and you have loved your family and your neighbors as best you could. I am very pleased with you. Because I am so pleased, I am going to give you an honor which I give only a very few. I am going to crucify you as I crucified my son. I give you the greatest gift I can give anyone on earth."

I was astonished but I was not so obtuse as not to understand. It was the contradiction and the paradox of the Gospel that was revealed to me then and there by this woman of simple faith. She taught me in an instant what all those theological tomes had never been able to teach me: what it was to be a Christian; to be crucified with Christ with nothing but the darkness of the surrender of faith in the agony and faith with Jesus on the cross. I had learned the mystery of the cross which is such a stumbling block to the whole world and to me as well. But there it was, the Christian paradox and mystery. At that moment, the scales dropped from my eyes and I for the first time, realized what it was to be a Christian: to be crucified with Christ in love for the whole world just as this bedridden, little old lady prayed and suffered with her crucified Lord for the salvation of the whole world. She died a few weeks later. I was called to her bed along with many of her family and friends. I anointed her and gave her a little of viaticum as we all prayed.

She smiled at me as if to thank me for all my stupid expressions of kindness to her. We prayed with her and when she opened her eyes she prayed these joyful words in Italian: "Signore Gesu Cristo, I thank you with all my heart for the gift of pain and agony I have suffered with you. Thank you for permitting your humble and unworthy servant to take part in that passion for the salvation of the whole world. Grazie di tutto mio cuore."

Then she stopped breathing. I could only hear the sobbing of her friends and relatives. And my own as well. But my tears were tears of thanks to God for having taught me through this saintly woman, what it means to be a follower of Jesus Christ. Even to this day.

CHAPTER 13

TEACHING CAREER

I held some of the greatest teaching positions which I dearly loved with all my heart. There is no greater function in life than to teach. Parents teach their children by word and example; judges teach by their opinions and decisions; lawyers teach their clients; the bishops and the Pope are essentially teachers of doctrine; universities, colleges and institutions of learning all teach; everyone teaches each other if nothing other than by their example to society, for better or for worse. The world is full of teachers, because each has something worthwhile to hand on to the next generation. The essence of the teaching function is that we are mortal and we want to hand down valuable information, research, and knowledge of all kinds before we die. We can write books which are also part of the teaching function but there is nothing like the person to person communication. Even lovers teach by the way they talk, relate to and, communicate with each other. You know a lot about a person just by the way he or she treats you. You can learn whether he/she loves you or not by the way he treats you. Actions always speak louder than any words.

Teaching was my first and deepest love. Perhaps my only one. I gave it up when it became too evident to me that I was really psychologically unfit to teach because I had a big mouth; and I didn't know how to control it. I actually said what I meant and I meant what I said which was not always pleasing to my superiors, religious and secular alike. Looking back, I really can see no difference between my secular educational superiors who were joyful, studious and honest. There was not yet some of that self improvement, self centering philosophy which would corrupt so many priests and seminarians in the 1970's and 1980's and which would ultimately result in their leaving not only the priesthood but the faith itself. Having given up on God, they accepted everything: psychoanalysis, Buddhism, re-incarnation, mystic contemplation, gurus from the East - you name it.

But those days in the early sixties before Vatican II were enthusiastic days. I don't know exactly when we lost our enthusiasm for the faith and why. Maybe we became too influenced by the despair of the existential world and did not rejoice enough in the joy of faith. I mean if you really do believe in the Creed which comes down to us from the very earliest days of the Church's life including the resurrection of Christ, how could you be overcome with the darkness and the despair of the world? How could its unbelief defeat you? How could joy not be a part of your believing? It's because of our present crisis of belief or perhaps better, our unbelief. The Creed and the New Testament are not just incredible; worse, they are just too good to be true and so deep down we simply do not believe. Not because faith is incredible but because it is too good to be true. Nothing like that really happens in life which is full of sorrow, tragedy and death interspersed with moments of joy here and there. But ultimately everything good must end.

But it was a joy to teach such dedicated young men. A seminary is the Church's West Point, Annapolis and Air Force Academy all rolled into one. But better because it is a matter of belief. In fact, it is better than all three combined because they train not for war and death but for peace, love and justice. That makes them very special people.

The early sixties were times of transition. In the middle of the first year there at the seminary, a decree came out of Rome that seminary courses had to be taught in Latin. So as to soften the blow, we were allowed to give the lectures in Latin (American Latin that followed English structure: Argumentum tuum non tenet acquam - Your argument does not hold water - a perfectly meaningless phrase to a good Latinist) and sum up the lecture in English so that at least they would get something out of the lecture. It was all terribly foolish of course and after three months (Vetus Sapientia - Ancient wisdom) it was quickly dropped. The students did not understand and we were wasting time, constantly repeating ourselves. It may have been an ancient wisdom but what was wisdom long ago was not necessarily wisdom today. Requiescat in pace. Now we have gone to the opposite extreme: none of the priests today even read Latin. How can you understand 2000 years of Church history without knowing Latin?

In any case, I tried to update my teaching by adding elements of religious freedom and ecumenism. My favorite Protestant theologians were Karl Barth, Soren Kierckegaard and a few others. I introduced the students into the thought and theology of these Protestant experts and assigned some readings. I also had other non Christian readings from the Veda texts, the Koran and the Sermons of the Buddha. Guess what?

You would have thought that I had tried to burn the place down. I was considered a theological pyromaniac particularly by two Dominicans who taught philosophy at the seminary. They were my enemies from day one. I personally thought they would have made great Inquisitors under Torquemada who also was a

Dominican in 16th century Spain. They were about as closed minded and racist as any two people you could find. It was pure heresy and danger to the tender minds of young people, to introduce them into the theology of the 20th century and into ecumenism so that peace could reign among the churches instead of the traditional hatred and distrust. After all, that is what Jesus Christ wanted for his Church – a union - communion of love - communion. Instead what we have is scandalous divisions among the Churches which .gives a terrible example to non believers. But in those early days of the sixties, this was not to be and when some ancient Methuselah was appointed bishop, out I went in a matter of months. I cried for weeks after that - something I never recovered from. I wanted that work more than my life. If I really had to specify the beginning of the end of my priesthood, it was that firing. It broke my spirit because of the injustice of it all. No one explained anything, told me nothing. I was just ordered to leave a job and a position which I had trained for years and wanted with all of my heart. Off I went to the boondocks of the diocese to become pastor in Whitesville. In five months I would have a nervous breakdown and I had to recuperate at the home of my parents in West Seneca. It took me all of a year and a half to recuperate but I don't think I ever fully recovered from that shock. But at least I had a good place to go.

While at home I attended classes in political science at the State University of New York at Buffalo. I always loved politics, government and foreign affairs. Since the local bishop had left me without a dime - not even the small salary of $100 a month which priests of my age and rank received - I had not the means to go to school. I just stumbled into the office of the dean of the department. Dr. Civatos, a

Greek, was tough and gruff but a most compassionate man. He happened also to be an atheist. When he saw my credentials he offered me a job on the spot as a graduate tutor (TA) for undergraduates and I earned my tuition and $150 a week - six times my diocesan salary. I could not get over the contrast: an atheist who helped a wounded Samaritan on the side of the road while the religious priests just passed me by. It was painful to see relived in my own case the Gospel story of the Good Samaritan. Clearly God chooses whom he wishes, when he wishes and is no respecter of persons. In any case he chose an atheist who helped me in my hour of terrible need while the religious ones passed by. It was all so incredible that it was happening before my very eyes.

I taught at the University for that year and a half of the next and earned my MA in Political Science. It has been a constant source of widening of my perspective on life. Theology and philosophy should expand to encompass the ethics of foreign affairs. Those were a few happy months because I was respected for who I was and what I was doing. I was available for the students very generously and they liked that very much. I had a sense of humor which was appreciated even more. In any case, I received from agnostics and atheists respect and gratitude which I had never received from the religious people in my life. God truly is not a respecter of persons and saves those who do good and therefore do his will. I don't know how my faith survived all that but it did in spite of those in the Church. In any case, I taught there until I received my MA and then another opportunity opened up for me that permitted me to leave that pit of pain.

For reasons I still cannot explain, I was offered a position teaching theology at Notre Dame University. It seemed like a godsend from Buffalo, a place I had come to hate and fear. Fear because there was no longer a future for me in Buffalo; and hate because I had been treated like a dog where I was more at home with non-believers than with believers. I guess if I had to give the real reason why I finally left the ministry, it was not sex and loneliness; it was simply because I had over the years found so little Christ like behavior in the Catholic church. The institution of religion had become so important for its priests and bishops that it had forgotten why the Church is on earth in the first place: to become like the person of Jesus Christ and that her faithful should become Christians. It was more important for them to become Catholics. That was an inherent contradiction in terms which 1 have never been able to understand. A scandal, really, for me and for many outside the Church.

In any case, I visited the Notre Dame campus in 1964 and started to teach there in August, 1965. The campus was beautiful except for the terribly long winter (November through April.) The buildings were spacious and there was a 100 million dollar building program under Father Hesberg who was a good administrator and a rather original thinker. He wanted a first class university and I suppose what he got was a second class one but he left it better than he found it. Were it not for the football team, no one would much notice Notre Dame as an intellectual dynamo which it was not and still is not. I do not mean to sound condemnatory but it was still a Midwestern school with small time values but with a great library. It was just behind the football stadium with a large fresco of Christ with his arms raised in such a way that it was called "touchdown Jesus."

The football team members in my courses were always serious. If they had to be away for a game, a tutor would come, get the material and make sure that the student was up to snuff in the learning of his lesson. I was supposed to make sure that they had learned the lesson by giving them an extra quiz which I always refused to do. The way I looked at things was that theology was a course of essential freedom - if you wanted to learn it, fine – if not, it was up to you. Enough forced religion in the lives of those students. And the football players were no exception. The coaches were furious with me including Coach Parsigean. We spoke once and he hung up on me. I think he confused himself with God Almighty.

The students were respectful and they seemed to be genuinely interested in the subject matter. I taught courses in social and moral ethics so we always had great conversation and participation in class. The laymen from Notre Dame had an extraordinary allegiance to the school so that the Notre Dame mystique was pervasive and deeply rooted. It was charming and in many cases taken to heart as a Christian commitment. Every once in a while it is really difficult to tell at that level of development you could see who would be a success as a thoughtful Christian. Simplistically, I thought that that was the criterion of success of a Catholic university or college. Credo ut intelligo.

The winter set in early that year, We had our first snow storm at the end of October. I genuinely liked Notre Dame although I was never accepted as one of the "boys" by the religious order which ran the place (C.S.C.) or Holy Cross Fathers. I lived in a few rooms right behind the Church of the Golden Dome just adjacent to Notre Dame du Lac about 2 1/2 miles around. I used to like to walk around the lake for exercise but I didn't make many friends among the faculty. The Fathers of the Holy Cross ran the place and they were not a very friendly lot. Why should they be? They were aloof and seemed to tolerate the rest of us. This was their show. You had the great honor of teaching at Notre Dame and that should have been reward enough. It wasn't. They had their own community and did not much fraternize with others unless you happened to be an established scholar at which point you were welcomed. I of course was not. The only other professor with whom I associated was a member of the English department. As I explained elsewhere, we organized the first Vietnam protest in January, 1966 at the height of the Vietnam War. This was not well received by Father Hesberg who in January, 1966 issued an order that was broadcast all over the U.S. "Anyone protesting the War at Notre Dame would be expelled." Guess who was the first to be expelled? Exactly. Hesberg effectively told me that my one year contract would not be renewed. That was the end of that and that was the end of my university career.

The rest of the year was a blur. I continued to teach but I do not know how I muddled through. I again fell emotionally ill but not quite a nervous breakdown. I tried to carry my teaching load so that at least I could get paid but that was about it. A nun who had befriended me helped me through those terrible days on the campus. I was there but since my days were numbered, I was a dead man walking. I had not felt so lonely, so abandoned and defeated even while I was in Whitesville. This was supposed to be a Catholic community and it surely was not. Once people knew you were fired, they avoided you like the plague. The only taste of Christianity on that campus which I experienced was a lowly nun who was so good to me and took care of me for six months. I knew I could not afford to break down again (even though I did but couldn't let anyone know about it) and it was that nun who provided me the crucial crutch I needed to survive the rest of that year. I could not have made it through the lonely days without her. She cooked me an evening meal when I could not go to the cafeteria; she washed my clothes, cleaned my rooms when I did not have the strength to do it myself. In short, God had sent me yet another angel along the long path of failure and defeat.

By this time, there was a pattern in my life and I was so thick that I couldn't see it or recognize it. The only thing I do know is that the final months were personally humiliating for me and I became a hermit in my room, going out only for classes or for some exercise. The sense of failure - again - was overwhelming. I spent a week at St. Peter's Hospital which was a good stay. They found nothing and I was missed on campus not at all.

But God was good. In May I met a Christian brother from St. Mary's College in Moraga, California. It seems that he told his people back there that, I was available and I was visited by the Dean of the College in June with hardly an interview because they were impressed with my resume. I look good on paper. I knew that I could not and would not go back to Buffalo. I had decided that rather than go back to such a place, I was ready to leave the ministry so I took the job immediately without even informing the Bishop back home. I was prepared to leave the ministry rather than turn down the opportunity. It was at least a way of holding on continuing my writing and I could get my PhD at Berkeley which was just over the hill from Contra Costa County. It was ideal.

So in August, 1966, I rented a trailer, loaded my things and off I went to the far west. The Christian Brother came with me and I dropped him off in Sacramento. I arrived at my parent's home because they had moved to Napa with my sister who in turn had moved there in 1964. It was a perfect deal for me because I could teach at the college and still be near my parents for weekends and holidays. They and my sister were a great consolation for me and it was one of the few times in my life when I was truly happy. Now I could write, speak and teach and make a decent living. And we lived in the most beautiful place in the world.

California was the end of a dream. The place was so beautiful - it was really breathtaking. You don't know California beauty until you have lived in the east or mid-west. You could understand why people risked everything to go there and why the Indians valued it so. The Bay Area is perhaps one of the most perfect living areas in the world and no one ever wants to leave. I didn't. It was heaven on earth: a perfect moderate climate, beautiful hills and mountains, the sea, the city of San Francisco with its own mystique, the many institutions of teach a colorful people to say the least. All those advantages naturally drew millions to that area and I was totally taken in by its beauty, its "laid back" attitude and its charm.

The Christian Brothers were at least tolerant of my presence; at least at the beginning. I lived with the young brothers in one of the dormitories for whom I said Mass and counseled. They gave me room and board and a small stipend. Many of the older brothers who lived in another community had their own lives but it was strange to see so many of them addicted to alcohol. As I became reluctantly - involved with civil rights and anti- war activity, the brothers became more and more concerned that I was bringing the wrong kind of notoriety to that small men's college nestled in the mountains and hills of Contra Costa County; I antagonized a whole group of them who hated who I was and what I was doing. Strangely they would come to me for confession because I was known to be "easy." I never condemned any of them and tried always to be compassionate to all who came to me, even those who I knew disliked me. I always thought that that was what a Christian was all about in any case. But the number of alcoholics among them was astonishing. Maybe it was because of celibacy or the whole notion of a group of men who were not ordained to the ministry but whose whole lives were taken up in teaching young people. Besides they had the whole Christian Brothers winery in Napa to feed their habit!

The teaching of these young people was laudable even though it was evident to me that many Catholics sent their sons to that college as a protection from the evils of Berkeley and the California scene. St. Mary's, safely out of range of the City by the Bay (Babylon, as Herb Caen called it) was seen by them as a "safe area" for their sons away from those evils of that city. They were willing to pay very high tuition for that peace of mind even though it was a complete illusion fostered by the Brothers. The dormitories were filled with drinking and women on weekends but on a quieter note. On Friday nights, you could feel the quake of fornication. There was as much fornication on that campus as there was over the hill in that place of iniquity called Berkeley. It was amusing to see how the charade worked: the campus looked calm and safe. The parents saw the Christian brothers in charge; they concluded that it was "safe" so they sent their sons there for protection, paying on the way large amounts of money up the kazoo. It was a charade because none of it was true. It was the same life as at Berkeley, only quieter and under the auspices of a religious community. That is why my presence and activity became such a scandal and a worry at such a place. The real world of war and civil rights now came on to the campus which was thought to be safely hidden away from "all that." I mean, thought the parents, why the hell are we paying so much money if the same corruption comes onto the St. Mary's campus as in Berkeley through a rebel priest? But Berkeley and all of its ferment were only ten miles away, just over the Caldicot Tunnel so how could it not be infected? It was difficult even during those days to understand the mentality of the Brothers and of the parents who sent their sons to that place. The illusion of security against the evils of the world is very great: it is called denial because you have to want to be a believer. So I knew immediately that turmoil was up ahead and so it was. Christ, here we go again! The reason I was not fired sooner is because I had received rank and tenure in one year - so anxious were they to keep me, at least at the beginning. It was considered the biggest mistake in the history of the College by some of the Brothers. It was a move the Brothers would soon deeply regret as I began a rather lengthy stay but this time with the protection of a tenured position which I had not enjoyed before. It felt good.

The students of course were not serious. I mean this was California! Is anyone serious in California? The college period was that interim between weekends and vacation which was separated by class time. I found most of the students to be no better than those in Berkeley with plenty of drinking and fornication in the dorms. This of course is not to condemn them since they were mostly young men getting their rocks off at a stage in life when they walked around with perpetual erections to see where they could put them.

I actually had one young man write a whole essay for a term paper on one of his visits to the Mustang Ranch in Nevada where prostitution was legal and much practiced. The specificity of the facts clearly showed that he knew what he was talking about and he had no qualms about visiting those places. Or about writing about them. They even had a menu over the entrance station with the prices for different sexual acts. They went something like this:

1) All acts to be done after proper inspection of the male's genitalia before services by the young ladies
2) A complete bath by the young lady
3) Regular intercourse $100 per hour
4) Masturbation only, $50
5) Fellatio an additional $25 but ejaculation in the mouth was forbidden
6) All intercourse was with a condom supplied and applied by the young lady
7) Double women partners was 50% more (50% discount)
8) No anal or perverted sex, no whips, chains, maso-sado. Intercourse under any circumstances
9) Overtime was by the quarter hour even if it was less than that
10) Simple conversation for modeling, i.e. nude was $75 an hour and a group of 3 or more was $200
11) After washing was included in the price done by the client

I swear that was in his paper and each of the conditions were posted "by law" and were annotated by personal experience.

In any case, I taught many courses but the student reading and understanding level was not great. Much less than at Notre Dame. In other words, outside of some good exceptions, the theological IQ was not high and the desire to learn very low. I thought it was mostly a waste of time since as one professor put it non-delicately, students were there for a "buck and a fuck." Get a degree to get a job to make money. Perhaps too hard on the students but their interest level was very low. I personally advocated that college should be postponed until age 25 during which time the students could do anything but go to school. It was otherwise a waste of time during which they learned nothing. Education is mostly wasted on youth, certainly theology was. And that was a shame because of the lack of maturity.

The stay at St. Mary's was enjoyable because I could teach which I loved, make a decent salary to survive, publish as much as I wanted and give time to organizing anti-war activities. Robert Brown of Stanford and I organized Clergy-Laity Concerned which organized protests and other forms of civil disobedience. We were arrested some four times in Oakland and San Francisco for anti-war sit ins and this infuriated the Brothers at the College. And the parents of the young men at the College. They were furious that such a man taught their sons.

The pressure to resign became greater and greater. The Brother President (Anderson was his name) begged me to leave and when I did in 1974, they gave me a year's pay as if on sabbatical after eight years of teaching. They were so happy to see me go that I think they did a jig. A few years later I heard one of the brothers malign me to this priest I knew. He must have really hated me because he told the priest some pretty awful things. I remember the Brother very well because he used to come to me all the time for confession so I knew all about him. As well as his darkest secrets.

I sent him a note informing him that I knew all about him and therefore those who lived in glass houses should not throw stones. And his house was made of very fragile glass. He got the picture because I never heard any word from him after that. Some Christian Brother!

By the summer of 1974 I had had enough of Catholics and their whole system. After negotiating a leaving package with St. Mary's College, I left, thinking that maybe I could do some good as a lawyer. I had always loved the law and I was happy to go to law school. I had been accepted at the University of San Francisco so I was set. I was determined to teach law so I spent three years there and then went across the Bay to Berkeley where I earned my MA and PhD in law. After graduation in 1977 and while in graduate school, I had to earn some money so I got a job teaching law at an unaccredited law school in San Francisco, Lincoln University School of Law. It was unaccredited for a reason. It took in students who couldn't make it in regular law schools. The dean liked me very much so he made me the assistant dean of the school. I really did get along with him very well because we had high hopes for our students. I taught con law, ethics, contracts and trusts. The students were not the brightest but they did make up for it by studying hard and trying to make the grade. The Bar passage rate went up from 15% to 35% during the years I was there and I like to think that I had made a difference. Night school made it difficult. I practiced some law during the day at the office of Charles Geary, the famous defense attorney for the Black Panthers, even though he was a professed Marxist. He was very kind to me. Once again it was an unbeliever who came through for me when I needed help. It was never the Church. I also planted and took care of gardens to earn extra money. I wrote my MA thesis on the removal of life support systems from the comatose and I passed with the highest honors. I knew that I had to stop being a full time student now and earn a living for my family.

My first big job offer was to the University of Florida in Gainesville. Even from the beginning there was an on- going dispute on that faculty between conservatives who did not want me and the liberals who did. In the first six months I was there I turned this directly around so that when I left, I had befriended the conservatives and alienated the liberals because I attacked homosexuality, abortion and affirmative action. That was and still is anathema to liberal thinkers. I didn't give a damn - I was far beyond that. Having had so many setbacks in life, one more was not going to make a difference.

I loved Florida. The University had everything you wanted. Research materials, secretaries, good students, light load of six hours a week and all the time doing good teaching and writing. I love to be near the ocean, the many sport facilities and the moderate (but humid) climate. I think I was a good teacher and the students were serious. They were receptive to good teaching and I really tried to give them the best. But alas! I think I was doomed there from the start. I loved the school, the state, the whole place. But in January 1980 when a vote was taken to give me a tenure track position, the vote split 22/22 and on a tie vote, you lose. I probably would not have taken the position even if it had been 23/21. There is no sense in being in a place where almost the majority of the faculty doesn't want you there. I had also had a run in with the acting dean who had accused me of coming a week late during the previous summer session and not telling him about it. Since I did not appreciate being called a liar, I rather stormed into his office and demanded that we talk with the professor whose place I had taken and who then in fact confirmed on a three way telephone connection that that was exactly what had happened. There is no greater enemy than a higher up whom you show up to have been full of crap. When I demanded an apology after the phone conversation, he simply refused. I departed after I told him what an arrogant and faithless bastard he was. He wasn't fit to tie my shoe. I added that he was ethically unfit to be teaching young people in a law school and that he would turn them into sons of Satan worse than himself. So you see that it was over before it even started. But I gave it the old college try. No way was it going to work.

So on September 1, 1981, I left Gainesville with a very heavy heart. I actually cried for hours after I left on the road of I-10 back to California to practice law. I had to stop at a few road stops so that I could get my eyes back into focus, swollen from the tears. I still get sentimental when beautiful things disappear from my life.

I arrived in Houston the next day and stayed for a few days with a dear friend, a former nun who was now a school nurse in Houston. I planned to stay a few weeks with her for a long deserved vacation. While there, she mentioned that South Texas College of Law was looking for professors so I decided to make one last attempt instead of going back to California to practice law. I was now sick of traveling around the country.

It was a difficult decision to make. I can now understand how the old become cynical and that is the great danger in trying to do good with your life. It's much easier to aim for power and money.

CHAPTER 14

THE FIRST MASS

The morning of the 29th of June, 1958 was exciting for me. Who would not be excited at the prospect of being ordained by the Pope in St. Peter's along with candidates from some 160 nations. It was truly a Pentecost when people from all over the world gathered in one place would profess their belief in the one unifying event of all human history: Jesus Christ is Lord, risen from the dead, conqueror of death of him who had died absolutely and who rose to divine life absolutely. For whatever reason, that was the central thought that went through my head on that day of days and the next day when I celebrated my first Mass at the Papal altar in St. Peters.

All this theology came alive for me during those two days. It wasn't just the majesty of the place and of the person of the Pope solemnly at the main altar. It wasn't even the beauty of the light reflecting on Bernini's columns through that window above which reflected the early sunlight on the main altar as a seeming descent of the Spirit on that place. That is what Michelangelo wanted to portray when he built the basilica at the end of the 16th century over 400 years ago.

It was the person of the Pope, successor of Peter on whose bones the whole edifice was built and constructed in more ways than one. I had visited the excavation under the Papal altar where Christians honored the burial place of Peter since the very days of Nero (66 AD). The whole truth of what was happening on that day was taking place over the tomb of a man who had seen the Word Incarnate, lived the testimony and who gave his life in the belief of the truth of that central belief; and whose profession of faith continued through the living mouths of each and every one of his successors, now in the person of Pius XII who was about to lay hands on me so that I too could continue that witness in the place where I would be sent.

All my joy was there as at a new Pentecost where I was soon to receive the Spirit for this task. It was all in faith of course. The ceremony was symbolic of this central event: Pius to Peter to Christ to God. Take away any of the lineage and you have a · gigantic fraud on your hands. The message is from God through Christ: the good news that we are now joined with the life of God, having overcome death in and through Christ. All the tribulations of life (and they would be painful, many and very real) would be endured in the Spirit of the crucified Lord in view of the resurrection for life with God even here and now. That was the good news, the joyful news with which the Church is entrusted, to be announced to the whole world. I was going to be a part, a very small part of that mission as it has come down to us through the ages. My emotions were full but guarded since I knew even then how weak a person I was. My life since then has proved what my premonitions told me kneeling there in the middle of St. Peter's as I placed my hands in those of Peter's successor and promised him obedience and celibacy.

My friend Msgr. Calliteri, Administrator of St. Peters was there next to the Pope. He was the best investment of good wine the world had ever known. For two good bottles of wine, the Monsignor took me down to see the excavations of St. Peters under the Papal altar - an honor given to very few indeed. But I was about to ask him for something even greater which no wine could bribe (before its time!)

I was all alone on that day - travel was too expensive for my parents to come or anyone else for that matter. So all my great moments were celebrated with this Italian Monsignor who could at any time get in to see the Pope. After ordination we went out for a good Italian dinner and during the meal I broached the subject. I said it plain and simple.

"Voglio dire la prima missa al'altare papale." "I want to say my first Mass at the Papal altar." Without batting an eye he said, "Dificile pero non impossible" "difficult but possible." I was to come to the back entrance of St. Peters where a Papal Swiss guard would show me to the sacristy. I was there promptly at 5:00 AM and just as promptly so was the Swiss guard all dressed in his Michelangelo suit from the 16th century, who snapped to attention and without a word led me in a double march to the sacristy. There was Msgr. Calliteri, smiling and glad to see me, holding beautiful gold vestments worn only by the Pope himself. Monseignor would serve my first Mass.

The light was just beginning to come through Bernini's window. Two candles were lit and in place. There was no other light in the whole of St. Peters. There were just the two of us. It was horrendously beautiful and I was awe struck. There I was looking up at the Papal altar, ''Introibo ad altare Dei" "I will approach the altar of God" ''Ad Deum qui laetificat juventutem meam" "to the God who gives joy to my youth" intoned-clearly and slowly by the Monsignor. He knew how much this meant to me, how deeply I was moved standing there where for 2000 years all the successors of Peter had given their witness, some in blood, others in the simplicity and sanctity of their lives. Others had not been so holy but that was the Catholic Church, mother and whore, saint and sinner, always human struggling to be like her savior and spouse, Jesus Christ, the resurrected Lord. And as the great emotions passed my soul upon ascending that mighty altar I lifted my hands and said "Dominus Vobiscum" – the Lord be with you - I just stood there not so much in awe (that too) but in such profound gratitude that God had been so good to me. I remembered all those who had loved and helped me and all those who world help and love me until the end of my short stay in this life. Even then, I knew that not all would come out well in my life – there had already been too many signs of rebellion and discontent but whatever time was given to me, I would give generously and in full freedom because I wanted to give it under the grace of God. I felt utter gratitude and perfect freedom. I was there as gift to God because I wanted to be there and not because of some stupid divine "push" or inspiration. God called in a way that not even I understood at that great moment but I felt he did and I responded in freedom.

I stood there so long that the good Monsignor came up and, whispered "No se preocupa. Quando sera Papa lei tutto questo to sera normale." "Don't be afraid. When you become Pope all this will be quite normal."

He was such a sweet, generous and optimistic man. I do not know why he liked me so much. It just wasn't because I always brought him good wine. It was because he saw something in me that few others, including myself, ever saw: a generosity which gave without counting the cost, the price of the true disciple. And at that time, it was all quite true.

Each prayer was so meaningful: "Oh, Lord, on this holy day of the witness of St. Peter, by his example strengthen us to give similar witness in whatever station you place us." No more appropriate a prayer could be found and I wept as I read it. The sight of a stupid, young priest weeping at the Papal altar moved the Monsignor whose tears I saw. Those were precious tears to me because he authenticated my sincerity. He could tell hypocrisy from the real thing in the twinkling of an eye. God always seemed to send his messenger when I most needed him and here in an empty St. Peters I was filled with the spirit of gratitude and thanks. I cannot explain it. My emotions were filled with that one word - gratitude - because isn't that what the word Eucharist means? My life had been a pure act of grace and it led me there in ways which I did not then nor now understand. Monsignor's tears confirmed that God wanted me where I was there and then. I know that sounds pretty dumb but I swear that it was his tears that confirmed who and what I was on that day. No one ever knew that and I never told anyone about it.

I don't know whatever happened to him. He must be dead by now - that was thirty five years ago and he was old even then. We embraced after Mass. It was a long and affectionate embrace because I knew I'd never see him again. We said nothing because we both knew that we would see each other only in God. I remember holding him and I tried not to cry but it was too much for one who had been so good to me. I gave a deep sob that reverberated through my whole body. He held me close and whispered in my ear "Ah, Angelico, se recorda Gesu crucificato e un vecchio qui sempre ti ama" - "Ah, angelic one, always remember the crucified Lord and this old man who will always love you."

I slipped away into the darkness of St. Peters and on to St. Peter's Square. I do not remember much more of what happened on that day. No matter. The emotions were enough for a lifetime.

CHAPTER 15

THE MISSION: NEW GUINEA

Some of the gentlest, kindest people I have ever known were from ferocious backgrounds. To this day, I do not know whether it was simply they who had been so ferocious or their culture and background that made them so. To this day I do not as yet understand which, even though I was with them for a year.

Such were the Papuan Indians of Papua, New Guinea. The island is just north of Australia, really a part of the Indonesian chain. In 1959 it was part of a U.N. Trusteeship originally from the Dutch whose colonial rule was destroyed by the Japanese during WWII. The island is incredibly beautiful, filled with thick jungles, open fields of swamps and marsh lands which were alive with every variant of life: crocks, monkeys, poisonous snakes of all varieties, leopards, tigers, some zebras and many more species. Rice was the staple farm product because of the abundant monsoon moisture but it was always dangerous because of the poisonous snakes who liked thick and moist vegetation that attracted a lot of mice and rats-the staple of these snakes. Mostly cobras and some green snakes - the most dangerous serpents in the world. Their poison is so powerful that death comes within a minute as the venom paralyzes the various sectors of the brain. The green snake was dangerous because they hung on low level vegetation, particularly the small rice plants. Ironically, the cobra is sought after because its venom used in small quantities is a powerful medical tranquilizer and is used in operations to relax muscles (curate). Not much farming was needed because fruit and wild rice grew naturally. Meat was killed from wild boar, zebra and some other wild animals. Fish was plentiful in the many rivers and inlets and so the fish were there for the taking. The only thing you needed was a net with a little bread thrown on the water. The fish would come to eat and the net was thrown, capturing three or four at a time. Mostly salt water mullet which was delicious. Since fish were so plentiful and so easy to catch, it was the staple of the island which had a million inlets and rivers. Fish was used in almost every dish. Fruit of the most delicious varieties was present the year round and flowers whose names I could never pronounce covered the island in a thousand shades of deep colors which cannot be described but must only be seen. Many of these flowers were treated and used as non toxic dyes for the colorful native clothing. Transportation was mostly by foot- at least it was in 1959. A few airport facilities remained from WWII.

It was difficult to believe that fierce fighting had taken place there between Japanese and American forces. But it was perfect for defensive warfare because of the hidden caves, thick undergrowth and hiding places. The Japanese had to be driven out cave by cave, hill by hill, almost tree by tree. Those who fought and survived were never the same because of the gruesomeness and fear of that fighting. It was mostly hand to hand with knives and flame throwers. There is something about killing a man whom you saw and heard die as you cut his throat or saw him die, screaming in the agony of napalm thrown by a flame thrower that changed your life forever. The Marines who fought there were never the same after that kind of fighting. Worse than the Civil War which also had been hand to hand. Even their souvenirs showed how strange they had become (e.g. ears, noses, dried penis and testicles taken from the dead.)

Except for some rusting barges and sunken ships along the coastline, the jungle had hidden and destroyed all the vestiges of WWII. Once in a while there was an explosion as some wild animal detonated a bomb or other explosive still alive on the island. Even in 1959 it was dangerous to go off the beaten paths. There were many unexploded munitions left there but there was no way to know where they were because of the thick covering vegetation which guarded the island's secrets until it was too late. Some of the children had missing limbs as a testimony to that residue of WWII.

I arrived there in October, 1959 by plane to Sydney and then by boat to the island. Since New Guinea was on the equator, there was no change of seasons and it was terribly hot during the day with a constant humidity factor of almost 100%. The only relief was ocean breezes and the daily rain shower that came in every day like clockwork. For about an hour after the shower it was cool and pleasant but then like the pouring of water on the hot coals of a sauna, it turned back to that high humidity which continued night and day. So the beauty of the island had to be balanced with this one terrible drawback. The natives of course were acclimated and they wore bright clothing covering the lower part of their bodies. The top was bare - both men and women - to keep cool. If you observed the women as they got older, you understood why Western women wore bras. The older native women had drooping breasts almost down to their navels and beyond! Hardly a sight that would sexually excite Western men, obsessed as they are with women's breasts. Here a woman's breasts were strictly functional – for babies. Only when the early missionaries tried to make the women cover their breasts did problems arise. Only then, hidden, did they arouse the curiosity of the man and became foci for sexual allurement and excitement. The missionaries soon gave up that practice and respected the customs of the natives. At Mass it was common to see mothers nursing their babies. Inadvertently, they had created occasions for lust. No one even noticed.

But the most interesting of their customs or at least their former customs was that of cannibalism and the shrinking of human heads. Of course the practice had been outlawed since the UN Trusteeship in 1949 and the islander's conversion to Christianity but the memory (and sometimes the practice) still remained.

I remember studying with a black African from Ghana whose teeth were sharpened into a V shape and of course I asked him why. He was from the interior of the country and his great grandfather had practiced cannibalism. I asked him what human flesh tasted like and he told me his grandfather said, like pork chops. The most tender part of the body - the palms of the hands and feet – were considered a delicacy and were reserved for the chief. The teeth of all young men were "V" sharpened and filed at adolescence. The practice was considered both a sign of manhood (like circumcision) and as a weapon for fighting animals and enemies during war. If you had nothing else, you could always use those razor sharp teeth to tear at the animal or your enemy. The Papuans did not sharpen their teeth but they were cannibals or at least had been in the past.

For these people, cannibalism was not a food need or dietary supplement! It was always a religious act and a form of communion. When you defeated an enemy, you ate him so that his substance and strength would flow into yours. You were then an even greater warrior. And to prove that that was so, *you* shrunk the head of the one *you* had eaten and hung it as a trophy in your tent. They continued to live but only through *you* who now are stronger and braver through having killed and eaten your enemy. In that sense, there was reconciliation with enemies! It was a pure form of communion much like the bounty taken from conquered enemies by Greeks, Romans, Egyptians, and Babylonians. While cannibalism was not unknown among these latter tribes, it was not widespread and seems to have died before the 3rd millennium B.C.

Such vestiges of cannibalism as a religious rite were common even among North American Indians. When the Algonquians captured the Jesuit North American martyrs, one in particular stood out: Father Jacques Lebeuf. He had been formerly captured, tortured by having his fingers cut off and told never to return. He did return and was again captured and tortured. Over a three day period, the Indians would bring him out each evening after the hunt and ceremoniously dance around him all the while cutting pieces of his flesh with sharp knives and eating it right in his presence. All through his ordeal he never uttered a word - neither of pain nor of curse. When he finally died of exposure, the chief ordered his heart to be cut out and a piece eaten by each of his warriors so that LeBeuf's great strength and courage would flow into them. Their modified cannibalism was a communion of strength and courage. The Papuans only added the ritual of head shrinking.

This process had to be carefully done because otherwise the head would not look like the original head. If that happened, then the strength of the defeated enemy would not flow into the eater because it would be a different person from the one who had been killed. So the process had to be carefully done. The head was severed at the base of the neck with one great chop from a very sharp machete carefully honed for exactly that purpose. Then they buried the head in rich red sand and continuously placed hot stones around the buried head. The stones would draw out all the moisture from the head which would be carefully absorbed by the rich sand. After about twenty four hours the head would be very small but would look exactly like the original head that had been placed in the sand. All the moisture from the head had been drained out and you had an exact look alike - only one eighth the size of the original head.

When Nelson Rockefeller's son came looking for such heads in 1959 he knew very well that there were none to be found. After the Trusteeship and their conversion to Christianity, the heads were ordered buried. He offered the natives trinkets in exchange for the heads, knowing full well that some of the Indians would go over the hills to neighboring tribes, kill some of them, shrink their heads and give them to Rockefeller in exchange for the trinkets. It was a terrible and vicious deed perpetrated on a very simple people. Sometime later it was reported that Rockefeller was lost at sea. But it was strongly rumored that some of the relatives of the ones killed, came, took him to their tribe, lopped off his head which now adorns some chief's tent. We certainly hoped so The Western press did not and dared not report this story for fear of offending powerful people in the U.S. But all of us were secretly pleased that the young Rockefeller had received the just reward for his iniquitous deed at the hands of the very people he had injured. And glory be - no lawyers or long drawn out trials. Justice was done and peace reigned.

Aside from this former custom, the natives were extremely gentle. In addition, they were naturally and profoundly religious. The presence of God in their lives was simply taken for granted and I never found an atheist or agnostic among them. They were a docile people who had a profound sense of right and wrong. Their sense of justice did the young Rockefeller in but there was never any stealing or rape or killing of tribesmen. They disciplined the young and boys and girls were severely restricted as to their access to each other. Contrary to some of Margaret Mead's nonsense about free and promiscuous sex among the natives of the South Sea Islands, the girls had to be virgins entering marriage and for her not to be, was a dishonor to her and to her family.

Each village was communal in work and in sharing the work. The men seemed to do a lot less than the women. The men appeared to talk all day while the women gathered, shook down fruit trees and fished. The men would gather when they went out to hunt large game (lions, wild boar, monkeys.) When they killed some game, they would set aside some of the meat for proximate meals and the rest would be smoked or dried out for use later on ("beef jerky.") Even the meals in the evening were communal, gathering families together, each family taking turns preparing the food of the day.

The priests always ate with the people. It would be an insult to refuse to share a common meal because that would be a lack of communion with them. That is why the Eucharist meal was so easily understood by the Papuas - so contrary to American congregations who have almost no realization of that sacrificial meal. They would sit in a circle and the chief would invoke God's blessing. That blessing would last quite a while - interspersed with holy stories and a lot of singing for edification. Then the first plate would be passed around starting with the chief and then the guests. Each person would take a handful and place the food on leaves which served as plates - big, thick leaves from banana· or pepper trees. After the meal the leaves were recycled back into the earth – they were environmentalists long before the West even knew what the term meant. Nothing was wasted and anything remaining was given to the animals, since there was no real "dog food" except for these leftovers.

But just before the meal, the chief would sprinkle a very strong smelling liquid over the food. I asked the pastor what it was and he said "later." I ate what was really a delicious meal (all with hands, no utensils) but I was still very curious about that liquid. On the way back to the mission I again asked the pastor what it was. I wish I had not done so.

It seems that when a relative died, the body was wrapped in very thick leaves and was placed upright underneath the hut. All The huts were built on stilts for two reasons: to protect from flash floods (monsoons) which could arrive very unexpectedly and to protect against meandering poisonous snakes which could endanger the populous while they slept - especially the young children. At the base of the corpse, the bodily juices were gathered, fixed with a form of deodorant and some spices and then it was used to sprinkle on the food. That also had a deeply religious significance. Again it was a form of communion with the dead because the community was a combination of living and dead people and they were reminded of this by consuming some part of the dead in liquid form. Rather disgusting to Western tastes but its theology was quite profound. The community gathers at the main meal and all share in that meal, both the living and the dead – all one community- some of whom were alive, some who were dead. I understood the meaning but my stomach didn't. I think I lost a great deal of weight while I was there on those islands.

The most embarrassing things about their customs was going to the bathroom. Of course, there were no bathrooms and the whole jungle was where they went, using large leaves for toilet paper. Once again, all purely recyclable. As a Westerner, I wanted privacy but such was not to be. These people were always curious and there was very little privacy even when they went to the bathroom. They wanted to see us defecate and consequently, I was stopped up for weeks in fear of being seen. The people asked the pastor if I were sick since I was not seen going to the bathroom. After a while, it was go or explode so I finally overcame my embarrassment and went, to the cheers of my congregation.

Another distasteful habit they had (for Westerners) was to burp and blow air - which was a sign to the hostess that the meal was very good. The louder the belch, the better the meal. I have got to tell you, I became the champ in both areas and the women were happy when I came to a meal they had prepared.

There really wasn't much to do except teach the children in the morning and visit the sick. Any marital difficulties – there were few indeed - were mediated by the chief whose word was like binding arbitration. There was no appeal from his ruling but everyone seemed to be happy.

The natives seemed to practice a natural form of birth control by lactation method and it was unusual to have a child except every four to five years since mothers milked their young for as long as two years. The average family had about six children which was about the child bearing years of a woman. I wish I had had time to look into this further but I believe lactation, natural living, natural foods of great variety, little meat and a lot of fish gave these people a healthy life. The UN had vaccinated the children against childhood diseases so the mortality rate among the children was very low.

I had never seen such happy children even though they had so little, at least in the eyes of Westerners. Their baptism was really a major event in the lives of these people who considered it an entrance into the life of the community. I must say I never saw any sign of depression and suicide was simply unheard of. It may all sound like a south sea paradise but these people were genuinely happy because there was meaning in their lives. I believe that that was due to their faith. They were part of a large, true community which excluded no one and which had a very deep religious sense for them. Why shouldn't they be happy? The only difficulty I had was two-fold: to speak their language (although everyone understood English because of the UN Trusteeship) and what to tell them in my sermons. I finally just told them biblical stories and what they meant. That made them very happy because I spoke in stories and people pay avid attention when you speak in stories. They were innocent like children and they loved these stories.

I wonder what the spirit of their community might be now that Western ways have begun to set in. The natural foods were becoming less and the terrible intrusion of the radio and television had already begun among them. Once you introduce people into the sparkle and glitter of materialistic Western ways – the really nothingness of Western ways - people begin to forget their natural goodness and religiosity. I wonder what has become of them now that their gods have been taken from them. Like King Kong. After he was taken from the people who worshipped him, after the mystery of the great Kong was gone, the natives became drunks, sexually perverted and debauched. When mystery disappears, people no longer have a will to live. Has the same thing happened to the Papuans?

Some day I'm going to go back and find out.

No ethics, no worry about the right thing. And that's why most people don't do it - it's much too painful. You end up with neither the good nor with any financial security which you could have built up during the years. So help me, when your marketability is gone and you reach the age of fifty and beyond, the feeling of helplessness and insecurity only grows. And unless you have a firm foundation in the spiritual life, a deep and personal belief in God, you will not be able to survive the cynicism of old age and its- insecurity. You become too weak to depend only on yourself; and too proud to admit that you need help. I mean if you're not going to succeed at the first, why not at least have the second? There is nothing quite so pathetic as an old do-gooder who has to beg for a living. Yet I must say, I am inspired when I attend meetings at various issues that benefit the public and I see old guys out there still swinging at the corruption of power and money. They have one foot in the grave and they are still swinging at power and corruption. God, that gives me hope and courage for the next day's battle. But those are the great exceptions because they are few.

At the College my interviews with the dean and professors went well. The dean could not believe that one with so many credentials was looking for a job. Something was wrong here which, of course, he would find out only later on. But it all looked good on paper. He put the assistant dean and two students on my case who then proceeded to call and check out every institution of higher learning, every article and book I had ever written, everything I had ever done. It all checked out 100% and I was offered a job teaching law in January, 1982. I would teach contracts and family law for $36,000 a year which for me and my family was a king's ransom. I had never made so much money in my whole life. I even got medical coverage- something I've never had again since I left the College in 1985 - a three year run.

Every day now when I wake up, I pray God that if I get seriously ill, that I die. It's much cheaper that way, comic as that may sound. In 1993 in the middle of a trial, they thought I was having a heart attack. I went to the emergency room at 10:30 AM, then to a special observation ward at noon, then to a regular room for further observation and a battery of tests at 2:00 PM. I stayed there on monitors until 6:00 PM the next day when I was released. The bill was $12,500 for 36 hours in the hospital - without an operation or other serious procedure. I paid the total savings I had ($1000) and $200 per month for 36 months and a special payment of $2000. They gave me a discount for the final bill and I was home free. Now imagine if I ever became seriously ill? You get the picture. That is now the constant fear I live on.

Teaching was good. The classes were about 150 students each and I enjoyed the rapport in teaching the "Socratic" method in law school by reciting from a case, talking about its reasoning and holding and then connecting it up with previous teaching from previous cases to conclude to a common law (judge created) doctrine. It was a lot of fun and I enjoyed the repartee.

One of the strangest phenomenon I observed at the school was the amount of flirtation by older women. It was a night school approved by the ABA and as such, attracted older students who had to work during the day. They were worldly wise and knew what they wanted but the competition for grades was so intense that some of the women really did come on to me - something I had simply never noticed before. And I must admit some of them were terribly attractive.

I'm a leg man myself. My personal sexual attraction is a woman's legs. If they are not good I stop right there and then. Of course, a woman is finally attractive in her heart and mind which is the final determination but as an initial attraction, it's always the legs. Well there was one student called Mary, an older blond woman of about 32 years of age. She was pretty but with a pair of legs that drove me nuts in class. I was glad there was a podium behind which I could teach and not reveal what I was emotionally feeling at the time. She would come in and sit about three tiers up, cross her legs in her short dress and drive me to distraction. Literally.

The class was contracts. One case had to do with the contract price for rope ordered from Java and the increased quality of the hemp actually shipped. Should there be a higher price than the hemp hose actually received as distinct from the hemp hose actually contracted for? My question to the student was what was the difference in price, if any, between the real hemp hose and that of the panty hose. Everyone knew where my mind was and after a few excuses, I dismissed the class early much more from embarrassment than of lack of material. I am embarrassed to this day but I still vividly remember those great legs on Mary.

I could also write to my heart's content. I would be there for the students from ten in the morning to after eight at night. It seems that the 22 other professors were out practicing law to make extra money. I considered it my duty to be there for students full time on a regular and constant basis. My classes were the first to be filled and I was quite happy. It wasn't a great law school but I could teach and write and I earned a living wage. What more could you hope for in this life? You did what you were good at and trained for and you got paid for it. Now that was heaven on earth. Of course, it could not and would not last.

It was too good to be true and, of course, I was right. In 1984 I wrote a series of articles on oil companies and their failure to pay a fair share of their taxes. In 1973-75 during the Arab oil embargo, Shell, Exxon, Texaco and other oil companies simply took the oil beyond the international boundary (seven miles) brought it back and called it "new oil" for which they could charge a different, higher price. This was simple fraud which if it had been you or I, would have landed us a stint in jail as well as hefty fines. Not so the oil companies. They got their taxes reduced by hundreds of millions of dollars which we other tax payers would be obligated to pick up.

All hell broke loose - again. The presidents of those companies wrote and threatened to take away their grants and students - remember, this was Texas where you live and die by oil. Well, the old dean called me in, read me the riot act and I knew that again, I was a dead man walking. In Texas you do not criticize oil companies without receiving a death warrant signed by the executives of the companies. I was dead meat.

Sure enough, some six months later, the same dean called me in, told me that the tenured faculty would not give me tenure and that I should be on my way when my contract was up in January, 1985. Like a fool, I actually believed the guy. I found out about three months later that he had lied to me and that every tenured professor wanted me on the faculty and would have voted me in if given an opportunity. I could have fought the whole thing in court - hell I taught that contract crap - but once again, I refused to remain where I was not wanted. I would not be at peace and those parties would not be at peace and that mixture spelled hell on earth. God wants our peace and we ought not to go around making war for ourselves. So I just left quietly and chose not to fight. I hate fighting. But I was in a hell of a profession for one who hated confrontation. It was like wanting to be a Quaker and a soldier at the same time.

So that was the end of my teaching career. Do I regret it? Not at all. Most of my difficulties were self made and I cannot and will not blame others for what I did with eyes open and with full knowledge. But someone who wants to teach and at the same time last in the profession should remember some very simple rules. The first is that you have to control your mouth and not give vent to every injustice. At least until you get rank and tenure. But that's dangerous. Time you get to that point; you might have sold out all your principles. Select your target, write and research about it and put it in heavy professional lingo. That way, higher ups who really cannot read will not be disturbed at what you are saying. Christ, they won't understand it. Secondly, write like that until you get rank/tenure when you are comparatively safe. Even then, you have got to be prepared for hard times, uncomfortable times, if you are going to speak the truth as you see it. The most important quality in a good teacher is truthfulness. That is, the determination to seek the truth with your whole heart and soul and to follow it no matter where it might go. And then, to be obedient to the truth which you have found no matter how much it costs you personally to live by it. But God, it's tough.

That's a mighty costly demand. But there is no other way to be a good teacher. Anything else and you are a simple ass-kisser and you will ultimately amount to nothing at all. Nothing. And when you die, no one will ever even remember who you are. In fact, you will be so unknown that your worst enemy won't even bother to come to piss on your grave. Now that's forgetfulness!

And that is what I always vowed in my personal and teaching life. That is, that I would always make a difference for better or for worse. You might pray for me, hate my guts, but you would
always remember who I am. You would always come to pray at or piss on my grave. But not ignore it.

The thought that no one would remember me after death was repugnant. One way or the other, people will remember and in that way, I shall have made a difference.

And I did, I think. If not, I gave it all I had.

CHAPTER 16

CANONIZABILI

In each of our lives there pass from time to time genuinely good people whom we consider 'holy". By 'holy' I mean people who give themselves without counting the cost, who treat each person they meet with courtesy, compassion and understanding, from the highest to the lowest. You feel elevated in their presence and without preaching, their example encourages you to be better than you are, to do better. They would surely object if you called them holy because being holy, they know how really unholy they are. The rest of us, mired in our selfishness and sin don't consider ourselves so bad ("I keep the Ten Commandments, I don't steal or murder and I go to Mass each Sunday") so we don't know what real holiness is. Only the saint can realize what a sinner he/she is without false humility because as he/she comes close to God, the source of all goodness, the more he knows he needs God's mercy and love. Paradox. The holier you become the more you realize you are a sinner and that all is pure grace.

But I have played a little game with myself. If I were Pope, who would I choose for my Congregation to investigate as to their holiness? I prefer the definition of holiness of Pius XI: "One who practices heroic charity on a constant and daily basis in his station of life." By "heroic" the Pope simply means constant, day by day, day in and day out. This calling to holiness by the grace of the Spirit is open to all, commanded of all ("Be perfect as your heavenly Father is perfect") in every station of life wherever we find ourselves at any point in our lives. This call to holiness, to be like the Father, is open to all, rich and poor, black or white, young or old, male or female, American or Indian, religious or layman. We may be confused as to whom we are; we are never confused as to what we are commanded to be.

There were four people I have encountered in life that if I were Pope I would give an order to the Holy Congregation of Worship and Rites to investigate. It so happens two were religious and two were lay women. Two were men, two were women (politically correct so far - but all this is irrelevant.) The following are my candidates.

Mrs. Edwin Berger. I was a kid in West Seneca and not a very pleasant one. Anytime we were hungry, anytime we wanted something, she was a soft touch. She never once complained that we used the Hell out of her because she was always there for any of us. She was religious without being overbearing. She and her husband had raised eight children and she had a temperament of kindness without sharpness. I never knew her to make an uncharitable remark about anyone. All the neighbors knew that they could count on Mrs. Berger if they needed anything. Her children grew up to be exemplary Christians, I still remember Kenny Berger, her youngest son. Once in the woods near the railroad tracks where we played a whole gang of 13-15 year olds beat the hell out of us and were in the process of stealing everything we had. There was Kenny, tall, courageous, who told the whole gang of about six bruisers to stop, leave our things and be on their way. His moral strength and his courage told them he meant business and off they went like dogs whose rear ends had been painted with turpentine. I'll never forget him as one of the few in my life who was there for me.

During WWII Kenny volunteered for the most dangerous job in the Army which accepted only volunteers - demolition, because he did not want to kill. I found out later that Mrs. Berger had taught all her children about Jesus, the non-violent, long before it became chic in various circles. He was killed by a bomb he was detonating on the day before VE Day in Europe. Mrs. Berger was the model of accepting the will of God. In spite of his non-violence, Kenny was one of the most decorated soldiers of WWII. Thousands attended his funeral at St. William Church. Mrs. Berger sat there in tears with her family but happy that even in the passions of war, her son sought peace through non-violence.

To this day her memory inspires me and encourages me every time I am tempted to leave the Church, filled as I have found it with hypocrites and Pharisees, starting with bishops all the way down to those in the pews. It is people like Mrs. Berger whose memory is ever present to me, people who were faithful and good to the end in spite of being considered a fool even by her own husband because she was generous and giving when those to whom it was given were filled with greed and ingratitude. No matter. She persevered in doing good day in, day out, to her husband (who was a constant old grouch) her children, her neighbors, to the famished kids who always came by just to get what she was always prepared to give. She would pray for us, constantly, with her rosary in her hands.

I chose Mrs. Berger for a simple reason. Anyone who is kind, gentle and charitable in old age has been so throughout his or her whole life. Old age changes nothing; it only solidifies and makes more clear what the person has been all his or her life. Old age only confirms what we have become throughout our lives. If Mrs.

Berger was what she was at 85, she was that at 15 and 25 and 55. There is nothing more Christian than a joy filled old Christian man or woman.

Mrs. Olivadadi. The second was a bedridden old Italian woman in Buffalo where I was first assigned as an assistant pastor. She particularly fascinated me from the day I arrived at St. Francis. It had been my "function" to take Holy Communion each First Friday of the month to all the sick of the parish, at least to those who had requested it. Mrs. Olivadati lived right across from the church at North Ogden Street so it wasn't far to go. And each First Friday, there she would be immaculately clean in her bed (she had been bedridden for several years,) terribly respectful and pious in a genuine sense.

She fascinated me over the weeks and months. I used to stop by frequently and she greeted me with genuine joy and openness. It was Leon Bloy who once said that the true mark of the Christian was joy and indeed, that was her constant mark. Once I happened to run into her doctor and asked what paralysis Mrs. Olivadati had. He smiled and told me there was no paralysis. Why, then I asked, was she bedridden? He smiled again and said: "Father, why is it that the priests understand so little?" "I don't understand." He smiled and continued to my dismay. "That woman, Father, has terminal bone cancer throughout her body. She's filled with it and the agony must be horrible. She refuses everything but some aspirin for her headaches. I have never heard her complain - not once - or be irritable or unkind to me or to the nurse who comes to see her daily. And that's the God's honest truth."

I was astounded. Terminal cancer? Of the bones? Agony? Refuses medicine? Cheerful and joyful? Something was wrong here and I was to find out the truth: I understood nothing about being a Christian even though I had studied its theology at the greatest Catholic universities in the world in Rome, Munich and Louvain. It was a sick, bedridden woman in cold Buffalo who would teach me.

Armed with that knowledge, I was determined to get to the bottom of things. So on one of my visits, I broached the topic as gently as I could. I asked her permission to speak of her illness and she readily granted it. We spoke of what the doctor had told me and she confirmed it all. But, why, I asked, did she never reveal any of this to me. She just simply said that it wasn't important. Finally, frustrated that I couldn't understand (what was finally not understandable) I blurted out: "But a woman like you. Kind to all the poor, who clothes the naked, never turns away anyone in trouble. You who raised such a fine family whose reputation for goodness and charity goes far beyond the confines of this parish, why you with such an agonizing death? Why you and not me?" I remember her answer vividly some thirty five years later. I shall never forget it. "I spoke to God about that once. Like you, I did not understand and told him that straight out. You know what he told me? 'Olivia!', he said, 'you have tried to follow my commandments and you have loved your family and your neighbors as best you could. I am very pleased with you. Because I am so pleased, I am going to give you an honor which I give only a very few. I am going to crucify you as I crucified my son. I give you the greatest gift I can give anyone on earth.'"

I was astonished but I was not so obtuse as not to understand. It was the contradiction and the paradox of the Gospel that was revealed to me then and there by this woman of simple faith. She taught me in an instant what all those theological tomes had never been able to teach me: what it was to be a Christian, to be crucified with Christ with nothing but the darkness of the surrender of faith in the agony and faith with Jesus on the cross. I had learned the mystery of the cross which is such a stumbling block to the whole world and to me as well. But there it was, the Christian paradox and mystery. At that moment, the scales dropped from my eyes and I for the first time, realized what it was to be a Christian: to be crucified with Christ in love for the whole world just as this bedridden, little old lady prayed and suffered with her crucified Lord for the salvation of the whole world.

She died a few weeks later. I was called to her bed along with many of her family and friends. I anointed her and gave her a little of viaticum as we all prayed. She smiled at me as if to thank me for all my stupid expressions of kindness to her. We prayed with her and when she opened her eyes she prayed these joyful words in Italian:

"Signore Gesu Cristo, I thank you with all my heart for the gift of pain and agony I have suffered with you. Thank you for permitting your humble and unworthy servant to take part in that passion for the salvation of the whole world. Grazie di tutto mio cuore."

Then she stopped breathing. I could only hear the sobbing of her friends and relatives. And my own as well. But my tears were tears of thanks to God for having taught me through this saintly woman, what it means to be a follower of Jesus Christ.

Even to this day.

Marty Martin *is* my third choice. He was a diocesan priest from Buffalo who taught me at the minor seminary. His name was Marty Martin, one of the most lovable priests in the diocese. He was one of the most honest, faithful, humorous and intelligent men I ever met. He taught Latin like it was his natural tongue. He had studied at Innsbruck, Austria before WWII, was a chaplain during the War (he never talked about it) and was - how shall I put it - saintly is the best word I can find. When he said Mass he was totally absorbed in the act of prayer so even that act mesmerized those who saw him. At least it did me. He was simple as a dove and wise as any serpent. But I never met a serpent but I did know Marty Martin.

He never uttered a harsh or uncharitable word against anyone. He even had a good word to say about the devil - "that poor bugger" - he actually felt sorry for the devil! He was there for the students at all times and he could entertain by telling marvelous stories. He was the greatest story teller in the whole diocese and he had a story for every occasion you could think of. He would even take his false teeth out to illustrate the details if he had to.

He was an extremely erudite man who never tried to show off with it or to use it to put anyone down. He could talk plainly to the street conductor as well as to the local bishop as to a Ph.D. at the University. Made no difference to him. He approached everyone with profound respect, consideration and charity.

He was a bit scrupulous on the fasting side during Lent and Advent when the old laws of fasting were at their height. He would actually weigh breakfast and lunch to see that they would not exceed the total of the evening meal. But whatever else he was, he was terribly hard on himself yet absolutely forgiving and easy on everyone else. You'd love going to confession to Marty Martin because no matter what sins you told him in confession, he'd find something encouraging to tell you to keep up your spirits. It was often said that if you ever confessed killing your mother, he'd emphasize that, well, you still got to think of your father who would now be alone!

And a sense of joy and humor always surrounded him. If you were depressed, you went to Marty Martin who would find a way to cheer you up. If you had difficulty with school work, there he was on his time to help no matter how long it took. If you wanted a word of encouragement, there he was. On the spot, drop everything and there he was for you, all the time, every time, always.

Old Marty Martin was hardworking, faithful, prayerful, joyful and giving. As I said, what had always impressed me most was his inability to say anything bad or uncharitable toward anyone; and always a word of joy, forgiveness and a story for anyone who came to him. If there ever was a priest who could be called Christ like, it was Marty. The only thing he ever got angry at was l) himself and 2) evil. It is difficult to believe that such a priest ever existed after the example of so many arrogant, power filled and angry priests and bishops I have met in my life. But it's true. God in his goodness and mercy permitted me the grace to know and love this man whose example has remained for me a paradigm of everything Christian. I no longer have the excuse that most of the priests and bishops were horses' patouts - all that just didn't matter and still doesn't. There were periods in my life when I forgot the precious gift which God had given me early in life in the person of this smiling, red headed Irish cleric who was profoundly joyous because he was profoundly Christ like.

Marty Martin physical characteristics never much changed. Even in old age he looked like Santa Claus - his red hair never whitened, his skin never wrinkled, his cheeks as rosy as an Irishman at the local pub with an impish smile at the ready anytime. If there was any word that characterized Marty Martin, it was joy. I guess I'm a sucker for joy because joy reveals deep belief and deep belief reveals love. The acts then of a joyous Christian are therefore always loving acts as well.

Honore Van Weyenberg is my fourth candidate. He was a bishop, the rector of the Catholic University of Louvain where I attended, from 1951-56. While I was there, he was clearly an extraordinary person. But it was only after I had done some research on his background that I realized what a truly great person he was.

Honore Van Weyenberg was appointed Rector of the University in 1936. His problems began in March, 1940 when the Nazis came to see him. The University had not opened that semester because of the real danger of war. After Germany invaded Poland and then Russia (1939) it was only a matter of time before war would come to the low lands. This happened in early 1940. Because the young men were not attending classes at the University it was difficult for the German authorities to know where they were and what intellectual qualifications they had. As it turned out, the Germans suspected more than they knew because some fifty divisions were thrown into the war with Russia. There was therefore a great need for men to work in German defense industries and other public works for which Germany was short of cheap manpower. The easiest, most economical way for the Germans to keep up with the great demand of defense and public works would be to indenture workers from the countries they came to occupy. It was in Hitler's master plan from the beginning to impose on each occupied country a quota of men to fill for shipment back to Germany for such work. In addition, there was the "traditional" Nazi roundup of Jews for "repatriation" to what amounted to concentration camps. All the Belgians knew the whereabouts of their young men as well as the Jews in their midst. Along with Denmark and the Netherlands, Belgium hid the most Jews during World War II and so the Nazis were particularly brutal in their discovery methods in Belgium.

Their favorite targets of course were universities, colleges, gymnasiums and other private places of learning for young men fifteen and above (who were all subject to deportation.) The Nazis fanned out over the whole country to fill their quotas. They came to the Rector in March, 1940 and asked him for a list of all the students of the University with addresses and academic qualifications. Those were the days before computers so the names had to be meticulously typed and reproduced from master copies kept under direct supervision of the Rector. Knowing full well what was coming after the invasion of Belgium and its defeat and surrender by King Leopold, Honore simply burned all the records so there would be no chance of discovery by the Nazi authorities. But having almost a photographic mind, Honore could reconstruct those names from a multitude of other files which he had at his disposal. But it could not be done by one unfamiliar with University rules and references. So it was imperative that Honore do it himself personally. The result was that without him, the Nazis could never find these young men.

The Rector's refusal was polite but absolute. He had no authority to release the names and their academic history to people who would use that information to harm them. He would not be an instrument of deportation to slave labor for Hitler's Wehrmacht. To do otherwise would be to betray the students, the University, the Church and his own conscience - something he was unwilling to do. The Nazis gave him 24 hours to consult with other officials, particularly the Cardinal Archbishop of

Malines. When he would not even do that ("There is nothing over which to consult. It is against God's laws and my conscience. I have consulted with a higher power and all other votes do not count.") He had a dry sense of humor which of course passed the Nazis by. They never smiled or laughed because they took their work very seriously. How else would a universal Third Reich be established except by very serious men with no sense of humor?

He was arrested on March 18, 1940 and taken to Central Nazi headquarters in Brussels some 25 miles away. There again he was interrogated but this time with more persuasive "methods."

These methods were the usual: electric currents to genitalia, to beatings, shock therapy, lack of sleep, purch ties, etc. They also tried sodium penatole but this was essentially useless since even under the serum Honore would only give them the contributing documents but it was Honore himself who had to creatively put them together to produce the results. So without a free Honore to combine the documents creatively, the penatole was useless. The torture and interrogation went on for six months. He was kept without proper food, medication and toilet facilities. He was not allowed to wash or bathe. His cell was 10 x 15 with a cot and a bucket as a toilet. He was fed once a day with thin soup, a few potatoes and two slices of bread. No sheets for a urinated upon mattress and he was allowed a bucket of foul smelling water with which to drink and bathe as best he could. He lost over 35 pounds and some of the open wounds from the beatings had become infected and full of pus. In short, he was humiliated beyond description.

At Bergen Belson, German scientists practiced particularly horrible experiments to see how long people would last when they were thrown into icy cold water. This was to measure the time it took to freeze to death so that the Germans would know how long they had to rescue their pilots who had been shot down in the North Sea and in other frigid oceans. This was a particularly horrible and painful way to die, shivering to death, because the Nazis always tried to revive the prisoners thrown into the ice water. This was part of the experiment. One froze to death with almost no pain but the revival by blankets and hot water was very painful because when the blood began to circulate again, the pain would begin with uncontrollable shivers.

The Nazi scientists always asked for volunteers - the ones who survived were promised extra rations and lighter work. Some actually did survive (about 1 in 15) so that the chances were not good. In fact they were terrible. But some prisoners simply didn't care anymore because their reason for living had long ago vanished from their souls. As philosophers say, if you have a why, you can endure any what. So they volunteered because most had given up on life. But the majority did not.

One particular Monday there were not enough "volunteers" so the Nazis simply chose at random. One of the men begged the Commandant not to be thrown into the icy water because he was the father of five children who needed him. But pity and mercy were not the virtues of the SS. So Honore stepped forward and asked the Nazi officer to let him take the man's place because he was a father of a family who needed him. He explained to the Commandant that he was only a priest, of need to no one and so it would be better if he were taken rather than the other prisoner.

The Commandant refused under superior orders because the authorities still believed that Honore would relent and give them the information they sought. His request was denied and he was told not to make such a request again. "What will you do? Put me in prison?" Honore had a sense of humor that never failed him, even in the terrible darkness of a death camp. The Gestapo were not amused.

Honore returned to receive the greatest honors from his countrymen and to his position as Rector of the Catholic University of Louvain. He was awarded his country's highest medal of honor while the Pope later made him an Archbishop. But those honors meant really nothing to him because he had seen too many men and women die horrible deaths who, he thought, were infinitely more worthy than he of all these honors. He was that humble and gentle. But he never spoke of his experiences again. What little we know of this man's courage, humility, and self giving in the midst of the most trying times and places, are known to us from others who had seen his witness in the camps. He did not consider himself worthy of telling their stories. Not even his own.

But people knew who he was and who he had become for them. His life at the University was the same and yet entirely different. The intensity of his humility and charity were legendary. He would even go into the street and let others pass on the narrow sidewalks - that was a standing laugh among the Americans at Louvain told not as a mockery but as profound respect. Honore would not be outdone in humility!

The only expression from the past which he allowed himself was his celebration of feast days with the American students from the American College whom he held in most special regard. The one thing he could never understand among Americans was the longstanding prejudice against blacks. To him, they were the incarnation of God's mercy and gentleness at a time when he had nothing to give to his saviors except undying gratitude. It was total grace and it came in the face of a black man. It is true, he thought, God is black! To him, God's salvation came in the face of a big, gentle black American sergeant. He never forgot. The Americans loved him as much in return because they recognized in him the incarnation of goodness but above all of hope. Hope that in the darkest of darkness, a man was faithful to responsibility at great cost to himself; who loved his fellow humans so much that he would not betray them in any way no matter what the cost; who forgave his enemies and harbored no ill will for anyone; and who now spent the rest of his life as the visible reminder that the only thing which matters in life are the three great theological virtues: faith, hope, charity. And the greatest of these is charity and forgiveness. Honore was charity incarnate. He had become a true Christian.

<u>Conclusion</u> Every once in a while in the history of mankind, there appear visible manifestations of self giving, of truth, of love of others, that so go beyond the common measure of even good men and women, that words are inadequate to describe them; and one's instinct is to simply wonder in worship at the mystery who deigns to raise up such men and women in our midst. These four men and women were just such a grace in the darkness of an undeserving world which treated them so painfully and so cruelly. And lo and behold: they give back only thanks and goodness, love and forgiveness, absorbing into their own persons the hatred and the violence of men. One can only worship the loving mystery who raised them up for our courage and edification.

CHAPTER 17

LOSS OF FAITH: STORY OF A CHAPLAIN

It was way back in 1962 (it took me forty years of therapy to even speak about this) that I was a fresh first lieutenant in the chaplaincy corps for the 101st Airborne Division, Sixth Company. I was excited about going to Vietnam to help defeat the godless Communists and defend the American way and the freedom of the Vietnamese. Training was done and I was anxious to get on to the work. We were supposed to be training members of the army of the Republic of South Vietnam and not be engaged in actual combat. That was simply not the case. A few Vietnamese officers accompanied us into the jungles each day or week from base camp but they were really ornaments for cover. Sometimes we were in those dense jungles for over two weeks when we searched for the enemy called then the Viet Cong in the field to destroy him. To this day I do not know why they even wanted me along since I was excess baggage who didn't even carry a rifle or ammunition. It was forbidden under the Geneva Accords. Only a Communion kit for Mass. I guess it was for the morale of the men knowing that whatever happened there was a priest present to console them and give them Communion and "the last rites" as it was still called back then.

We slept and lived in the jungle day after day with heavy rain every afternoon, nowhere to really wash and no change of clothing for weeks at a time. We really stunk. No one noticed because we all stunk alike! But that was not the worst of it. We would lay in wait after info from headquarters that pinpointed the supposed place of the enemy coming through. Sometimes the opposite happened; the Viet Cong lay in wait for us in hit and run operations. We would lose t soldiers a week but most of the wounded did not die because of their quick evacuation by Huey helicopters which landed quickly and ferried them to the base hospital and from there to hospital ships or back to Hawaii for further treatment. Most survived. I don't know what the Pentagon told the families of those who were killed.

My job was (when feasible) to say Mass each morning on the back of a jeep or tree stump, hear confessions from the men, console and anoint the dying and close the eyes of the dead. These men really appreciated that and it was during those moments that I didn't feel like excess baggage but rather like a spiritual member for the team or platoon, depending on the operation. But the results of the fighting really got too me, especially picking up the pieces of a soldier who had attended services that morning. The fighting was intense and when we really needed, help, the officers in charge called in the Phantom jets and artillery. We prayed that these death machines would bit their targets with the napalm and 105 artillery shells and not us. Many died from "friendly fire." I would simply shake with fear in the hole each of us had dug with bullets whizzing all about and explosions from small arms, band grenades and RPG fire (later used with great effectiveness in Iraq and Afghanistan}. When we could we lay those deadly claymore mines all around our location and the first sign of the enemy was when one of those exploded and we could hear the cries of agony of the enemy wounded and dying. Funny how the dying on both sided would invoke God or their mother- mostly their mother. Maybe that was because that was a throwback to the security and warmth of a mother's embrace. In any case, the dying always died with their eyes open at least when the soldier was not killed outright. It was the last attempt not to lose sight of the light before the darkness of death closed in. I held many of them back there as they breathed their last, happy to be in the arms of their priest as their last companion on earth. And it didn't matter whether they were Catholic or not. When you are dying, accidental things like denomination make little difference. The only thing that mattered was the warmth of a brother close to you as each of the dying took his adieu from this life. I anointed them all irrespective of who they were.

I thought every buzzing bullet; every grenade explosion had 'Riga' written all over it. As a priest I should have been more courageous and not show my fear to the men in the field. But I was deathly and continuously afraid of death, of course. Maybe because I had so little faith and that little faith was being exhausted in the fields and jungles of Vietnam. The country was so beautiful and what we were doing so terrible that I finally did lose my faith amidst the screams of agony of the dying that I heard in the jungle almost on a daily basis.

The "real" event was a day in July when I lost my faith. We had approached a field of rice paddies right there carved out of the jungle. The point men were about seventy yards ahead of us when we were hit by cross fire from the tree line where the enemy was hiding. We were too close to call in the Phantoms and the artillery fire which would have killed us, friend and foe alike. I didn't know whether those two point men were alive or dead - and I didn't care, as I dug deeper into that paddies pit -which were always dug for irrigation for the rice grown everywhere in Vietnam. We were caught in a cross fire and we couldn't move until base camp could send us some helicopter gunships to strafe that tree line. In the middle of the fire fight the medic crawled up to me and shouted that we had to go out there to bring those men back from the line of fire. "Are you crazy? That's fifty yards and we will never make it," I said crouching deeper. He insisted with growing anger: "We've got to try, goddamn it, and you're a Catholic priest. What's the matter with you?" The medics in the armed forces were the most courageous soldiers in the field. You knew they would never leave you behind. Most of them came from pacifist churches and they never carried a rifle- only their medical kits like I carried my communion kit. Their casualty rate was almost forty percent. He shamed me into following him through that mud and gook with bullets firing and explosions from that tree line. *Kyrie Eleison!* I thought we were doomed then and there. Just before we got to the men, a bullet took the head off the medic in front of me and I was there alone in no man's land. I was shaking with fear but I kept crawling. *Kyrie Eleison.* I still don't know why I was spared among all those flying bullets and explosions but I was. Upon reaching the two Marines, one was clearly dead but the other was still breathing. I swear that at that moment I stopped being afraid and I didn't shake. Why? Because I had lost my faith right there. I just didn't care anymore. Funny how faith and non-faith can come in a split second. I mean, what good is a priest without faith? He is nothing at all since his whole life is to witness to a reality that no one can see without faith. If you lose it, what do you have left? Nothing really. I no longer cared whether I lived or died. I took the wounded Marine on my shoulders and began walking down the hill to the ditch. And you know why? I wanted to die. I had lost my will to live because I had nothing to live for. I hoped that the bullet · with the name 'Riga' on it would hit me and kill me. I wanted to die but in what seemed a major miracle to the rest of the company, I didn't receive a scratch.

They company thought I was a hero when I was a coward of the first class who simply wanted to die because without faith, I had nothing more to live for. I was decorated with a bronze star even as I protested and tried to explain to the captain what had really happened. He didn't believe me because he thought it was a ritual of humility that Catholic priests are supposed to practice. So I was the only soldier in the United States Army who was decorated for cowardice! It was that courageous medic who deserved that medal, not the one whom he had to shame to go along with him. No one knew that except me. I lived with that for forty years. Even today.

This of course is only part of the story. There is much more to be said because later on by the grace of God, my faith was restored in a way that was almost as marvelous as when I lost that faith in the mud paddies in what was then the Republic of South Vietnam. That story is for another day. It took me forty years to tell my story. I do not know even not why I feel a need to tell it. Maybe it's because no matter how dark our lives become, there is hope. Even for a chaplain in Vietnam amidst dying and death.

CHAPTER 18

A CHAPLAIN'S STORY II

It should be clear that my lot in life was faith and its loss. My life was spent vacillating between these two poles. It was by faith that I became a priest and by its loss that I was so deeply wounded to my very soul. It was the sight of death, of bate, of brother killing brother, of the dying crying for their mothers- all together that became the tsunami that ripped my faith from my very soul. I could not believe in this God of love when so much hatred surrounded me. It was almost instantaneous as I was helpless before the marine that I lifted on to my shoulders and hoped against hope that the enemy would kill me as I made my way down the hill in the broad openness of that day. In spite of my desire and hope, it was not to be and it was from there that I had to make my way back to faith in God's not my own. The hound of heaven never gives up on me. This is the rest of the story.

I had become reckless as I thought to take the place of the medic who had shamed me to go after the two wounded marines and who was killed along the way as we crawled toward them. His memory became my memory, his courage my courage, his willingness to face death for his brothers became my own. I swore that like that medic I would leave no man behind even if I got killed doing so. I had no more fear. I was no longer afraid to die. So now what did it matter? My life of faith was over, my priesthood empty. The longing for death intense. I did what previously I was deathly afraid to do (no pun Intended). The men of my company thought I was a man among men, a hero in their midst who went where they feared to go whereas it was an intense desire to die. What did I have to live for? What I had prepared for all my life was gone and my life was as St. Paul put an empty gong, empty brass. I could reveal it to no one so I kept hearing their confessions, console their dying, encouraging their spirits and closing their eyes in death. I remember in the study of the Fathers of the Church how they opposed the Donatist's heresy. Even if the priest is sinful and unworthy, they said, it was the faith of the church and of the recipient that created the sacrament, that worked by the Holy Spirit to become real in the fruitful love of the soldiers. I never had any doubt that my own lack of faith had anything to do with the living faith of the simple soldier who knelt before me. I felt so ashamed, so unworthy of his faith in me as representative of holy church that I would cry myself to sleep right there in the hot jungle. But I was a soldier who had to do his duty. But that duty was now empty of meaning for me.

This situation lasted for some four months and my own spiritual and moral life deteriorated significantly. Then as from on high one night we were shelled with large mortars. Some of the men had been hit and since I no longer had any fear of death. I actually welcomed it. I'd crawl out to the wounded and administer any consolation I could bring. Some of them were dead before I got there. I'd close their eyes because I had nothing more to offer them. Except if there were others there, I didn't bother with the anointing and the prayers for the dead since I had no faith and the words would have been empty in any case. But in a flash as I closed the eyes of one Marine, I was blinded by some explosion just above me and that is the last thing I remember. The blast was so great that it must have rendered me unconscious. When I woke up, I was being carried out on a stretcher to a waiting medivac helicopter that had landed in the jungle. My back felt like someone had simply lifted me off the ground, slammed me down and left me for dead. Later I found out that I had been hit with about fifteen pieces of shrapnel so that they had to lay me on my stomach. I could not feel my legs so I had to feel if I had any left. I felt them but they were numb and immobile. My God, I thought, I'm going to be a paraplegic for the rest of my life. They rushed me to a naval medical facility at Danang and I was put out almost immediately. I woke up in a dark room on my stomach with excruciating pain in my back where the shrapnel had lodged. What seemed an eternity before the doctors finally came to tell me the news? I had been hit by one of those mortars that exploded above me. If it had landed, I would have been blown to bits. One of the doctors remarked that God had saved me for a purpose. He sure did but then I didn't know why. They had removed most of the metal but three pieces were so close to my spinal cord that they were left untouched for fear of a paralysis from the waist on down. They would hurt but in time I'd have the full use of my legs. Even today it takes me ten minutes to get up. They kept on saying how lucky I was when the only thing I wanted back in that jungle was to die. But I was the coward who would not speak.

God does have a sense of humor. The nurses would come in each day to give me a sponge bath and to make sure I was as comfortable as possible. One had a good sense of humor: "Well, Padre, I've washed down as far as possible and I've washed up as far as possible. Now you wash possible." We had a good laugh but it was painful to even laugh. I could watch a little TV and a hook up from below so that I could read books upside down. Reading is a great analgesic and I did a lot of it. I did a lot of sleeping from the pain pills. It was then that the local commandant came to read me another citation for a Purple Heart and bravery. This time I did not bother to tell him that not only did I not desire that second honor but that I didn't deserve it. But in the Army it's "Yes, Sir" and "No, Sir" and that is the end of it.

After a month I started to be ambulatory. They put me in the same room with a soldier near death. He had been hit by one of those road side bombs while driving his jeep through one of those jungle roads. Doctors had done all they could do for him so they thought that the presence of a wounded chaplain would help him die. I didn't know what to say so that for the most part I simply held his hand. It is surprising too many how much the dying are consoled just by the presence of another human being who cares. He didn't want to pray but I asked him if it was okay for me to pray. He said yes. We were both being taken care of by one of the kindest, most considerate doctors in the United States Army. His name was Fitzgerald and he would come some three to four times a day when it was clear that he did not have to. He'd check the tubs, take our pressure and kiss the young soldier on the top of his head. How many doctors do you know who do such things? I know of none. In any case, after one of the doctor's visits, the young soldier asked the doctor whether he believed in heaven. "Why yes, I do." "What is it like?" "I don't know." The young man was shocked. "How do you believe in something which you don't know?" The doctor thought for a moment and responded. "Outside that door is my dog. When I open that door, he will fly into my arms and lick my face because he loves me and knows that nothing evil will befall him as long as he holds on to me. That is how I see heaven. I don't know all the surroundings and I could care less. What is important is that I will fall into the arms of Jesus Christ who loves me and gave his life to prove it. Nothing evil will ever befall me. That is heaven."

The answer was so simple and to the point. I think I learned more theology from that doctor than I had learned studying in the finest institutions of Europe-Louvain, Munich, Rome-but never had I heard such a beautiful definition of heaven. The young soldier smiled even in his pain. After the doctor left, I held him for awhile and then he died. I do not know whether the tears on his face were his or mine in my complete helplessness to do anything for him except to hold him as he died. I hope and pray to this day that he felt my love for him as he lay dying. No one should die alone and I gave him all that I had. And you know what? I began to believe once again. I wasn't there yet but I could feel the beginning of belief arise in my soul. God had used a doctor in a far away hospital in Danang, the Republic of South Vietnam and a dying soldier to begin my long journey back to belief. I was not there as yet but at least I could again start to pray. "Oh Lord, if you do exist, have mercy on me as you did on that poor young soldier who died in my arms." That was my prayer, simple and to the point because it was all the faith that I had. I gave all I had and I hoped against hope that from a small mustard seed, that faith would grow by the grace of God.

A few months later I was given my medical discharge. I had contracted malaria as well so my days as a soldier were over. They even had a band to see me off from Tan San Nut Air Base. Maybe because they still thought I was a hero. I know different but God has his own ways for which I had to patiently wait. I landed in California, visited some friends -and went back to my old diocese to await further assignment. What do you do with one thought to be a genuine hero? Why you put him in a mountain parish, make him pastor of some thirty families and about three thousand jersey cows. Whitesville, New York was nestled within the Allegheny Mountains near the border of Pennsylvania where he can't make trouble, where the winters were long and the loneliness extreme. You can read just so many books and visit so many parishioners when there were only thirty of them, all farmers. No intellectuals here. But it was a peaceful place - something I desperately needed in those mountains where you had to talk with God or go crazy. It's just that it seemed God never answered. Maybe he did in the howling winds of winter or the slight breezes of spring or in the hot days of July and August. The way of nature is beautiful when even the weakest, smallest plant breaks through the huge weight of ice when the spring comes and the birds sing. I had learned to be at peace with my tiny mustard seed of faith.

My habit from the time I had studied in Rome was to take a nap between one and three in the afternoon. In Rome, nothing moved during these hours - only the crazy American and English tourists. You could die of a heart attack and no one would notice. In any case, it was spring with the windows open with a fresh breeze. I had begun my afternoon nap and just then, a loud knock on the door downstairs. I mean, who the hell could it be in the early afternoon in a parish of less than thirty families? Abruptly I opened the door to find a young girl of no more than twelve or thirteen years. I was really angry to be so disturbed and I almost shouted, "What do you want?" She calmly said that she wanted to be baptized. "God Almighty," I told her in harsh terms, "Don't you know that you have a lot of studying and preparation for that great day? Do you know that?" I could see the tears whelming up in her eyes in response to my harsh language and angry tone which was almost a shout. "Why do you want to be baptized?" Now I had her. Through her tears she gave her simple act of faith: "Because Jesus is alive." There it was in all its nakedness calling to me from a messenger sent to me from God. I chocked on my own tears and excused myself. I went to the kitchen to weep and sob. I had hoped that the little girl did not hear this unworthy recipient of his restored act of faith because at that moment, it was God who had restored my faith through a young girl. There it was from the mouth of a simple peasant girl, "Because Jesus is alive." The very core and heart of what it means to be a Christian. Upon my emotional recovery, I invited her in and after she promised to come back for instruction for some weeks, I took her over to the church and baptized her. I wanted to baptize myself but that would have been foolish. Another had done that years before. It had only to be renewed. We hugged in a holy embrace of people of faith and I didn't want to let go. She was my angel sent from God to Whitesville, New York, to reveal His Son crucified and resurrected to a man who was so unworthy of the grace of faith. We are all unworthy but God's love envelops us and never abandons us no matter how we stray. Even from Vietnam to Whitesville, New York – the hound of heaven who never ceases to seek the lost sheep and once found, carry him on his shoulders as he rejoices that the sinner had found his way home or rather, that the Master had found him and brought me home.

There you have it all. The story of the chaplain who lost his faith which by God's grace was restored to him via the two messengers of his love... a doctor and a dying soldier, and a young girl of thirteen who proclaimed to him the truly good news of salvation: Jesus is alive!

Alleluia! Alleluia! Alleluia!

CHAPTER 19

SENTENCED TO LIFE

The irony of war is that it is never over for the combat soldier. It is a reality that never really dawns on the ones who send him to war. If he survives, they think, he comes back to where he left off and no one realizes the agony and the pain he must endure for the rest of his life. The reason? The horrible scenes of death and suffering which he has witnessed in combat both of his friends and comrades and what he has done to the enemy when he soon finds out that he is flesh and blood like himself. Is it guilt or is it that he survives when so many around him are dead? Why does he deserve to survive while so many others no better than himself did not? It is a question bored into his soul which can never heal. No one on the civilian side ever seems to realize the life changing reality every combat soldier must endure for the rest of his life. What it really is, is a sentence for life. No one in our prisons who serves for life can ever imagine what the combat soldier must endure for his sentence of life. That is why it is so important that we send young men to battle only for the most serious of national needs.

In my case, it was for me a long list of shame and pain. It was bad enough to try and cover by denial that you had anything to do with the Vietnam War for fear of further condemnation and humiliation. So you simply never talked about those days. What is worse is not being able to talk about those experiences, that you really couldn't speak to anyone who would ever understand what you went through. And still go through.

There were the awful desires to kill yourself many times during the day; the cold sweats and nightmares in the evening. How many times did I wake myself up screaming or wetting my pants in the bed? I often became so cold that no amount of blankets could keep me warm. And the images and flashbacks of the dead and dying and the screams of their agony echoing in your ears that never went away. And you couldn't tell anyone about it because of fear and shame.

None except a Houston police officer who picked me up on Westheimer Avenue in Houston as I was walking in my sleep in my underwear. Thank God he was a vet and knew exactly what was wrong. He held me like a baby in his squad car as I told him of the horror and the pain of those days. Like the medic who shamed me into crawling with him to rescue two Marines who were wounded under fire from the tree line. I was a chaplain and I was deathly afraid, trying to dig deeper into my hole to escape all those bullets and bombs that I thought had "Riga" written all over them. I was a coward and he shamed me into following him. Halfway there bullets ripped his head off and his life's blood covered me to my horror and my fear. Thank God it was not my blood, I shamefully thought. I crawled to the two Marines. One was dead, the other was dying. I didn't care anymore whether I lived or died because it was at that moment I lost my faith in God in the midst of such pain and horror. How could a God of love permit this for his children? It sounds so juvenile until you face the God awful reality of a friend's blood being spilled all over you. There can be no God who would countenance that and still be a God of love. I lifted the Marine on my shoulders and started down the hill. And you know what? Without faith, I only wanted to die from one of those bullets which would rip me open as it did that truly brave medic.

Would you believe that I made it without a scratch? The Colonel thought it was the greatest act of bravery he had ever seen and awarded me the Bronze Star in spite of my protests trying to tell him that what I wanted was not to save that Marine's life (he did make it after all) but to simply die with (I thought) both of the Marines. So I had to live with the hypocrisy of award to a coward and the pain of all those days in the field. There was really much, much more to tell but you have a glimpse of what I have to live with for the rest of my life. I was sentenced to life in my prison of horror, cowardess, pain and shame. Until God sent that Houston police officer to begin my healing.

Lucky for me that the police officer brought me to the local veterans hospital where a group of former vets could actually talk about all those terrible days of pain and shame - precisely because they had experienced the same thing as I did. They warmly accepted me even as I cried like a baby for finding a few people who actually understood and did not condemn. For the first time in thirty five years I could actually talk of those days and begin to heal even if you never fully heal even after that talk therapy. But it was enough to live by. What I (and they) had experienced was what we later found out was post traumatic stress syndrome (used to be called "shell shocked" during WWII) but there were no facilities or personnel then to help us overcome it or at least to live with it. You never overcome the trauma; you only get to live with the pain that never goes away.

I am so thankful that those soldiers coming back from Afghanistan and Iraq now have facilities and personnel to help them when they get home. They will still be sentenced to life but the trauma and the pain will be less. Most can then live with it.

No one ever remembers all those of my generation who committed suicide because the memories were so vivid and so bad or who simply gave up and became homeless without direction and meaning in life. You can see them all across the cities of this nation. You have only to look. Now soldiers have at least a realization of what hurts them and others who can help them deal with the memories and the pain. I am deeply grateful for them; I only wish that my generation could have been reached and helped. May God console them and give them peace which none of us experienced during all those days after that awful war. We are all sentenced to life.

CHAPTER 20

DENNIS THIBADEAUX 1933-1963

In each life there is one or another person who stands out for good (and even for evil). Such a person gives us strength and courage as exemplary, that is, one who gives us all the reasons to continue in life. If you are religious, such people can be thought to be sent by God at a particular time and place to be a lifeline at a time of trouble and distress.

In my life, there have been a few such people, three in number: a bishop, a nun and a captain of the 101st Airborne Division. I recount the third here because of his courage and bravery at a time in my life when fear almost overwhelmed me and I thought I was a lost soul. For him, I went from fear to lasting pain.

I was stationed in the Chaplain Corps assigned to the 101st Airborne Division. Our assignment was to train troops of the then Republic of South Vietnam. Our duties were to train ARVIN or soldiers of the South to defeat the insurgency of local militias called the Viet Cong or patriots of Vietnam. The regular army from the North had not yet entered the fray but in 1961-62 the Cong were plentiful, courageous and deadly. They were subversive as farmers by day and soldiers at night. They were really agents who took orders from the communist North after the declared peace after the defeat of the French at Dien Bien Fu. The military demarcation line was set at the 17th parallel and was supposed to be temporary until the election in 1956.

President Eisenhower thought differently so that the South would not become communist along with the North. He canceled the election and set up a temporary government under local (mostly Catholic) leaders (the Diem brothers) in the South who declared the South a separate country. In order to insure the survival of the independent South, Eisenhower sent military supplies to the South's government and "advisers" who were supposed to train the ARVIN as a competent army to insure the South's survival. Our soldiers of the 101st were sent to do just that but while the buildup of the ARVIN was only at its beginning stage, we (surreptitiously) engaged the enemy as well as trained the army. We were not supposed to be fighting according to the 17th parallel agreements. In fact we did most of the fighting in tracking down the enemy and sought to destroy him as a fighting force before the North could engage. That called for multiple patrols in those jungles along the Mekong Delta, the coastal region along the military demarcation line and the supply route along what was known then as the Ho Chi Minh trail that led from the North through Cambodia and enter via the plains. We were to set up patrols all along these demarcation lines to subvert and ambush the enemy and cut off their supplies from the North. We would go out on patrols almost every day and return to various base camps along these routes. But then, sometimes we were gone for weeks without showers, warm food or change of clothing.

The jungle was a frightening place with its deadly snakes, leeches, daily rains, heat, swamps, paddies but most deadly were the Viet Cong who were locals who knew the terrain and set up their own deadly traps. Their favorite strikes were from the tree lines as we passed open fields of rice paddies and other jungle openings. What were more deadly... leaches or the Cong? The latter! Leaches crawled into every orifice of your body and you could get them out only with lit cigarettes. We had to inspect each other every time we waded through those rice paddies.

The one in charge of the patrols in our sector was a Cajun captain who had already served in Vietnam for a few years. He was a graduate from Loyola University in New Orleans and a West Pointer all the way at its officer training sector. He was a deeply religious Catholic who attended daily Masses even in the jungle where I said Mass on top of a jeep or on tree trunks. Those Masses had to be done early and quickly because to stay in one place for long was to insure observation by the enemy. He saved my life once as I said Mass. The motor shell destroyed all my communion gear so that from then on I said Mass with a canteen, with whole bread.

Before each foray by the patrols, he would give pep talks about why we were there: to support freedom in the South against the communist tyranny of the North. The Vietnamese had a long history of defeating the foreigners who came to occupy the country: the Chinese, the Japanese, the French and finally the Americans. We had come, he said, not to occupy or colonize but to help the people of the South become free from the communist tyranny of Ho Chi Minh from the North. It was up to us to train the southern army so the country could protect itself after which we could leave. The plan was simple but the situation would become a full scale war with the North starting in 1965 once they realized that they had been defrauded (no election, creation of a southern army, an independent state or Republic of South Vietnam). But full scale war would begin only in 1965 when hundreds of thousands of American troops landed to defeat the armies of the North who came South after the defeat of the Viet Cong. That was the unexpected future. In 1962 our American engagement was limited in fighting and in training the ARVIN and destroying the local militias.

Captain Thibadeaux had been decorated with a Silver Star for bravery in the field and two Purple Hearts for wounds he received in the fighting. Each time he returned to the field, convinced that the American mission there was noble and worthwhile for the people of South Vietnam. He told us that it was okay to be afraid so long as we did our duty. Who wouldn't be afraid with death coming each day from those tree lines and ambushes in the jungle? To this day I do not know why I was there in the field except to give courage to the men that a chaplain was there no matter what. The chaplain and the medic - the men knew this well - would never leave any of them behind even if they died trying (the casualty rate for medics in the field was forty percent. I don't know what it was for chaplains. I only knew that I didn't want to be one of them).

The patrols surprised the enemy but sometimes they would surprise us with mortars and heavy machine gun fire from the tree lines as we crossed open fields. How many eyes did I shut in death in those days? It is strange how so many of the dead die with their eyes open so as not to be deprived of the light. The light is the last thing that leaves us and we strain that it not be lost. Their last petition was for their mothers.

The Captain never asked anyone to do what he was unwilling to do. He was a leader of a man's man because he led by example and not simply by orders. His first concern was the safety of the men and that no one is left behind. I alone saw him weep for those whom he lost and he blamed only himself for their death. What more could he have done for them? What a burden to bear and what a privilege it was for me to see such a strong man shed tears for those soldiers killed in his command. But he never cried in front of the men; only in front of me because he always thought a priest was special. Each evening he came over to kiss my hands and, embarrassed, I asked him why he did that. He said it was because those hands consecrated the bread of life that nourished his soul and gave him the strength to carry out his duties such as they were. He loved the army. He hated the killing. Paradox? It is a paradox every real Christian must deal with. But he never failed the mission.

David never underestimated the enemy. In fact, he admired his courage. When he was a lieutenant earlier in the war, his company had cornered two enemy Viet Cong who had already killed two of his company. They advanced slowly up the bill and when they finally reached the enemy, only one was still alive. The enemy had expended all his ammunition and that of his companions. When the Captain and his men came upon him, he was throwing rocks until he was killed. Such courage only came from a deep belief in the cause he was fighting for and it made David think about such courage. After that, he never again took the enemy for granted.

In addition, he was no patsy. Courageous me, I wanted to ride point in case something happened to the men. He nixed that idea outright. I would only be excess baggage since I did not carry ammunition or guns *or* supplies (chaplains were forbidden to carry them by the Geneva Accords). When I insisted he ordered the sergeant to put me in the center and if I made my way to the front, to put me in chains. Here was the guy who served my Mass each morning threatening to put me in chains! No special privilege with him- His was only the safety of his men including the chaplain.

He was a person of character in and off the battlefield. He didn't smoke or drink and never used coarse language. One day when we captured two prisoners, contrary to so many in the field who would torture them for information, the Captain bound them but then shared all our food with them. Being Catholics, they asked to attend my Mass the next morning. Then they sang like canaries. They warned the Captain that their companions were lying in wait at the turn of the Mekong River a few miles down the road. We found out later that their information was absolutely correct. Thibadeaux's kindness really saved our lives... so goodness does pay off. I'm alive today because of that man's humanity. The reason the prisoners gave for turning information? They didn't want the priest hurt. To this day, I think it was due to the kindness of the captain not the safety of the priest.

There was so much more to tell about this good man that I could tell you but I hesitate to say more lest I break down and weep. It has been over forty years and his memory is buried in my soul. Never a day goes by that I do not pray for him. He was killed a few months after my tour of duty was over (I was medically discharged early because of the wounds I had received). I learned that from a letter from a lieutenant in his command. He told me that the Captain was killed reaching one of the wounded. No one was to be left behind and he gave his last measure of devotion fulfilling that promise. To this day his image and example of bravery and fidelity to duty still overwhelms me. Why is it that such good men must die and deprive us of their courage and goodness? But all is a grace from God and I am profoundly grateful to have known this man and to have served with him. May the kindness he showed even to the enemy be given to him as well. "Blessed are the merciful for they shall receive mercy." May he rest in peace even as I await to join him in Heaven.

CHAPTER 21

THE WAGES OF WAR ARE DEATH

It comes as no shock to any combat soldier to hear of the massacre of the civilians by Sergeant Robert Bales in Afghanistan. The American people are shocked because so few of them have ever seen combat (and its fewer by the day). In Vietnam we had our My Lai even while most soldiers did their duty in a very confusing war. During my service in Vietnam as chaplain, we did not know who the enemy was among the population. Who would be friend to you during the day and who tried to kill you during the night. They would simply disappear into the population after the rising of the sun. In Vietnam, we didn't know who our enemy was especially when those we were supposed to be helping turned out to be our killers at night by planting bombs, betraying information to the enemy, selling weapons and tossing hand grenades into our tents. This created terrible tension between the American and Vietnamese soldiers, officers and civilians. This showed up clearly as Americans harshly treated villagers, burned their villages and mistreated many more because of fear, even of our friends. Even torture was used to get information about ambushes, strike places and other betrayals which never worked. You could not tell friend from foe.

You can see these parallels in Afghanistan. Afghans have always hated foreign troops in their country from Alexander the Great through the Mongols, the French, British and Russians and finally the Americans. Our soldiers do not understand their culture, their religion, their language, their history. The only thing they know is that among our so called friends, they may turn on you and kill you. Their leaders, corrupt as they are, steal our billions, do nothing for their people and attack Americans in speeches to please the people. You simply do not know what side the corrupt Karzai is on when he makes demands for U.S. troops to withdraw from the field. You can't trust the ones who are supposed to be on our side. This creates a fantastic amount of tension on both sides so that it is not at all unusual or strange for one or another serviceman to blow his gasket by killing those who are creating that tension. You get sick and tired of seeing your fellow soldiers betrayed, killed and maimed by people who are supposed to be your friends. In fact, you have no friends among the people because you never know who is plotting your death since AI Qaeda and the Taliban are at home, are among their own and people know very well that when the Americans leave, these Islamic groups will be here at home, marking for death each one who is cooperating with the American enemy who will soon leave that country. They are even given the date of their departure by the President of the United States. They betray Americans because they must betray Americans as the foreigners and infidels who must leave. If we had another hundred years to build up the new nation that might do the trick but even that is unsure and is a long shot. Why? Because whole groups have tried to do it before from Alexander the Great in 350 BC down to the modem army of the Russians who were defeated and had to leave in 1989 after losing over 100,000 of their troops (twice the number we lost in Vietnam) and after over nine years of war. Sound familiar?

As a great American general once said, "There is no substitute for victory." Now after ten years of war with no victory, the Commander In Chief of the U.S. is withdrawing in humiliation as did the Russians and Mongols before him. The combat soldier is left frustrated, bereft, defeated that all his efforts and that of his companions have been in vain. Sacrifice until victory. It simply is too much for many of those combat soldiers. The only thing left is another panel in Washington, D.C. with the names of the fallen from Afghanistan in another lost war. Under those circumstances, is it any wonder that one or another of those combat soldiers snapped?

Thus the tripping point for Robert Bales was the same as that company of American soldiers at My Lai who simply murdered hundreds of innocent men, women and children by machine gunning them in one big long ditch influenced by the same confusion as Bales - different culture, language, religion, motes, mixed enemy-friend in the same population, death of comrades by so called friends, etc. We can begin to understand Bales as one of those American soldiers who "snapped" under these contradictory and confusing circumstances. We cannot approve of what Bales did but we can understand why he did it. The question finally becomes for the combat soldiers, "What are we here for? What are we fighting for? What are my buddies being blown to bits for?" The confusion of our leaders is telling. One day it is to kill terrorists to keep American safe. The next day it is nation building. The combat soldier fights to win. When he sees his commander in chief about to leave the filed by 2014, the depression is great because he has lost his fighting edge. This is utterly confusing for the combat soldier when he doesn't know what he is fighting for. Explosion of irrationality! The only thing that keeps him fighting is that he is fighting for his buddies in the field with whom alone he has loyalty and trust. He can trust no others.

Every combat soldier knows this even if few combat soldiers do in fact "snap." But some do. The only wonder is that there are not more of these terrible instances. Why? Mostly because American discipline is strong among the military and restraint is asserted by senior officers who will not permit such behavior. But once in a while, one soldier is lost and snaps with scandalous results (250 dead civilians at My Lai; 16 dead civilians in Afghanistan- and others that never come to light). Afghan soldiers also "snap" for other reason (e.g. their faith commands the death of infidels, the burning of the Quran) and turn on their American trainers. We saw this a short time ago among Afghan trainees whom we were trying to help. Six Americans were killed by trainees who turned on their own trainers.

In the opinion of so many former combat soldiers now returned to civilian life is that there are so few such incidents. But it does not stop in Afghanistan. Time and again we hear of former veterans committing suicide or opening fire on groups that had nothing to do with the enemy. It is simply a result of reenacting the fears and memories of combat for which thousands of retiring veterans who suffer from Post Traumatic Stress Disorder. That will be one of the residues of war which we as a society reap in our own lives, perhaps for the rest of our and their lives.

We should be very grateful that the My Lais and the Robert Bales do not explode more often in this country. Most of the self hate and memories of death in soldiers that suffer PTSD are not directed to others but to themselves. That is why we have such high numbers of suicides among returning combat veterans. We must be prepared for many more Robert Bales, here and abroad. That is the price we pay for war.

CHAPTER 22

VETERANS DAY 2012

November has always been traditionally a month for the remembering of the dead. The Catholic Church begins the month with All Saints Day on November 1 and All Souls Day on November 2 to commemorate the memory of all the ones who led exemplary lives to be imitated by the faithful. Above all a commemoration of all the fallen since the time of Abraham Lincoln's famous address to remember the fallen at the battle of Gettysburg and the dedication of the cemetery of those who had died at the battle. Congress in 1920 then set aside November 11 both to recall that dedication and the armistice that ended WWI - 11-11-11, the 11th hour of the 11th day of the 11th month of November. That date was extended to commemorate all the veterans who have given their last full measure of devotion. It has come to be known simply as Veterans Day.

Every Soldier who has served has his own story to tell, particularly those who have fought in combat. Most do not want to speak of it because the pain of those days has forever sheared their consciousness so that many do not speak of those days. In my case, as a chaplain at the beginning of that Vietnam War; it took almost forty years to even speak of those days. The intervening years were full of pain, thoughts of suicide, sweats at night and nightmares because I could not speak of those months. Only after l came across a group of former veterans united at the local veteran's hospital could I begin to even speak to others about those days with those who had experienced what I had experienced. One recollection is particularly painful. I shared it with the group of former veterans and I would like to share it with others who might profit from my experience. It is not edifying but it is real and I was encouraged to write it down by that group of former veterans of the war because they thought that would encourage others to have some hope even as we read about the suicide of so many veterans who have fought in Afghanistan, Iraq and Kuwait. People should know what effect war has on the hearts and minds of the combat soldiers whose pain is so great that it leads to suicide. This is my story and I hope and pray that it will help others.

The "real" event was a day in July when Host my faith. We had approached a field of rice paddies right there carved out of the jungle. The point men were about seventy yards ahead of us when we were hit by cross fire from the tree line where the enemy was hiding. We were too close to call in the Phantoms and the artillery fire which would have killed us, friend and foe alike. I didn't know whether those two point men were alive or dead- and I didn't care, as I dug deeper into that paddies pit - which were always dug for irrigation for the rice grown everywhere in Vietnam. We were caught in a cross fire and we couldn't move until base camp could send us some helicopter gunships to strafe that tree line. In the middle of the fire fight the medic crawled up to me and shouted that we had to go out there to bring those men back from the line of fire. "Are you crazy? That's fifty yards and we will never make it," I said crouching deeper. He insisted with growing anger. "We've got to try, goddamn it, and you're a Catholic priest. What's the matter with you?" The medics in the armed forces were the most courageous soldiers in the field. You knew they would never leave you behind. Most of them came from pacifist churches and they never carried a rifle- only their medical kits like I carried my communion kit. Their casualty rate was almost forty percent. He shamed me into following him crawling through that mud and gook with bullets firing and explosions from that tree line were everywhere. The fear was overwhelming but the example of the medic led me on. *Kyrie Eleison!* I thought we were doomed then and there. Just before we got to the men a bullet or some explosion took the head off the medic in front of me and I was there alone in no man's land full of blood. To remain there would be sure death. I was shaking with fear but I kept crawling. *Kyrie Eleison.* I still don't know why I was spared among all those flying bullets and explosions but I was. Upon reaching the two Marines, one was clearly dead but the other was still breathing. I swear that at that moment I stopped being afraid and I didn't shake. Why? Because I had lost my faith right there. I just didn't care anymore. Why such death and agony? What kind of a God was I serving that permitted such hell, such agony, such death? It came and went in a split second. It was like the heat of a malaria attack. One that sooner or later would kill you. You shake in pain and then it is gone or you are dead. Funny how faith and non faith can come in a split second. Then I thought, what good is a priest without faith? He is nothing at all since his whole life is to witness to a reality that no one can see without faith. If you lose it, what do you have left? Nothing really. It really does happen that fast. It was then that the realization came that I no longer cared whether I lived or died. I took the wounded Marine on my shoulders and began walking down the hill to the ditch. And you know why? Because I wanted to die. I had lost my will to live because I had nothing to live for. Priesthood had been my whole life, everything I had aspired to, hoped for, desired with my whole being was gone. I hoped that the bullet with the name 'Riga' on it would hit me and killed me. I wanted to die but in what seemed a major miracle to the rest of the company, I didn't receive a scratch. I heard the whistles of death meant for me but like a divine protection, none came near. I desired what was not to be.

The company thought I was a hero when in reality I was a coward of the first class who simply wanted to die because without faith, I had nothing more to live for. I was decorated with a bronze star even as I protested and tried to explain to the captain what had really happened. He didn't believe me because he thought it was a ritual of humility that Catholic priests are supposed to practice. So I was the only soldier in the United States Army who was decorated for cowardice. It was that courageous medic who deserved that medal who had given everything in an act of mercy, not the one whom he had to shame to go along with him. No one knew that except me. I lived with that for forty years. Even today after I could speak of it. Most even today refuse to believe my story. Reality is infinitely stranger than fiction.

This of course is only part of the story. There is much more to be said because later on by the grace of God, my faith was restored in a way that was almost as marvelous as when I had lost that faith in the mud paddies in what was then the Republic of South Vietnam. That story is for another day. But it still took me forty years to tell my story. I do not know even know why I feel a need to tell it again. Maybe it's because no matter how dark our lives become, there is hope. It is my question: how do I reach out to all those retiring veterans whose only thought of relief of this pain is self slaughter? Oh God! I How I wish I could tell this to every one of them. About a chaplain in Vietnam amidst dying and death. Yes, hold on! There is hope.

CHAPTER 23

THE WOUNDS OF WAR

For years after my service in Vietnam with the 101ST Airborne (Chaplaincy Corps), I wandered the streets, had cold sweats and woke myself up with my own screams because I did not understand what had happened to me. No one told me that what I was suffering from was a syndrome flashback to all the horrors and guilt I had experienced during those combat days even if I never fired a gun in anger. I did not recognize that the wound of war was embedded in my DNA and I did not know how to deal with it. That is, until a local Houston Police Department officer picked me up while I was sleepwalking. He was a combat veteran himself so he knew and he directed me to a discussion vet group at the local Veterans Hospital. For the first time in almost forty years I would talk about the pain, the horror of war, the terrible flashbacks of the screams of the wounded and dying whom I could not help except to hold them. Now I could speak with those who suffered the same as I did and I felt free. I still suffer from the memories but these memories were shared and in sharing I could speak about what had happened to me. But the wound of war is still with me after all this time which will be with me till the day I die. But at least now I can live with it and there is a voice speaking to me in my darkness. That is true of every combat soldier who survives battle.

People seem to think that when they send men to war, they do their duty only to come back (if they come back at all) and continue what they had left off in family, in work, in country, even in church. The wound does not show as if an arm or a leg had been blown off. The wound is within, too deep to even talk about so the combat soldier seldom even talks about it. If he does it's usually because he's lying or had never really been there in combat (only one in three soldiers sent to Vietnam actually saw combat while the rest were mostly backup or a supply person). The real combat soldier does not want to relive what he went through for any number of reasons: he was a coward in some way; he suffers from survival syndrome. It is too painful to relive; he knows no one would really understand except the one who was there, smelled the rot and the blood, saw the pieces of companions he was with, heard the screams of the dying for whom he could do nothing. Whichever of these reasons fit, they leave a scar, a wound of war that never heals. He tries to forget in many ways and some survive it better than others. Others get lost in alcohol, drugs, become homeless because no one understands and he goes off into his deadly silence. Why else do you think that the number of suicides is so great among them, even today with all the psychological help they do receive? Even so, they are overwhelmed and often rid their pain by ridding themselves. While we recognize this syndrome better today than we did in my day, the wound is the same and it is the way we handle it that matters. Better today than in my day.

This internal wound has really three sources for the combat soldier. First there is the guilt of survival. Why did I survive when so many of my fellow soldiers did not? Was it only fate that some go and others do not? Fate is really irrational when about five to ten percent of soldiers die in combat. This syndrome is real and long lasting. It really destroys our sense of fairness of which Americans are so fond. It simply is not fair that this man dies while the man next to him survives. As I said, there is no rational or spiritual reason why this is so. That's what made my task as a chaplain so difficult not to say almost impossible.

The second source is the horror seen at very close range - even in the enemy whom the combat soldier recognizes is very similar to himself...the screams of the wounded and dying which he is afraid to attend to as he shivers in his own foxhole. That too may be a source of guilt for not tending to the screams of the other paralyzed in that hole in the ground. That fear is so deep, so all consuming that often it paralyzes. He fires his weapon when he does not even see the face of the enemy. Such killing is contrary to our nature, to all that we have been trained to respect and to love. All this must now be destroyed by command on command.

The third source of guilt is the reason for all this carnage. That is why it is so important for the combat soldier to be convinced that what he is fighting for is worth the sacrifice of death and pain, his and his companions. When this is not clear, he lives and dies for his buddy with whom he develops an intimate friendship. Even when the rationale of war is missing, there is the responsibility for his fellows which gives him courage to fight on. This bond can be so strong as to overcome the fear and horror of combat.

But once that war is over, the horror and memories remain nourished by that silent wound which never goes away. That is also why it is crucial that when we send our young men to fight and die, that we clearly explain to them how important the mission is and to know that even when we do so, the wound of war will always remain. But if the mission is strong and clear, that knowledge can alleviate the pain as it did in WWII when this nation was fighting for survival. Yet that was not the case in wars in Korea, Vietnam, Iraq and certainly not in Afghanistan. The rationale for war is much less the further we get from the war for our survival (WWII) and the guilt increases exponentially. How does the combat soldier feel when he visits that black wall in that ditch in Washington, D. C. with the names of 58,000 soldiers all of whom (it seems) died in vain? That sacrifice seems to be worthless. That deeply depresses. Mistakes will always be made. But they should be at a minimum so that when we send a soldier into combat, that there is truly a vital interest of our country involved which has been clearly explained to him. We can no longer believe that we must trust the wisdom of our leaders. Too often they have lied to us. The reasons must be firm, clear and that important. They must be spelled out for all to understand. Otherwise we might as well start building another ditch with its black wall for all the failures in Iraq, Afghanistan and whatever is next.

CHAPTER 24

DEATH

Death is the one thing that is unanswerable in life whether we think about it or not. It comes inexorably with each fleeting second and those seconds are all finite in number, some will have more, some will have less but always mortal, finite and ending. For everyone. Death is always at the horizon of our lives against which everything is measured. Its comparisons are numerous. One author describes death as if we are all chained together as in a chain gang. Every once in a while, the keeper comes up without warning and slices one of your companions throats - Doctor Death as he is known. You may always do the same to yourself for there is always a knife available for self disposal in case you can't stand the wait. Or it is as if we are on a conveyer belt with some falling off all the time and which finally compasses us all. There are none alive today who witnessed the Civil War. Our mortality is our inevitability. We try to prolong our life by medicine, good food and exercising habits and even by the quality of our genes. But no matter: one or a hundred to one, death grasps and embraces us all. We are all beings for death. In fact, there must be death or the world would be overcrowded in a hundred years. In the words of Zorba the Greek, "if all your learned books cannot tell you why we must die, I spit on your books."

Death is the core reality of religion which attempts to give an answer to this inevitable mystery in each of our lives. Religion tries to answer the mystery whether there is any life, conscious or not, on the other side of that divide: reincarnation, eternal life, transmigration or nothing (atheism). There is no way to prove any of this since no one has ever returned after death. Communication with the dead is completely bogus. There really is no empirical proof that there is life after death. Nor is there that there is not. This gives rise to faith in such an afterlife or faith that we simply enter or re-enter into the nothingness from which we came. I say 'faith' since there is no real proof one way or the other. Death is a leap of faith both for the believer and for the unbeliever since no one can "prove" the reality (if any) which exists once we have thrown off this mortal coil and tasted death. Any afterlife is governed only by faith. We all desire to be saved at the end. The famous story of Job is precisely that. Job was a good man but his fidelity to God is tested (with God's permission) by progressive misfortunes that overtake him but each time he is loyal to God. All is taken from him: his goods, his children, his health. Yet he is faithful to God in all these troubles and all these things are restored to him in the end because of his fidelity. The seventh cavalry comes to his rescue at the end and he lives happily ever after. But that is usually not the case in our lives. Someone with a horrible disease, e.g. Alzheimer's disease- will be saved only when death liberates him. The example of Christ in the gospels is also instructive in this regard: "My God, my God, why have you forsaken me". A human cry to one who had the power to save him but who remains silent. No seventh cavalry to come at last to save Christ on the cross on which he must die in agony. Only death will free him. And that is the lesson that will happen to us all. No matter how many times we are rescued by medicine or other means - there will always be some morbidity or accident to finally claim our lives. We may have a "war" on cancer or Alzheimer's but finally there will be some other disease or malfunction of body or accident that will claim our lives. There is no seventh cavalry that will save us in the end.

There are other ways in which the Greek, Mediterranean and near eastern religions tried to escape by union with their gods. For example, some religions even went so far as sacred prostitution in various temples of the gods. In uniting themselves with these prostitutes by sexual activity with them, the faithful could be united into the realm of immortality. Sexual pleasure would be the premonition of final union. The basic truth here is that in sexual union the future is guaranteed then there is the survival of the tribe which would not totally die. Their future would continue in the children of the tribe. Eternal life lies in the procreation of the tribe. Early Hebrew survival was not predicated by a personal resurrection but survival in the tribe which would carry the tribe forward. Only a few centuries before Christ did personal resurrection make its way into Jewish belief and then not completely. Some called Sadducees did not believe in personal resurrection while the Pharisees did In Christianity, the resurrection became complete with the death and resurrection of Christ which was essentially of a personal nature along with the whole tribe of believers in that resurrection event.

Christian faith is unique in the basic claim of the death and resurrection of its founder. If death is defeated once, it is defeated finally and cannot claim that person again. The resurrected one has defeated death by taking up his life again. But the life of Christ is different after the resurrection because he lives in a new dimension. It is the same Christ before and after death. "He showed them his hands and his side" but his life now is of another dimension which we cannot grasp. Christ returns to the

God-head that paradoxically he both never left and had to leave and return with his glorified humanity which is the mystery of the incarnation of Christ. Belief in Christianity is built squarely on that historical event. Without the resurrection of Jesus Christ, the Christian faith is false and a lie. Everything depends on the Pascal mystery of Christ in whom we are incorporated.

Why is it that Christ had to die since he was both God/man and had both natures? There is the utter comparability that being human, he could not escape the reality of death because death is part of our nature itself. He would not be like us if he could escape the reality of death. If Christ did not assume every human reality, said the early writers of the church, that reality could not have been saved. Therefore Christ had to die in his human nature as we must die: "He was like us in all things except sin" *(Hebrews).* It was in the exact moment of his human death that he rose gloriously in the final redemption and victory over death. He died and rose immediately.

But death in Christian faith is also a complete trust and surrender to God in whose hands the Christian gives himself. If God is the God of life and not of death, after the real death of the Christian, God could raise him from real death just as he had done with Jesus. Humankind had to traverse that door of death and thereby enter into the very life of God which is not possible if the human remained only in the human. In death, death's mystery is traversed by the resurrection of Christ which is the perfect work of God and is proof that the living God is operative in the life and death of mankind following Christ's victory over death.

Of course for the atheist, all this is nonsense since he has seen nothing but the natural. For the atheist all is restricted to the natural who sees nothing but the natural. He therefore remains in the natural that by death he believes that he goes back into the nothingness from which man first came. No one ever saw Christ's Resurrection or Christ himself. He appeared only to the disciples who proclaimed this event to all men and women who would believe their word: that they had seen, touched, and experienced the resurrected Lord. They were all martyred in witness to that event. As I have said, no one has ever seen or experienced any of this but what has been handed down by the community of faith who received it from the apostles who were the eye witnesses of these events and for which they all gave their lives. Only faith can reveal the reality of this supernatural reality which atheists deny. Who can blame them since they are without faith? They experience only the natural.

That is why death is so frightening. The veil through which we must pass can be traversed only by faith; there is only a proclaimed word handed down to us by the historical church from the apostles. It may or may not be true as seen by the outsiders. The only real testimony or "proof" of the reality of the afterlife is the quality of life of those who do believe. All this is quite true but much of death's agony and anxiety comes from the fact that we cannot be sure of what lies beyond the grave. We are afraid that it might not be true. Is it a glorious and loving reality who welcomes us or is it, well, nothing at all?

Thus the mystery of death (and it will always remain a mystery because it lies beyond our reason to really understand) is presented to us at every moment of our existence. Some try to forget this inevitability by work, profession, acquisition of money, sex, power, prestige but finally, that mystery gnaws at our consciousness as we see more and more of our relatives, friends and strangers all tasting death, knowing that soon it will be our turn as well. We have but a limited time to give answer to this mystery while we as yet have time to do so. At every moment, we hear and feel its overwhelming reality coming to meet us. Inevitably.

CHAPTER 25

WHY MUST WE DIE?

The mystery of death has haunted mankind from the beginning of recorded history. Every country, every civilization, every religion in history has struggled with it. They all knew that sooner or later all would die. No one is alive, say, from a hundred fifty years ago. Most ancient civilizations did not really ask this question directly but simply developed rituals for the dead. From all recorded history, the radical difference between humanoids and the rest of the animal kingdom was the presence of rituals for the dead. These have been found in the earliest excavations of humanoids. Never of any other species. These rituals served various purposes: communication with the dead, communion with the dead, helping the dead in the afterlife, an afterlife itself (intercessions by the dead and for the dead, helpers for the tribe by the dead, fear of the dead (e.g. headstones, arrows into the air to hold the dead down or to attack evil spirits) etc.

But no one asked why they must die. They really did not know. They simply died and they knew that they had to die. More modernly, if we did not die, we would enter a dimension of complete boredom, repeating over and over the same activities going nowhere finally and wishing that we could die! The ancients called it the *circuitus eternales.* It would be *Groundhog Day* all over again until the dimension of love and its growth comes on the scene as it did for the main character in that film. Only in love did he escape the boredom of a repeated life; love alone gives meaning to life. Everything else is marked with death or repetition which is another word for death.

Islam and Christianity have a clear notion of the afterlife which is in relation to this question. Islam's after life is nothing more than a continuation of the pleasures of this life (best foods, wines, sex with beautiful women but no relation with God). This is unsatisfactory because it simply continues the boredom of this life for which we become tired and ultimately desirous of death. When you do something over and over again you reach a point of exhaustion and want it to stop. For those who do not believe in a living God, only suicide will end it. On the other hand, in Christianity the afterlife begins in the here and now and is based on the concept of love since for Christians, God is love. We are made in the image and likeness of God; therefore, only love can make us like God who is eternal. This deserves an in depth explanation.

For Christians eternal life does not begin after death but it lives and develops in the now each time that we advance in the love of God and of each other because of who God is (he is love). The "beyond" (heaven) is not a place but a relationship, an encounter, an alliance, a commitment. In Christ Jesus, Christians believe that God has come to share his life with them which is one of love with us. Since God is love, love is life that is, what makes God a living God. To share God's life, therefore, is to share God's love. That was the reason for creation. That is, we are made to participate in the life and love of God. This "beyond" escapes all definitions but is inscribed into our humanity. In Christianity, it is Christ, who has given us the new commandment, that of the new alliance of God with men: "I give you a new commandment: "Love each other as I have loved you". (*John* 13:34) To love is to exit from our closed universe of repetition, to go forth from ourselves, to make a journey that never ends, to respond to that appeal of love to always go further and deeper, to always go ''beyond'' in the increase of love. That is the name of eternal life. This "beyond" begins here on earth in the measure that we love God and each other. "By this shall all men know that you are my disciples, that you love one another." In other words, mutual love of Christians is the sign of God's presence among us. Every act of love is an experience of God, of eternal life. The more we love the more we become like God. That is why life is an everlasting journey begun on earth and continued for all eternity because our union is with God and with each other in our growth in love who is God himself. God is infinite love and that growth in love is eternal life which can never be exhausted. One is never bored when one loves because in love we enter a new dimension of existence when time is no more. The character in *Groundhog Day* could escape the death of repetition only when he began to love.

Thus the "beyond" begins now, in the here and now. That is why and how we can grow in love by and in the Holy Spirit of Christ who with us form one body, the mystical body of Christ. That is really the communion of saints in this one mystical body of Christ composed of both the living and the dead and all those in the future will come into that one mystical body. Past, present, future all in one. In that sense, *the beyond is at the heart of the present as a commitment to love more and more as Jesus has loved us, that is, to give his life so that the other may have his life and love. The "beyond" is growth now and forever in love.* Simple living is boredom and ennui; to live without love is hell now and in the future. The definition of hell is to live without love.

The "beyond" does not speak to me of a world found outside my understanding. It is manifested as demands of life, of respect, of equality, of solidarity, of liberty, of dignity- to put these in operation now in this world which are all the manifestations of love. In all this, we attempt to change the city of man into the City of God. That is summed up in the one act of love which sums up all the law, the prophets and the commandments. Who loves God and the neighbor truly and authentically has fulfilled the law and all the commandments. In the words of Augustine, "Love and do what you wish" *(Ama et jac quod vis).* Love does not hurt or injure the brother; it only builds him and her up. Each day I learn that the beyond is the kingdom that Christ has come to inaugurate and which I have the responsibility to manifest and build in my life by my words and acts. The participation in that kingdom begins here on earth. The beyond is neither a time nor a place to attain. *It is my existence lived with God and my brothers and sisters here and now in Jove.* That is heaven begun here on earth. My present is manifest as a future to be accepted in the now. To believe in the beyond is to live the present in becoming the future in that act of love. When we love, time is no more. By our love, we have already entered the beginning of eternity.

Then what happens to our beloved deceased? Where are they? How do they live? What relation do we have with them? This faith in Christ's resurrection triumphs over death but does not eliminate here below our tears nor our mourning. We remain fully human with all of its vulnerability and lack of a perfect vision of who God is. But this faith permits us to give our beloved deceased a new meaning. It is here below on earth that by continuing to love each one, we mysteriously rejoin all at the heart of the kingdom rejoining all those who have left us. We have become one body in Christ by the workings of the Holy Spirit, some of whom are still on earth who live by faith; some are finally with God who sees him as he is and all those who will come after us for all time. All live in Christ, the first born from the dead, because we have all risen with him. If we have the eyes of faith. We were there with him as he rose from the tomb: some who now see God as he is; others still on the journey as pilgrims; and all those yet to be born whose numbers we do not know. Only at the end of time will the mystery be complete when Christ will deliver all to the Father.

Therefore the notion of eternity, life after death is not simply a projection of this life. Our eternal life is begun in this life, in the here and now in the measure that we love God and each other in the one body of Christ. If love does not begin here on earth, there is nothing to celebrate in the afterlife. That is the definition of hell. Love is not boredom but a relation of growth, a union and communion with God and with each other. Nothing is lost, nothing is destroyed, no one can perish if he/she begins to love here below which will only continue in union with God when time is no more. As the liturgy of the dead puts it. "Life is not ended but changed." It was the same Christ who lived, died and was raised from the dead but changed. What was begun on earth is continued in the beyond in love's growth because God is love. We need know nothing else about the afterlife. When time ceases there remains only the eternity of love which can only grow since God, being love itself can only continue what he is, in itself an eternity of love because time is no more. God gives us what he is which is love because that is all he is. It is almost too good to be true. When time is no more, only love endures. Death is that door through which we enter that absolute relationship. But die we must to reach that life of eternal love of what was begun in time. As the preface of the Mass of the Dead puts it, "Life is not taken away but changed". Changed because we will see God as he is. Because he is infinite love, we enter the beyond time to the eternal growth in love.

CHAPTER 26

THE LAW

After I negotiated a departure from St. Mary's Collegein Moraga in August, 1974, I knew that it was time to leave the ministry. My personal life had disintegrated beyond belief and I suffered from shame beyond imagination. I could no longer endure the hypocrisy of a ministry which would not get more tolerant or less rigid and the divided life I was leading. I blame no one but l (myself for all the turns in my life). As I have often remarked, my scandal came from the hypocritical life of a public ecclesial life which did not conform to the Gospel and a private life which conformed to that Gospel even less. Others scandalized me. I scandalized myself even more. I blame no one but each must give an accounting before God.

So with heavy heart I just decided to leave it all and I wrote the bishop of Buffalo accordingly. I simply told him that as a bishop he would never hear the truth because socially, he could not hear the truth; that I had exhausted myself in every way trying to bring the Gospel and the institution together and that I had failed miserably. I had failed institutionally which had been vindictive and confrontational with someone who was extremely difficult to live with; which in turn led to my personal disintegration of which he had ample knowledge. I was therefore - not surprisingly to anyone - leaving the active ministry. I was leaving as freely as I had entered and I would apply for no dispensation to leave the priesthood. I had entered freely, I had served freely (although miserably) and that I needed no one's permission to leave what I freely entered. I had married no one so I wasn't hurting anyone in leaving the ministry. Sex had never been the major reason for leaving the ministry, not then not now. That was a myth of a society so enamored with sex that it can't see or understand anything beyond its own whizzer.

That man tried in every way to get a letter to me. Trying to get me to leave officially. I guess it was important to him. It wasn't to me. I refused to accept every letter so I do not know what he said. Probably granting me a dispensation which I thought dishonorable to ask for and receive. I freely give. I should have the dignity of freely leaving without the ecclesiastical shenanigans. I had a little self pride so I would send each letter back marked "refused." I would have put a more obscene mark on the envelope but I owed the man respect and dignity which his office had never shown me. I was bitter, angry, dejected and defeated. But then if you treat people as badly as Catholic superiors have treated me, then I'm no better than they. And my pride would not allow that. Not that I felt superior to them in any way. God knows how I despised myself then as I despise myself now for my own failings, my own shortcomings and hardheadedness. I freely admit that I have done so little with so much of what God had given me that I had no reason whatever to feel superior to anyone. And I did not, as I do not now, just recognize honestly who I was but also who others were as well. But given what I was and what I had done, I was the last to be able to throw stones at others for fear of a huge boulder that would come crashing down on my head. But the inability of those men not to admit their own wrongdoing has stayed with me even to this day.

In any case, my thoughts went to law school where I thought I could do some good. I still had this idea that our lives are given to us on loan, as talents given so that we had something to show God at the end of our lives. You have got to give a response for what has been given you. Since law was so intertwined in everything American, I could think of nothing better to do with the rest of my life than to teach future lawyers. That would necessitate at least five years of more schooling which was daunting all by itself. I had been going to school for almost my whole life and I was getting sick of it. After a while, they don't teach you much of what you already don't know. I already had two doctorates and other various master degrees so my apprehension was warranted. But I was changing my career in midlife so I thought that one last push had to be made. I was lucky. I had some time to do something else with my life. I had to be well prepared for what I was about to do, so it was resolved in my heart: five more years of study for the last push. I could then be prepared for the second half of the drama. That too was to prove a mighty disappointment.

I wrote a novel once about a lawyer-soldier who entered law school to do good (it was never published.) He was inflamed with the passion of a young man who wanted to change the world by and through the law. He tried to the point of endangering his own life - through excitement and danger. He was a "warrior for justice" from the Book of Revelation. The moral of the book was finally that, yes, you can do some good but as you get older you tend to get more mellow and sanguine about what you can do in life. You are lucky if you can just change yourself. The hero comes to the conclusion that justice in this world is partial at best and that in the final analysis you must leave all things to God who alone can bring about the kingdom of justice on earth. When man tries, it's a disaster as we have seen so often during the 20th century. This does not mean that you should do nothing - on the contrary, we must do all of which we are capable. We must struggle and not give in to despair. But in the final analysis our justice and truth seeking are partial at best and failure at worst. I was to learn that painful lesson only after many years of teaching and practicing law. The guy in the novel was me. Maybe it was better that it was not published.

My first years of law school were at the University of San Francisco whose law school (for the sake of government money) had to take down their crucifixes from the walls which I thought very strange for a Catholic university. I soon discovered that this law school in its anxiety to become a "real" law school had to discard all things Catholic and Christian. That was even stranger. It thereby became like every other law school in the nation: secular, sealarized and separated from all things which are truly profound which only religion and transcendent thought can grapple with. Law separated from transcendence is tyranny as we are beginning to see in American law. This was all out banned and the school became like every other law school in the country. Not a bit different: same texts, same curriculum, same methodology, same thinking, same nothing. It was strange that I spotted this from the very earliest days of instruction. I realized that there was something missing but I managed to keep my mouth shut so I could at least make it out of law school.

I had to learn a new language, a new way of thinking, "to think like a lawyer." What it really was, was nothing more than good old fashioned logical thinking with a lot of history from the common law and some major principles of legal analysis. You could learn the whole thing in about six months but the union (ABA) makes ·you stretch it out over three years. All this could have been broken down into simple English but instead it was translated into complicated legalese so that no one could understand it. Maybe because we wanted to keep it to ourselves. The moment people found out how really easy it all was, we would be out of a job. Something like the priests of Rome who had their sacred language (Roma spelled backwards is Amor - the secret of the foundation of Rome) so that they could keep their jobs. It's a little more complex than that in law and you do need some training. But today all the forms and pleadings are on CD ROMs and disks which can be popped into a computer and there is everything you need. Just feed the computer the necessary information and bingo! You have all you need. You then have to have the gift of gab to get it across.

In any case, it took me the darndest time to master the language. Even after ten years in law practice, I still tend to speak in logical English and tend to avoid legalese much to the dismay of judges. One time after docket call, I asked the judge if the other lawyer and I could "huddle." The judge looked at me and said "you mean converse." "That too, your honor." He must have thought I was nuts and so did all the other fifty lawyers in the courtroom. I suppose I am nuts but lawyers should be able to speak simple English so as not to confuse people, much less themselves. Whenever you hear words like "heretofore," "know or should have known," "due process," you are in the presence of a lawyer and you better be on your guard.

The humor and put downs surrounding the legal profession was even then in vogue. The Irish had a limerick for which a classical education comes in handy.

There was a young lawyer called Rex
Who had miniscule organs of *sex?*
When accused of *exposure*

He said with composure

De minimis non curat lex

The students in law school were mostly pompous asses. They were either the sons or daughters of lawyers or of professional people. They loved the power which came with knowledge and it became clear to me even then where the profession was going. They practiced on each other when called upon in class "to recite." You were given 10-15 cases to read in any given day and if called upon to recite, you had to give the facts of the case, the law governing the case, an answer and a holding. It was preferable to be able to place the case in the line of cases which led finally to yours and its advance in the law. The articulate ones would shine when called on but you never knew who would be called on so you had to be prepared for everything. Never learned a thing through such a "Socratic" method. But it was good practice for being on your feet and thinking quickly while there. Ironic since Socrates hated lawyers and thought them hypocrites who for money would represent anyone. The original lawyers were called "the cynics" as befits their profession. When I would try and bring up the ethic of the law - was this right or wrong? This was simply not thought about because the law was interested only in results, in a legal analysis so it could fit in other previous cases, not in right or wrong. So a lawyer could argue an antebellum pro slavery case as he could argue a post Civil War rights case - it is all the same to him or her. The truth or falsity of the matter simply did not count - only whether the case was procedurally correct and whether it developed judicially created law. I could never get across to my professors that these were secondary issues to right/wrong, truth/falsity. In my mind, everything else fades into insignificance and indeed became a facade behind which one could actually escape truth. The professors after a while would try and avoid me and my questions because they thought I was in the wrong place.

I also quickly learned about women at the law school. Normally I was so busy and had to study so long to get down the new language that I had little time for the opposite sex. Most of the women at the school were from second careers - who were either divorced or they were bored with their lives (it was also a good second job making a lot more money than selling panty hose at Sears.) Most of them were ugly and mean. I know that that is not politically correct, but life's frustrations and pain had gotten to most of them which explained their cynicism and just plain meanness. Some of them actually hated men and given what most of them had gone through, I did not blame them. The expression was "hard eyes, hard heart, hard ass" and you didn't want to have anything to do with them. But they were as horny as hell.

There were exceptions of course. One was an older student about forty two who sat behind me in evidence class. She was sensitive and intelligent and I enjoyed talking with her. She had recently been divorced and had a few teenage children. Until I met her, I had had no time for women, much less the money to take them out. In fact, I was so busy that I must have sublimated my sex drive. My former profession had left me rather bashful with women in any case. She brought it to life again. I was genuinely interested in her, in law school education and the law for reasons that will become evident. We hit it off emotionally right away, we studied and researched together. She was interesting, warm and she had a good mind. We would have made a good law firm and become good friends had I not let sex get in the way. And so it was.

One day she asked me for a night at the philharmonic (Conductor Osana was magnificent) and dinner. I told her I had no money. She just laughed and said that her husband had left her beaucoup bucks so she would spring for the tab. I was embarrassed I because I thought that it was the man who would have to invite and pay. The world had radically changed since last I had dated. So I let it be and went along with the times.

It was a wonderful evening and she had become a new and real friend. But I was to confuse friend and lover and that would be a fatal mixture. I drove her home and she invited me in. She disappeared for a few minutes, then came out in a really sexy negligee. She just presupposed that was what I wanted. I had given no indication except hold her hand. Instead of being honest with her - that I valued her as a good friend only - I took off my clothes and made love to her. When I could not reach climax she gently asked me why when it was quite clear that she had done so several times. I had been very considerate of her for over an hour and I satisfied her a number of times. When she asked what the matter was, I told her that it was difficult for me to come to ecstasy with a woman I was not in love with. I thought I was being honest, perhaps too honest. She became furious and in no uncertain terms ordered me out of her bed. Even if you don't love, she all but screamed, you are supposed to pretend that you love when you sleep with a woman, she informed me in no uncertain terms. A woman wants to feel loved and told she is loved, even if you don't. It's a game that has to be played at the present stage of the sex revolution. I thought that was dishonest and cruel so I could not do that. She actually threw me out of the house and no matter how hard I tried to explain my feelings to her; she would have none of it.

We never talked or worked together again. Even when I said hello to her at the school, I was given no response. Sex had come to ruin a perfectly good friendship and I would never try that again. Never. She and I had both felt used and humiliated but I could not pretend to what I did not feel and consequently, could not do. In fact, it was one of the most embarrassing moments of my life which I did not want to repeat. Why this was so strange to her confounded me.

I was helped economically and learned some practical law working at the law firm of Garry, Drefus and McTerrnan. They were a Marxist firm - I think the only one in the U.S. I was not a Marxist but because of my involvement in anti-war, civil rights matters and for the poor they were the only ones to be there for me when I needed legal help. So I was impressed with their legal expertise as well as their dedication to the down trodden. I was to learn some value lessons in such service. There was a dedication above all from people who were non believers but who gave of themselves without cost for their ideals - erroneous in my opinion - which I did not see among the Christians I knew. It was the same old story: the example of dedication and idealism came from atheists and agnostics while believers, well, let's just say that I could not count on them when I needed them then, before and after. Why is it that the more religious people become the more they forget what it's really all about? In spite of all this, I remained a believer and a Catholic. Maybe it was because there are so many sinners in the Catholic Church that I was so much at home with them. And the Catholic Church is full of sinners. I'd never make a good Baptist even though I came to love them very much.

I worked in trial preparation for the Black Panthers, and The People's Temple, both clients of the firm. The People's Temple case was the most interesting. All their records were in the law office - some fifty boxes of them. We often met with Jim Jones and his wife and at the time they seemed like genuinely good people. I attended some of Jones' church services in San Francisco and almost immediately discovered that he was not a real preacher who believed in the transcendent but one who believed very much in the here and now, almost a Marxist ideology. I don't remember exactly when I found it out but it was more an intuition than anything else.

Maybe that is what made me so uneasy about him, his ministry and his experiment in communal living in Jonestown, Guyana in 1974-75. I could not explain my feelings of unease and when I discussed them with Charles Garry, he simply pooh-poohed them as misgivings from a Catholic who couldn't stand that Jones was closer to the Gospel than the Pope. When I pointed out to him the ideas and concepts in his sermons, I was accused of taking them out of context. Only later, when it was too late after the stupendous event of November, 1976, did I go into the records more profoundly and confirm what I had only suspected all along: Jim Jones was a self serving autocrat who fooled poor people to come to Jonestown and become (in reality) his slaves for the kingdom of Jim Jones. I wrote all about this but only when it was too late. In fact, Charles Garry barely escaped with his life after three days in the jungle as Jones and the 380 people at Jonestown drank the strychnine laced Kool-Aid in an act of mass revolutionary suicide. What that meant was simply that the suicide of all those people would be the beginning of a new view of reality, giving others all over the world the courage to rise up from their death and ashes and so begin an act of worldwide revolution. The only thing it proved in reality was that death conquered and that the only thing which death brings, is death itself. It was a massive piece of brain washing for all those poor people from the San Francisco Bay Area but which convinced the vast majority of those poor people at Jonestown to commit suicide intentionally and willingly (except for the children who were, of course, murdered.) What struck me most is how Jones had fooled even bright people like Charles Garry who was never again the same about revolution and overtaking the system. After October, 1976, the firm was never the same and it began to quite literally, die. Shortly after, I had no desire to work there.

Everything changed after that November including the idealism and commitment of the firm to the poor and downtrodden. After that date, the idealism died and Charles was never again. Three years later the firm broke up in a squabble over money and control. When the idealism died, so did the firm. Jim Jones had driven a stake right through its heart. Even Mr. Garry's secretary, Pat, lost her spirit after that date - a woman who was filled with enthusiasm for the poor and the downtrodden and who had become very close to me during that time. All that died and from then on, they became like all other firms - bottom line for money. One could almost trace everything back to that point in history which changed even the leftist idealism of the San Francisco Bay Area. Jones' revolutionary suicides proved that any idealism and movement no matter how laudable and worthwhile for others, without roots in transcendence is in continuous danger of losing its way and becoming runaway cannon in the body politic and social. Among the dead at Jonestown were Jim Jones and his wife, people whom I knew and actually liked. That event was so traumatic for me that after that I lost all enthusiasm and desire for all causes of the left. Not that I became a fervent right winger, only that the left did not recognize evil in the world, that human nature is fundamentally good, that we can of our own power find a cure for all our ills by our reason and our own efforts. If ever there was an empirical proof of original sin, it was Jonestown. The intent of Jim Jones was good and pure but separated from a sense of God, it ended in a grotesque cascade of history, without meaning and without sense.

I think my work and research on the terrible event of Jonestown destroyed my confidence in reason alone and in most causes of the left separated from the transcendence as well as even the law because dedication to the law without ultimate meaning was doomed to corruption and failure. You can see this today as you are what the law and the legal profession have become: laws anywhere on everything but nowhere effective and a legal profession empty of meaning and dedicated to the bottom line whose idealism of seeking justice through the discovery of truth has long since been consigned to the dust bin of history.

After Jonestown I should have realized that the law separated from the foundation of truth would ultimately be corruptive, deprived of meaning because it is deprived of truth. In fact, truth is constructed in such a way that when you distort it, it comes back to destroy the prevaricator and the liar. Anyone and everyone remains then without foundation, meaning and direction in life so that any law, any profession built not on truth is doomed to failure and despair from the beginning. That is what

Jonestown was all about: it was built on the lie of false messianism, a kingdom of justice on earth separated from its roots of transcendence (God) which, looking back, had to fail precisely because it was built on a lie. It was an overwhelming lesson. I still do not know why that simple lesson had not entered my mind and heart.

But the lesson didn't sink in till much later. I graduated from law school in 1977, got my LLM and JSD at Berkeley and off I went to teach law.

I passed the Bar in California and practiced some law in the Bay Area as I went to graduate school at Berkeley. Since it was the Bay Area, some of the cases were very strange. But after the Peoples' Temple case, nothing much seemed strange anymore.

The first case I ever got was that of an undertaker who was accused of taking liberty with the dead body of a young girl in the mortuary. The evidence against him was weak because no one had ever seen him <u>in flagrante delictu</u> and above all, who would want to believe that anyone would want to have sex with a dead body? I certainly didn't and what I believed or not, I could convince a jury of the same. (Of the fifty cases I tried, I lost one and I still don't know why I lost that one.) I refused to take cases when I was convinced the person was guilty because if he couldn't convince me, I could not convince a jury. I never could understand the patent nonsense of not judging a case. If anyone is in a position to judge a case's truthfulness, it is a lawyer.

The problem here as in all criminal law is what does the lawyer do when he knows his client is guilty. I know all the traditional answers: you defend your client because he has a constitutional right to the best defense available. Yes, as long as he has the money to pay for the best defense available. But what if by your talents you get a criminal off to walk the streets and then hear he harms another person? That is the perennial question for all defense lawyers. I could not answer it to my satisfaction so I took only the cases I was convinced were not guilty.

The problem with this whole system is that we have forgotten that truth alone is the thing which protects us against corruption of the system and of the individuals in that system. And the moment we deviate from that central truth, at that moment we have led ourselves and the profession down the prim rose path to destruction. And since law is so important as a unifying factor in American society (there really is nothing else) the corruption of the law gives scandal to every other profession in America with the result that we have a meltdown of the managerial class in America. The meltdown is from a belittling of the truth when we do not seek it as our mistresses. In any case, I was convinced the guy was innocent and I convinced the jury of it in less than twenty minutes in my jury summation. One of the jurors told me after the trial that he had been laying next to a stiff for twenty five years and never touched her. So jurors can be somewhat misunderstanding of what you are trying to do but in victory, you don't really care how they come to free your client.

Perhaps the most exciting legal morass I was involved with was that of the Oakland Raiders franchise in 1980. Al Davis wanted to move his franchise to a more lucrative market of Los Angeles. The owners of the NFL turned him down and he sued. He won in court so the other owners could not stop Davis from moving. But the city of Oakland desperately wanted the team to stay in Oakland.

There was only one way to stop him from moving and that was by condemning the team, its assets, its contracts under the regal doctrine of eminent domain, pay Davis the fair market value of the team and have the people of the city of Oakland and Alameda County buy the team so that it would remain in Oakland. This was much easier said than done.

While the loyalty of Raider fans was great, unfortunately Oakland fans were comparatively poor. The FMV of the team in 1980 was 100 million dollars, a huge sum, and there was no way in hell that that much money could be raised by the sale of public stock so that it would be the people who owned the team. I thought this was a really neat idea seeing how the NFL owners blackmail every city so that they can reap more benefits from-the public. If not, the team threatens to move with the local taxpayers to pick up the tab on stadia and complexes that are only half paid for. It really is inter -city warfare for the benefit of the owners with poor people picking up the tab in case of dissatisfaction of the prima donnas.

So I came up with the idea of eminent domain of the city and county condemning the team in the public interest. I forget now all the BS I conjured up about harming the local pride and deeply offending the sensitivities of fans who had been loyal for decades and who would suffer irreparable damage (that's the magic word) if the Raiders moved. Not to mention the terrible economic loss for citizens who now had to pay through the nose. The result is that it was owners versus hard working Tom Q. Public and it was in the latter's interest to keep the franchise just where it was for the benefit of the local public.

The federal judge in San Francisco bought it and we were on our way. However, we crashed when the city of Oakland and Alameda County couldn't come up with the money. But it was and remains a good precedent sitting there for others to use. It was a personal source of pride for me that I had a hand in the litigation even if we lost in the end. It was time well spent because I thought I had done some good. And I actually got paid for that case.

The next case was even more perplexing because it involved incest. A young man came to my office (which the Garry firm had allowed me to have) seeking a divorce. Nothing unusual except that when I asked him why (I usually tried to get them to see a counselor so that perhaps the marriage could be saved) he told me he wanted to marry his mother-in-law. I was stunned. He calmly explained why he wanted to do, so she was beautiful, sophisticated, intelligent, owned her own business and she was articulate and sensitive. I asked whether I could speak to her. He agreed.

She came in the next morning and I knew why he wanted to marry her. She was everything he said she was and more. Her beauty was literally astounding. I explained to her what it could do to her daughter but she simply said that she had not planned it that way but that it just happened. She fought it for months but ultimately she just admitted that she loved the young man and she was tired of fighting it. If her daughter would not understand that was her problem and the mother said she could live with it. She had fought it as long as she could but her mind was made up. Five hundred years ago they would both have been stoned to death for incest. But times have changed and there was nothing to be said. Besides this was the Bay Area where everything went. I did not take the case because my conscience bothered me: how could I participate in a charade which would destroy a human being? You could say that almost every divorce destroyed someone but somehow this case was different. I would have no part of it even though I knew I was giving up a big chunk of money.

That was one of my biggest problems from the beginning: I didn't know how to collect money. Deep down, I don't think I was worth anything. People put lawyers last on the ones to be paid except when they need you desperately. Only then can you get paid. I made the fatal mistake of always trusting people, finished the work and never got paid. I just didn't have the heart to take them to court- most of them didn't have anything anyway so what was the use. I was a monk in a dog-eat-dog world. That's the reason why I was constantly on the verge of bankruptcy and had nothing to give my kids. It was a constant humiliating experience and I had only myself to blame. The first thing a professor in law school once told me was to get your money up front because when they no longer need you, they spit you out like melon seeds. That was a pretty graphic way to look at it but it was true. Everyone hates lawyers until they need one but after they use you, they still despise you. Besides all lawyers are rich so it wasn't really like stealing. It was like taking from the rich - a Robin Hood syndrome. So all during my legal life I was always broke and I still do not know how I paid my bills each month. Each month was a miracle. It still is. The clients mostly lied to you and you had to protect yourself on a constant basis because they would simply sue you if you lost the case. I was really a queer bird: I would win the case and still never get paid. Just like at college: I published and perished. It was the worst of all worlds. As one lawyer once told me: "If you want justice go to a whore house. If you want to get fucked, go to court." It wasn't all that bad but the legal system was getting further and further out of the ability of people to pay (except if I it was a contingency case and then it had to be a sure thing for most lawyers to take it.) I took about 20-30% of my cases pro bono (for nothing) but that was already too much. Since I counted on the others to pay, when they did not, I had neither the money nor the time to help others in need. The iron law of wages always catches up with you.

The worst cases were the spousal abuse cases. Houston has a very large Hispanic community and the macho of that culture almost required them to beat up on their wives. The men are notoriously promiscuous but let a simple suspicion of the wife be even suspected by her husband - no matter how irrational - and the blows reigned down upon her like in a heavy rain during a hurricane. And if you ever lived in Houston, you know how hard that rain can come down.

There was the case of Mrs. Garcia (not her real name.) She came to my office and for two hours told me a tale of horror and violence such as I had never heard in my life. I had heard a lot here and abroad but not one quite like this one. She showed me the cigarette burns and marks from other burns. She had been to the hospital five times for a broken nose, torn ears, split lips, broken ribs from kicking, fractured skull from getting banged against a wall and a huge scar now covered by hair from being thrown out of a window of the second floor. No one at the hospital ever asked about her total person and why she came to the ER so often ("I walked into a door.") The hospital personnel were too willing to believe her fabricated stories because they didn't "want to get involved." Everyone is afraid of getting involved, getting sued and no one thought about this poor woman covered with scars.

With her permission, I called the police but their unconcerned, nonchalant attitude was almost as horrifying as the beatings: "We've seen this a thousand times before" was their response. But this man is insanely jealous and violent, I told him. I begged them for her protection and said that he would come after her sooner or later. When they wouldn't do anything I explained to her that I could get her a TRO but paper does not protect against bullets if he was determined to get her. No one can stop another from killing you if he doesn't care what happens to him. I begged her to reconsider but she insisted I get the protection for her which I did. Even at the hearing, I begged the judge to incarcerate and to give him no visitation but she insisted that nothing had been done and that therefore she could do nothing. All my fears were speculative and, of course, she was right at the time.

Two days later, he walked into her place of work. He shot her five times in the face, shot three of her co-workers dead before putting a bullet in his own head. I was shattered. Four dead but there was nothing I could have done to prevent that slaughter. I felt bad but not guilty.

I couldn't work for weeks and the guilt still follows me all days. I had done all I could but it wasn't enough. I weep to this day and vowed never again to take such a case. So far I have kept my word.

I really tried to reform the legal system, held meetings, gave talks on the legal system, wrote op-ed pieces, visited legislators all to little avail. The Texas legislature finally passed some tort reform (limits on pain and suffering) but that hardly scratched the surface. What was needed was a whole reform of the whole legal system, how to choose judges, campaign contributions, the way law students are taught and what they are taught. In reality, reform of law required a whole reformation of society, of ethics both personal and professional and a hell of a lot of courage. The situation got so bad that in one survey of California lawyers, fully one half of them would change professions if they could. That is poor commentary on the most influential profession in America not because of the quality of its members but because of the position of law in American society. Since we have no common tradition or religion, we are joined by one Constitution and one set of laws which hold us together for better or worse. When the moral foundation of these laws is gone or corroded by guardians called lawyers for money, there is nothing holding the American community together as a community. That is why the legal community in America has become a business rather than a profession, a job rather than a vocation for whom the search for truth that justice be done was either irrelevant or naive.

I started to practice law in earnest in Texas in 1986 after I knew my law school teaching days were over. I remember my very first case in Houston because it was the day the shuttle blew up over the Atlantic. My client was a transvestite who had been beaten up by the police because he/she was wearing women's clothing as she waited for her operation which was to transform her from one sex (male) to the other (female.) She was pathetic and with no money (of course, why else would they come to me?) I managed to settle her case for $5000 but under one condition: that I could have none of it. I agreed but I did get $500 for my out of pocket expenses.

One of my first cases and an omen to come was when I also obtained a divorce for a Cajun coon ass who left without paying me my $350 for the divorce. I was desperate. No pay from paying clients and on the other hand, no pay from my poor clients. How was I going to pay for my office in the executive suite? In the very nick of time I got a few more small change cases and an insurance slip and fall. I made $1500 that month and I had enough to pay for the rent, my apartment and at least one meal a day. God was good to me and I was grateful. Even for just being able to pay bills. But to go from $47,000 a year to $18,000 a year was a deep fall but the money was not really that important. I would seem to be helping people and that was important for me. It all wasn't much and I was not very happy but it was work and a feeling that someone actually needed me. I felt that no one had ever needed me. Even the women in my life had been there only for a while and they ended up never really needing me. That was always very important in my life: to be needed by someone even though deep down I knew I was full of crap. They used me - not needed me. But one must have some illusions to survive in life just like a woman wants to be told she is loved even though deep down she knows that she is not and is being f..ked. We all need illusions so that our lives can have the semblance of meaning and a new direction in which to go. Without that, we must just as well blow our brains out and not just wait for the end which will be slow and painful in any case.

There was not much excitement in the rest of the trials in the practice of law in my life. I was overwhelmingly successful but there was always that empty feeling in the pit of my stomach. An ache and a pain that would never go away. Even in the happiest days it was always there throbbing just below the surface. I tried every which way to cover it, work it out, write, study, read, even have some women in my life. But it never went away. What struck me in the law practice was the lack of humility in the judges who actually thought they knew a lot and how they lorded it over others in their courtrooms. Humility was not their forte and they would be forgotten before their coffins are covered with dirt.

I was always reminded of the painting in my office just behind my desk which always reminded me of who and what I was: "You can tell the measure of a man by the way he treats those who can do nothing for him in return." It was really the Gospel in small writ. When you do that, you know all about yourself, who you are and what you are up to. You don't need others to tell you who you are. In all those ten years of practicing law I tried to follow that motto religiously. That was always hope filled. In Chekov's phrase, "Every saint has a past and every sinner has a future." I don't think that I accomplished very much in that decade but I did keep my integrity and fidelity to the truth. I kept my word to all, I was loyal to my clients, payer and non payer alike, and I tried to be a good person and a good lawyer. They were not happy years but then there were few happy years in my life. Outside of the time with my children, there were few happy years. But "happy" is relative and perhaps not the correct word to use in this wasted life of mine. The better word is "peace filled" and I did have peace because I followed my conscience and the truth wherever it led. At the end I was mostly mistaken in my search but that matters very little. What matters is the search for truth which is only another word for God. A life spent searching for God, mistakenly perhaps, but always a faithful search makes life successful and fulfilled. Only that can be truthfully put on my tombstone if I ever get one. As things go now, I'll have neither a grave nor a headstone. That doesn't matter. They got to bury me somewhere. What matters is the good we have done by the grace of God who will judge us by standards other than those used in courts or churches or society.

"Here lies a nameless bastard who tried to find and follow truth in obedience to his conscience. RIP."

CHAPTER 27

THE FIRST CLIENT

David was now ready to practice law. All the theoretical stuff from law school was about to become a waste of time. They didn't even tell him where the courthouse was. He knew even from the beginning that he would never make it with a large firm because his bottom line was not and could not be the bottom line.

His first case walked in the front door. He was an undertaker who was accused of the criminal desecration of a corpse. It was such a terrible offense that David could hardly believe it. It was technically called necrophilia or taking sexual liberties with a corpse of a young girl who had died in a car accident. She had been killed instantly by a truck carrying long steel rods for building construction. When the semi jackknifed to avoid an obstacle in the road, the rods came loose and a few were hurled like javelins on the incoming lanes of the freeway. One of the rods went through the passenger side of the oncoming vehicle and drove right through her heart. Instant death. Death happens when we are preparing for something else. We are like men on a chain gang from which we cannot be released. Every once in a while one or another of the men has his throat cut and there isn't a thing the other prisoners could do about it. Except to know that unbeknownst to each of them, the day most assuredly will come when each will have his throat cut.

The undertaker was called, of all things, John Totemplace, which loosely translated from the German means 'the place of the dead.' A most appropriate name for his profession. Strangely, Totemplace hadn't known what it meant until David translated it for him and they both had a laugh. He brought the indictment from the grand jury with him as well as a picture of the alleged victim. The young girl had been blond, blue eyed and stunningly beautiful. She had been a model for various clothing stores on her vacation days so her name was well known in the community. The case had therefore some notoriety so it seemed strange to David that a few criminal lawyers whom John had interviewed had turned him down. Why? That was the first question that came to my mind.

I think they were afraid for their reputation. A kind of Saturday night horror show," John remarked. "Cases will do that to you. You get a reputation for defending a certain kind of client and people begin to identify you with the crime", I said rather sadly. "Who recommended you to me?"

"The last lawyer said that you had no reputation to lose, so I might as well try you."

Insulting,, but given that the rent had to be paid, I couldn't really afford to be choosy. Or offended. "The indictment says that an embalmer saw you in the room with her as she lay naked after the washing and that you were acting suspiciously. What does that mean?"

"I was trying to adjust the body so that the blood would flow correctly when it was drained. I did touch her body but it was in the process of my work. I can't help it if the guy had a dirty mind."

I didn't have a clue about the undertaking business so bethought that what John did was appropriate. "Could you demonstrate it to a jury?" "Sure." "Anything else?" John asked.

"The embalmer also claimed that after the body was dressed, he came in for a last look and saw the body's clothing had been ruffled. He claims that he lifted the skirt and found her panties out of place."

"Isn't that strange?" I naively asked. "I mean, why would a dead body need panties?"

"Not really," John responded, "when you move a body about trying to get the best position for viewing, that can happen. The parents had requested that she have her panties on so they must have been displaced as I did the moving of the body. It's unusual for us to put underwear on a dead body. I mean, what need is there for underpants? All the fluids have been drained. But that's what the parents wanted and I was not going to disappoint them."

Logical explanation, I thought.

"Then why do you think the embalmer would make such an accusation before a grand jury? That's a pretty terrible thing to say about a fellow worker in the profession."

"Because he has been trying to establish his own business and my location is perfectly positioned in the city. Right in the middle of Place John Paul II near St. Louis Cathedral. Cajuns are very superstitious and they like to view the body, the casket, the grave. The location is ideal for my kind of business. With me effectively gone, because I'd lose my license forever, he could buy me out for nothing. Maybe he even thinks that if he refuses to testify, he might make a deal by saying on the stand that he probably was mistaken. He could cover himself well, if we could strike a deal."

"Is that what you want me to do?"

"Never. I'm innocent and my reputation is at stake. A deal would besmirch my reputation. Will you take the case?"

I could hardly believe that anyone would have sexual commerce with a dead body. It was so awful a thought that I never even hesitated. I agreed to defend John Totemplace precisely because I did believe the man and could not believe the crime. And what I believed in, I could convince another of his belief. The secret of the good attorney as opposed to a great attorney is belief in his cause, in his client. The second is almost as important: eye contact with the jury. People are juries and juries are people and what they want to find is belief and fire in the belly of the attorney.

The trial was scheduled soon as requested by the defendant. Now my time had come. It was my first case. I was kind and humane while choosing the jury and so won their initial attention. That's all you can do at that point in the trial. Keep them with you. Get them to like you and you carry them for a while. But only for a while. After twelve have been chosen (plus alternates) it was the time to strike at their will to believe. The evidence was rather brief. The testimony of the embalmer was as told to me by Totemplace and cross was brief. He was the sole witness. Totemplace took the stand, gave his resume of a perfect reputation and how he proceeded with his work. The DA's cross followed the testimony of the embalmer and that was it. It was up to me to convince the jury in the summary.

"Ladies and gentlemen of the jury. The worst death possible is to be talked to death. Contrary to rumors lawyers are not paid by the word, so I shall keep my remarks short. This trial has to do with a shameful crime, a crime about the desecration of a dead body, that of a beautiful twenty two year old coed who had been killed tragically in a car accident. My client here is an undertaker and he is accused of sexually abusing that body by fondling, caressing and touching that dead body indecently. I cannot tell you how painful all this is for him that after a twenty five year career without so much

as a whisper of impropriety, he stands before you utterly ashamed and chagrined by being accused of such an unspeakable crime. Twenty five years of unblemished reputation - that's almost as long as some of you have been alive. Think about that. As long as some of you have been alive this man before you has carried on an immaculate reputation as care giver to those who grieve. He has handled literally hundreds of dead bodies of all ages and sexes. Perhaps some of you have lost loved ones and have experienced the ministrations of someone like my client. You remember the kindness of other undertakers who served you, helped you in grief in your greatest hour of need and who were there for you. My client has been there for thousands of people like you in their time of need. Without a whisper of misdeed."

"Today this man stands before you in his need for you to be there for him. We have shown not only an unblemished career but also that the person who is the principle witness in this case had everything to gain from his testimony and that the evidence against John Totemplace is purely circumstantial and in reality, is perfectly explained and understood as part of his care giving business. Just keep in mind, ladies and gentlemen, as you listened to the evidence, that the one who accused my client had every reason to profit from this man's conviction. My client sits before you today, with his whole past, present and future in your hands. As he gave much care during his twenty five years of service to the community, may you give him that care in return by being attentive to what he said to you. The evidence showed you that such an unspeakable crime could not have been committed by my client. Whom shall you believe? A man of impeccable service or one who has something to gain? Thank you."

From that point the trial was over. The rest had been sincerity, credibility and eye contact which David did in spades. The evidence was such that they could pin their decision on the two witnesses. David had given them rational reasons to cover the emotional ones. He believed that an undertaker could never commit such a crime. That the accusation was so detestable that the jury did not want to believe it either and would look for ways to find reasonable doubt (whatever that means anyway) and so release David's client. David had given the jury the basis of every trial which is the will to believe and giving the jury a hook on which to hang their verdict of "not guilty". David had that unique gift right from the beginning and the result was a foregone conclusion. It was simple because he had the key to being a successful trial attorney. The jury returned quickly.

"How say you?" intoned the judge. "Not guilty" chimed the jury foreman. "That say you each and every one?" "We do." That was it. David had won his first case and the jury was anxious to congratulate him on his brilliance - brilliance because he had made them want to believe and he gave them the opportunity of finding for him in the end. Ironically, it was the jury who was grateful.

One juror volunteered an intimate moment of his own. "Hell" he said, "I've been sleeping with a stiff for twenty five years and I never dream of touching her."

Humorous note but a larger commentary on his marital situation. But then maybe they are both happy that way. Who knows? "Judge not..."

Six months later in the *New Orleans Times Picayune,* the headline read: "Undertaker caught in the act of desecration." It seems that John Totemplace was guilty after all: now they had their eyewitness *in flagrante delictu.* David prayed that John wouldn't come a second time. Fool me once, shame on you. Fool me twice, shame on me. Totemplace didn't come back. *Deo gratias.*

CHAPTER 28

FORGIVENESS

All during the celebration on the tenth anniversary of 9/11, there was the constant theme of forgiveness for those who had perpetrated the horrendous deed. This theme was restricted to the United States and I know of no Muslim country, official Muslim organization, etc. that asked for forgiveness for what their co-religionists did in the name of their religion. Not a one.

We do know one thing about the opposite of forgiveness, that is, a continuous hatred of those who did the monstrous deed. Hatred eats the soul and only perverts the one who harbors that sentiment. But forgiveness? That is really a very hard thing to do because it comes from letting go of the hatred (negative) and a form of loving (positive). More of this later.

But what is forgiveness? It is a voluntary act by the one who has been unjustly injured in some way, by which the injured restores the relationship with the perpetrator of the injustice. It is not something that can be demanded by the guilty party but one that must be asked by him and freely given by the injured party. Forgiveness can even be given without the apology of the guilty party. That is the meaning of hope.

One of the first observations to be made is that forgiveness is beyond the law and cannot be mandated by law because it involves love and love cannot be mandated. Forgiveness must come freely and lovingly from the injured party for reasons that are proper to him or her. That is what makes forgiveness so difficult and so mysterious since it must come freely from the injured party which makes it so difficult and cannot be demanded by law. This makes the perpetrator of the evil at the mercy of the one whom he/she has injured no matter how sorrowful and regretful he may be for his unjust action. It becomes even more difficult for the injured party to forgive when the one who injured him does not repent or is not sorrowful for what he has done.

It should be noted that since forgiveness is so difficult that a certain time must elapse before true forgiveness can be given - if at all. One must be terribly suspicious of one who almost immediately forgives the injustice perpetrated on him. Since the wound is so deep, it takes time – if at all- for any kind of forgiveness to be authentic and real. Perhaps that time will never come because certain people cannot forgive the hurt that has been done to him or her. The injured party will have to live with that any way he can. He can refuse to forgive because forgiveness is a voluntary act which can be mandated by no law and must be a species of love and restoration of a common humanity.

Some claim that they are to forgive because it is mandated by God in an example given by, say, Jesus, who was unjustly put to death. That too is not only difficult but it depends on the nature of the God who is worshiped. What if one's God is vindictive, hurtful, vengeful? Then his followers not only will not forgive but in imitation of his God, cannot forgive. It is important to understand the nature of the God we worship which will influence the decision which we may make on our own forgiveness. It will be easier for the injured party to forgive if his God is loving, merciful and forgiving in his relationship to his worshiper. If that God forgives only if he wants to or who can simply withdraw forgiveness if he wants to, that makes the decision of the follower ambiguous and in the sense that his God does not demand that he forgive just as that God has or has not forgiven. We become imitators of that God whom we worship.

Perhaps the most difficult situation is the following: how is a guilty party forgiven if the person from whom he asks forgiveness is dead and cannot humanly forgive? Only the injured party can forgive and no one else can stand in his place. If the injured party is dead, we have a very grave situation for forgiveness. The guilty party cannot be forgiven and can only ask for forgiveness for which no answer can ever be given, positively or negatively. It is like the former Nazi soldier at Buchenwald who asked a rabbi for forgiveness for his participation in the slaughter of his fellow Jews. The rabbi responded that it was not his to forgive because it was not he who was injured by that soldier. He could only pray with the soldier for what he did and encourage the former soldier to do works of repentance to show the sincerity of his sorrow for what he did as a lesson for those who see him doing such penance in good works. But his forgiveness will have to wait for the time when the soldier enters eternity where the God of love resolves all contradictions.

A final difficulty comes after forgiveness and the guilty party continues to injure that party. In such a situation, the injured party must fall back on to the limits of the law that demands retribution and self defense of the injured party (e.g. the law, penal punishment, jail, legal process). The law is that limit beyond which we may not go. To continuously be hurt and continuously forgive the same fault is really infantile and is going nowhere. The one who injures must then be restrained from further injury on the injured. Forgiveness cannot really take place if the perpetrator of the injury continues to injure. The very first requirement of true forgiveness is that the perpetrator of evil stop the evil. If not, that is a matter of justice meted out by the law and the consequences of the law for evildoers. Forgiveness is still possible but only after the injury ceases.

Finally, forgiveness is really an act of love to reconcile or to attempt to reconcile the perpetrator of evil back to the common humanity which both victim and perpetrator of evil share. Forgiveness is an act of gratuitous love that reaches out to the perpetrator of evil- while not for a moment justifying the evil done - for him to come back from and recognize his evil deed and be reconciled to the common humanity of both. Forgiveness is an act of pure grace to bring the perpetrator back from his evil ways to their common humanity of both through the grace of forgiveness from the only one who has been injured. In Christianity, the act of forgiveness is to act like God who is open and welcoming to the sinner, always there even if that grace is rejected. After all, the perpetrator of the evil must freely recognize the evil he has done, repent of it and ask forgiveness of the one offended. The grace of forgiveness remains within the freedom of the injured to act like God in grace or he remains within himself and refuses to open himself to the one who has injured him. In Christianity, forgiveness is the freedom to act like God who forgave the murder of his only begotten Son. Forgiveness is always free, a grace and love on the part of the one who was unjustly injured.

CHAPTER 29

CORRUPTION FROM WITHIN

I must admit that as I look around, it is not the country for which I once fought in Vietnam. That war clearly dispirited me by our betrayal of friends who fought alongside of us and many of whom we condemned to death and to a civil fate under communist rule. We won that war and could have made it another South Korea, democratic and free but the radicals among us betrayed us for which they never apologized for the death and enslavement of millions of Vietnamese, Laotians and Cambodians.

Now that corruption has come to roost as the moral corruption of betrayal comes now to betray us. This corruption can be seen everywhere in this society from families to entertainment to government and to foreign policy. I list some of the elements of that corruption which follows.

On the other hand, it is important to know the thinking of our enemy which today is Islamic fundamentalism which is a literal reading of the *Quran.* It is also important to know the thinking of two of modem Islamic thinkers who gave us insights into the Islamic thinking of fundamentalist Islam. After all the celebrations of the tenth anniversary of 9/11, it is important to understand the reasoning of the Islamic revolution and why it is coming about. The corruption of the West is seen very clearly by Islamic thinkers who believe that the West will become Islamic without Islam firing a shot. Why? Because of our deeper and deeper interior corruption that becomes more corrupt.

Both Sayyid Qubt writing in *Milestones* and Hasan al-Bana (founder of the Islamic Brotherhood) in his own writings in his independent newspaper *Al-lkhwan al Muslimiin* claim that the reason Islam is so popular today and is making worldwide converts is not because of violence or self immolation but because of the growing corruption of the West, Europe in particular, but growing rapidly in the United States. This moral collapse will be followed by a great Islamic victory. Al-Bana has simply given up on violence among the Islamic Brethren which he founded in 1928 in Egypt. Why bother, he says, because places like the United States are morally rotting from within.

Are these Islamic thinkers correct? Have we lost our Judeo-Christian spiritual roots? And what have we replaced it with? We know that Europe has already lost her spiritual roots. At this point I am not sure but the corruption within the United States grows by leaps and bounds and there seems to be nothing we can do to counter it. I do not mean to be pessimistic but I would suggest we look at the facts and see if Qubt and Al-Bana are correct in their observations. Here are a few of those corruptions affecting the West.

The massive use of drugs -legal and illegal- grows exponentially in America. Thousands of tons of cocaine, marijuana, methamphetamines are consumed every day by millions of Americans. In addition, some five to ten percent of Americans are alcoholics. There would be no drug wars in Mexico were it not for the voracious appetite for drugs by Americans. Every dollar spent by Americans for all these illegal drugs is a contribution to the death of Mexican soldiers, policemen and citizens caught in the crossfire. There have been over 35,000 Mexican deaths in this drug war. Guns are shipped from the United States are paid for by the billions made by the drug lords who feed this voracious American appetite for drugs. Cartels corrupt officials at every level. This is not to count the millions of prescription drugs that are used every day to calm nerves and so that millions can operate effectively. Already some states have legalized marijuana for "medical" purposes when everyone knows this is a pure cover up of another habit along with alcohol. Why do we need such drugs to get high? Why do we need an escape from reality for so many in our society? The use of drugs is in reality a form of escape from reality. But what is so bad about America that we must escape it by chemicals both from abroad and amphetamines made right here in the United States.

The replacement of the foundational ethical standard of Judeo-Christian morality by one of relativism, consumerism and materialism. There are no longer objective truths that can unite us as a nation and each one is left to create his or her own values and truths. "We hold these truths" of the Founding Fathers is no longer operative in America. It is only what each individual believes and holds that matters and nothing can really bind us as a nation.

The marriage situation in America grows more dismal by the year. Some states now recognize - for the first time in human history- same sex marriage under the Equal Protection Clause of state and federal constitutions (rejected however by every referendum voted on by thirty one states). Almost forty percent of children today in the United States are born outside of marriage and growing. This number increases to 72.5 percent for black and Hispanics. Millions of couples live together without marriage and some twenty five percent of children live with only one parent (much higher in minority communities). To grow up without fathers presents a corruption that affects the whole way of child rearing and instability for children. The number of children per woman in the white community is 1. 7 when you need 2.1 to sustain the same level of population. The absence of fathers has a deleterious effect on young males who do not know how to act like men with responsibility. The result is gangs, criminality and violence. *See* Chicago. Besides same sex marriage, there is talk of legalizing polygamy.

The entertainment industry grows more coarse by the year. Language is debased and most of the sitcoms on television are sexually orientated. Even the commercials are political. What used to be called "fornication" or sex between the unmarried is now simply taken for granted. Sex among the young begins as early as fourteen years and one in four teenagers are infected with some form of HIV or other venereal diseases including herpes, gonorrhea and syphilis some of whose strains are no longer controlled by the medicines we have. Such diseases last a lifetime and infect partners so that there are now one million people in this country infected with HIV. This also affects the ability to have children later on in life.

Experimentation on human embryos is now taken for granted as a source of stem cells for the possible use for the cure of diseases affecting adults. Human embryos are now a source of possible cures for adult diseases that make the ancient sacrifice of children look good. In addition there are 1.3 million abortions each year in the United States and in some areas like Washington, D.C., there are more abortions than live births. Abortion is now the back up for contraception failure now acceptable in American culture. Even the U.S. Supreme Court has said that is the reason why *Roe*

V. Wade cannot be repealed. Abortion is now employed for sex selection when we thought that this practice was restricted to China and India where this is exercised. What the future holds for such a practice remains to be seen.

College sports at almost every level are seen as farm teams for the growing number of professional sports. The corruption of college sports is growing by giving money and other gifts in order to insure that a team wins which produces millions for the universities. Professional sports have become so polluted by drugs that testing on a frequent basis affects almost every sport. Whole teams have been suspended for these corruptions (e.g. USC, Ohio State - even Notre Dame has had its recruitment troubles). Players have been suspended for being paid to injure another good player to make winning easier. The whole of football has become a real problem with the discovery of head trauma at every level of the game. The question today, is this game, like boxing, ethical *per se?*

The economy is headed for a debt collapse with over sixteen trillion in debt which can never be repaid and is growing. This will require large cuts in all areas including entitlements which most Americans refuse to even consider. In Europe, riots have followed austerity measures to pay for the interest on debt. Europeans have lived beyond their means and have had to cut back in almost all areas. This is a premonition for America. We have spent the future of our children/grandchildren who will be paying the interest on our debt (up to fifteen percent of the federal budget now and growing) for which they will receive nothing in return because it has been spent to sustain entitlements which they will never see. It has been spent by their forefathers in a form of a ponzi scam. This is called a form of generational theft.

In addition there is the corruption of the housing market where lenders and banks made loans to people whom they knew could not afford them. They counted on housing to increase in value until the bubble burst. When the housing bubble burst, millions of people suffered foreclosures. Banks had to be bailed out in the hundreds of billions and no one has gone to jail for all these manipulations. Those who profited from this mess have simply walked away with the profits which will never be returned. This alone has increased the national debt by the federal government by trillions. This accounts greatly for one sixth of Americans who are now in poverty.

The internet is polluted beyond belief. Some two thirds of the hits on the internet are for pornography. Child porn is popular even among professional groups who have been caught using this form of pornography (e.g. doctors, teachers, lawyers, business men, even clergymen). This is not to mention the sexual corruption of children by some of the clergy and political officials in Congress and other state houses. More and more we hear of teachers having sex with their students the priest scandal has brought great shame on the Catholic Church for the lives of victims ruined and the Church economically depleted. It is almost impossible to believe any of this.

In spite of huge amounts of money spent on education (about thirteen thousand per pupil in our public schools) the level of achievement grows worse by the year. Whole districts are caught cheating (e.g. New Orleans) on tests to raise the level of "education" in their districts (e.g. Houston. Texas and Atlanta, Georgia). In many schools, more time is spent in controlling classes than in teaching or in preparing for tests and not in real learning. Many who enter college lack basic skills to do college work so that remedial classes are at an all time high. We graduate few students in areas which are needed (engineers, teachers, scientists) and many we don't need, e.g. lawyers and CPAs because they are financially profitable. More alarming is that the workforce is not prepared to meet the real needs of a high tech economy.

The churches have suffered continuous losses of church goers, particularly in the main line churches. Some have accepted the practice of marriage of homosexuals- not to mention the number of priest sexual abuse of children in the Catholic Church (about five percent). There are now about four out of ten former Catholics who have either left the church or who no longer practice any religion. The loss of prestige of the church is a growing phenomenon with fewer and fewer people who in fact go to church. The only exceptions are evangelicals and Muslims in this country. Many of the main line churches are more into social justice than they are in purity of doctrine. This is because we have abandoned our traditional Judea-Christian value system.

Many Americans no longer believe in objective moral norms such as contained in the Ten Commandments as in the Declaration of Independence -"We hold these truths." These were truths and not opinions. This has been replaced with secularism and relativism as well as materialism and consumerism since there are few if any absolute truths. Everywhere in public there has been a war on God: prayer in public schools, sports events, and in other public areas God has been eliminated in the name of separation of church and state. The Ten Commandments are no longer seen as absolute moral truths but as simple *desiderata* or suggestions which may be accepted *vel non.* There is even a movement to eliminate God from the Pledge of Allegiance and from our money. Secularism and relativism grow as our belief in God grows weaker. There is a true cultural war on God and religion.

In foreign policy we see more and more forms of appeasement even for those who have vowed to destroy us as they did on a minor scale on 9/11. The great enemy of the United States, Iran, is building nuclear weapons and already has missiles that can reach the Middle East and Europe. Our politicians want "to talk" with people who by their religious faith have vowed to kill us and are building the weapons to do so. Our leaders do nothing to stop this except forms of material punishment via trade embargos for which our enemies care nothing at all. We fail to see the religious nature of their intent to kill us because of our secular vision of the world. Deterrence means nothing for these people who are not afraid to die unlike the old USSR who feared death and annihilation. No such fear among the mullahs of Iran because they believe that they are doing God's work. They welcome death if it means the coming of the machti.

Finally, *there is the crushing and all pleasurable hold on people called consumerism.* We live to shop until we drop. The whole economy is built on consuming more and more goods which we do not really need. Consumerism is everywhere, in advertisements, on television, newspapers, flyers, etc. A slow down of consumption means a recession of the economy. The simple life is gone. Instead of ways of paying for the war in Iraq for example, the President told the American people "to shop" instead of sacrifice on the part of all the citizenry. No added taxes to pay for a war conducted on borrowed money, increasing the debt exponentially. No draft. No sacrifice of any kind and this was war which is left to a small group of volunteers who must be deployed again and again, resulting in a great amount of mental breakdowns and suicides. Only a small portion of the American people fight our wars,"voluntary army." The rest simply leave the fighting to the small group of volunteers.

Conclusion: Our Islamic enemy is correct in seeing the deep corruption from within of western culture in general and the United States in particular. They need not fire a shot or commit an act of terrorism. They need only to wait until this society - like the Roman Empire – collapses morally, economically, politically and socially. The corruption grows more coarse by the day and there is not a civilization in history that has suffered these dimensions of corruption particularly in the sexual area and has come back to virtue and discipline. The Romans, for example, in the second century could not field an army of their own because of the amount of venereal diseases among so many Roman males. Compare this with our youth whose number of infected people are already one quarter who suffers from some form of venereal disease which may last a lifetime. Given this growing sexual corruption, could we fill a vigorous and patriotic citizen army? I have profound doubts because the young have been infected deeply with the philosophy of relativism and consumerism. What would such people be fighting for since they believe in nothing profound or lasting? The Romans had to use mercenaries and many wonder whether we are doing the same thing in giving up the patriotic soldier and substituting a volunteer army. Even there, open homosexuality in the ranks is now approved.

A dismal picture? The question is whether all this is true. Two thirds of London was destroyed by fire in 1666 and rebuilt by Sir Christopher Wren.

Londoners placed on his tomb the inscription *"Si vis monumentum requiris circumspice"* - "If you seek my monument, look around." We may do the same with American culture -look around and see what America has become. If you seek our monument today, the most telling could be that hole in New York City which took us ten years to fill. Officials at the site actually excluded religion and prayer on the tenth anniversary of 9/11.

CHAPTER 30

IN JESUS, NONVIOLENCE FLOWS FROM LOVE

The merchants who were expelled from the temple by Jesus using a whip is rather disconcerting *(John* 2: 12-28; 4: 5-12). Jesus had nothing to do with violence. Jesus overturned tables of the money changers but he only told the poor who were selling pigeons to simply remove themselves from the temple area. Not only did he preach non-violence when he commanded his disciples that when one is struck on one cheek, they are to turn the other cheek to the assailant. Jesus even practiced non-violence against those who were unjustly killing him on the cross. Moreover he commands Peter to put up his sword who only sought to defend Jesus from injustice in self defense: "Put up your sword. Those who take up the sword will perish thereby" *(Matthew* 26: 52; *John* 18: 11). Most of the ancient writers of the early church came to the same conclusion: violence in self defense is forbidden.

We must ask ourselves: what does this episode tell us? First of all that the cult of God is incompatible with every other cult. Only God may be worshiped and all other lesser gods that men worship (e.g. money) are incompatible with the divine worship. It is here a question of cult: the place that was destined for the cult of God whereas for these merchants it was the place of the cult of money. We have the illusion that an abundance of what we possess gives us an advantage of being, of status, to be someone honored while Christ tells us that our being is measured by what we give not what we have. Here God himself in the temple and his cult are used to make money: God is sacrificed by idols. God is, therefore, in a sense placed outside, chased out of our lives by other cults deemed more important (money, sex, power, prestige, honor, etc.) than God. Putting God outside, it is we who exile ourselves from the temple, from the residence of God. At the beginning of the public life of Jesus, that is, at the beginning of the announcing of the "good news," Jesus gives us a kind of parable which recapitulates all that which is to come. In the end, he will be sold for thirty pieces of silver but which will purchase the victory of God for and in our lives by the resurrection.

Secondly, the whole Bible is a history of fragility and weakness. The fragility of creation is submitted to the unforeseeable turns of nature, the fragility of man who is often characterized by sickness, poverty, despised, excluded or prisoner of his own passions which devour him. At the core of our existence, fragility is king. God himself announces that he becomes fragile and vulnerable for our sake: the birth of Jesus is completely dependent on others; his precarious life is threatened by enemies ending in a painful and shameful death. He does this to bring life to us and more easily come to our encounter. To be one with us to the very dregs of our death of our humanity. Finally, we are happy that the Christian God is a fragile God who becomes one like us in all things but sin. How could he otherwise show us that we are loved?

Thirdly, there is the constant theme of scripture which refers to Christ as a lamb. In nature, God has given each species the means of protecting itself from enemies: snakes bite, deer run, fish swim, lions are fierce, elephants have size, birds fly, and rabbits are prolific. Only one animal has no defense: the lamb which the Bible uses to describe Christ. He comes to us as the immolated lamb and invites us to accept him as a child: "Whoever receives a child in my name, accepts me" *(Mark 9:37)*.

We must open our arms and hands to receive a child who comes freely to us. The child is like the lamb. The lamb is both defenseless and loving and open to our freedom. Just as is the child.

The lamb has no defense mechanism. Even when it is in grave danger, it does not run but willingly accepts the knife of the killer and gives voluntarily of his wool without a struggle and never uses force to protect itself. If you have ever seen the slaughter of lambs, you know how true this is. The whole life of Jesus is one of absolute non-violence and does not resist those who desire to kill him. What more human instinct is there than one of self defense? But why is this? He who is Master of heaven and earth, who created all that is, omnipotent, omniscient, all powerful comes to us with open hands, vulnerable to us. Why? Until his "hour" of passion and death comes, he counts only on his Father to deliver him from his enemy. He submits to his enemies because that is his Father's will, to show how deeply God's love really is. When his enemies have him he does not resist them but submits to their humiliation, torture and death foisted upon him with not even a harsh word- contrary to one of those two thieves who were crucified with him who cursed and made demands on Jesus. Jesus even has mercy on the good thief who was repentant of his sins and appeals to the mercy of Jesus. Jesus prays for his torturers and killers with not a word of rebuke or cry of vengeance. Jesus even rebukes Peter who desires only to save Jesus from unjust attackers. We would normally call this an act of self defense which Jesus rejects because that would be an act of violence which Jesus refuses, root and branch. Why? To show anger and violence would show what kind of God his Father really is. If he is love, there can be no violence in Jesus or in his actions. He commands Peter to put up his sword and let his enemies have their way with him even if he could call on twelve legions of angels to protect him. He therefore refuses even divine help to save him from an unjust suffering and death, if that is the desire of1esus but that is not his will that must be done but that of his Father. That is the ultimate form of non- violence - a refusal even of a justified self defense against unjust enemies. Instead he prays for his killers to be forgiven, makes an excuse for them because "they know not what they do." Later it will be the same non-violence and forgiveness as practiced by Stephen the martyr in Acts of the early church who puts up no defense against unjust enemies and equally calls on God to forgive them for their unjust attack and killing (Acts 7: 60). Stephen's passion and death is modeled on the passion and death of Jesus with its non violence and his refusal to defend himself. Even when Jesus humanly knows that his Father can deliver him and does not know why he does not, Jesus submits to that divine will even when humanly he does not understand and does not hesitate to give his life even when he does not humanly understand. His last breath is surrender in love and peace to the Father: "Into your hands I commend my spirit." Even in his human ignorance. But at the moment of death, God responds in the reality of the resurrection.

But here we go from the beginning which is also the end. When Herod sought to take the child's life the angel tells Joseph to flee to Egypt rather than put up any resistance to Herod's murderous intent. Flight is better than murder. For three years in his public life Jesus is threatened and hated by his enemies but God his Father protects him rather than counting on swords and clubs. Having asked his Father to deliver him from that terrible "hour" at Gethsemane, the Father refuses and Jesus willingly (humanly, Jesus does not know why) and lovingly does his Father's will by non-violently submitting himself to his enemies who will kill him without any violent resistance on his part.

The teaching of Jesus goes in that same direction from the beginning. He not only rejects killing, he commands his followers to turn the other cheek to the ones who strike him. He commands his followers to love enemies and do good to those who hate them so as to become like their Father in heaven who causes his sun to rise on the just and the unjust. He not only forbids killing, Jesus commands his followers to not even be angry with those who are their neighbors and companions. He noted the goodness even in those who occupy his country (centurions) who also have faith instead of hating them as occupiers as many of his countrymen did. All this is in the Sermon on the Mount, the basic foundation of the kingdom of God. In fact, to enter the home of a pagan was to be excommunicated from the community. Jesus risks condemnation to come to the aid of one who is hurting even if he/she is non Jew. The same as the Good Samaritan who comes to the help of an enemy (a Jew).

Thus from the beginning of his birth, through his public life to the very end when men will unjustly kill him by hoisting him on a Roman gibbet, Jesus is utterly non-violent and more – he forgives and loves those who will unjustly put him to death who is without a word of hatred or vengeance but dies in surrender to his Father with love and forgiveness on his lips. That is the utter example, the paradigmatic example of Christ for his followers to follow. That shows us who God is because that was the mission of Christ to the world. He is the incarnate image of who and what the invisible God is. To show hatred and violence is to show a God who is hateful and not a loving God. Jesus' God is a loving God who loves his children even when they go wayward in their lives (prodigal son, good shepherd, Good Samaritan, admiration for a centurion and a pagan SyroPhoenician woman), Jesus commands his followers to love and do good to them, etc. Followers must follow the nature of the God they worship. In the teaching of Jesus, God is Abba, Father, who is always loving, merciful, forgiving because as St. John notes, "God is love." How can there be violence in one who loves? One who is pure love? That is, in the one who by nature is love itself. God is not by nature loving but one who is love itself through and through.

Conclusion: Perhaps in all the history of religion, there has never been a teaching so loving, so forgiving, so uplifting as the teaching of Jesus of Nazareth. Not one word of hatred, violence, vengeance because the God whom Jesus reveals is a loving and merciful God who loves all his children, good, bad and who never ceases searching for sinners, forgiving and loving all of his children. If the whole world acted as such, there would be peace immediately in the world, throughout the world. Unfortunately there is much evil in the world and self defense against evil is often necessary or at least permitted. But it is still evil. In the early church even the soldiers who killed in self defense had to do penance sometimes for years before they were again admitted to the sacred Eucharist. That being so, non-violence flows both from Christ's teaching of love, from his person and his example to the very end of his life; "By this shall all men know that you are my disciples, that you have love for one another." He even rejected a justified self defense. That is the core of Jesus' teaching which really goes beyond "non-violence" to the nature of love itself. Non-violence is only a means mostly in political terms; the teaching of Jesus goes beyond non-violence as the way of fostering love even of enemies which is the core of Jesus' teaching for one reason and one reason only: because God is love through and through. Not that God is loving but because God is love and his followers must act like God. To be perfect is to love. Those who desire to be God's children must love as God loves: absolutely, unconditionally, in perfect forgiveness. "Be perfect [in loving] as your heavenly Father is perfect." Thus non-violence in the name of Jesus is a result of love and not visa-versa. Love does not kill but forgives, endures, hopes.

> "Love is patient, love is kind and is not jealous but does not brag and is not arrogant, does not act selfishly; it does not seek its own, is not provoked, does not take into account a wrong suffered, does not rejoice-in-unrighteousness but rejoices in the truth, bears all things, believes all things, hopes all things, endures all things; love never fails" (I Corinthians 13: 4-12)
> "God is love and the one who abides in love abides in God and God abides in him" (I John 4: 16)

Non violence flows from this love not visa-versa. The non-violence of Jesus is not a political or social exercise but a reality that flows from the core reality of God who is love and our imitation of him. We should not confuse this love of God with political non-violence. The former gives birth to the second and not vice versa.

CHAPTER 31

THE LONELINESS AND MAJETY OF MAN

All my life has been a struggle between majesty and humility and the resulting failure of both. I would call it constant glory or at least reaching for glory and constant failure to achieve that glory. Let me explain.

Scripture tells us that we were made in the image and likeness of God. The original fault instigated by the serpent in the garden was that God was a jealous God and if Adam and Eve ate of the forbidden fruit, they would be like God, knowing good and evil. The result of the fall is a double pull in life: the majesty of man to be like God in discovery, wonder, development, success in creating by continuing the creation of God. But in man's nature there is the everlasting hubris because he wants to be God. This is the original hubris. To be like God or to be God. The result is that man returns to dust to remind him that he is not God. Both are present in majesty and humiliation, success and failure, life and death. God's breath and dust all combined in fallen man, triumph in life and humiliated in death which has the final say as man's last end. "Who will deliver me from this body of death?" What is needed is redemption which cannot come from himself who is perpetually tom between majesty and humility resulting in the lonely man. Death is the perpetual reminder of dust, failure and loneliness. Majesty to be like God (likeness of God); humility that it ends in death (dust).

In Christian theology there is also something like" Adam the first" and "Adam the second." Both scripture passages of creation show us the problem. God made man in his image and likeness (Genesis 1:27) so man could create, wonder, explore and continue God's creation as God's lieutenant. That is his majesty. In the following chapter, Eve succumbs to the serpent's temptation (Genesis 3 :7) that if they ate of the forbidden fruit they would be not just like God but they would be God, knowing good and evil. It is both creation and the fall. The first Adam is made in the image of God (not God himself) so he can aspire to greatness. The second Adam is fallen man that he be mindful that he is not God, forgetting that he is not creator. Trying to take God's place is hubris, fallenness, namely all that man does ends in failure and death (Adam means clay-dust to which he must return). We reach for the heavens with all our strength, all our mind, all our abilities in every profession (not just sports) but always on the horizon is death which comes inexorably. If we reach to heaven knowing that we are not God in humility, we may reach as far as we can. But the knowledge that all will pass because we are beings for death is known as humility. Only God can bridge the two known as redemption which is exclusively the work of God who delivers man from death. Man is majesty and humility, greatness and fallenness, life and death. Only God can reconcile this seeming contradiction in whom all contradictions are resolved. Memeno homo quia pulvis es" as a cautionary note.

Reach more but remember your end. To make things clearer, let me give you a short resume about this in my own life. As my readers know, I used to be a priest for decades. When I was in the minor seminary, I strove to be the best (majesty) and succeeded. I got the highest grades of the graduate class but failure came fast and furious. The rector said I did not deserve the honor because I had spent three years in a public high school before coming to the seminary (humiliation). How was this possible? We had the same courses, the same texts, the same exams and I won! I reached for heaven and was pulled back to the dust in not getting the reward I thought I deserved. I was dragged down to earth because I was not God. I tasted the dust and I was angry because I could not be God.

When I was sent to study at the most famous Catholic universities in Europe (Louvain, Munich, Gregorianum) I achieved what no other American had done: summa cum laude cum honoribus and I won the theological debate with students from sixty countries participating (majesty) but was shamed by my superiors for not having humility in my success (humiliation). I received rebuke not praise. I could not understand that after all my efforts, study and exhausting work, no one of my superiors did not appreciate my glory and chose to put me down for a lack of humility. From the heights to the dust. Again, anger because I was not God to be honored as I deserved.

Instead of a life of learning and scholarship (majesty) to which I felt entitled, I was sent to Vietnam as a chaplain soldier in the 101st Airborne (humility). As a soldier I received medals for bravery and wounds (majesty) when I knew that I did it from cowardice and shame (humility) and considered myself a failure. I had saved the life of a Marine in the midst of a firefight in walking, carrying him in the line of fire but it wasn't bravery- it was sheer despair because I had lost my faith (humility). What good was a priest without faith so I really wanted to die, be killed hauling that Marine down the hill to safety. My commander thought it was a great act of bravery when I knew it was nothing of the kind. From majesty to the dust.

I wanted to be the greatest preacher and achieve that status in the estimation of others (majesty) only to be ostracized for theological suspicions (humility) even if vindicated later by Vatican II. I wrote dozens of books and articles (majesty) but instead I was called to Rome for investigation because I was under suspicion for deviance of doctrine (humiliation). I got fed up, told them to go to hell and left the priesthood (hubris, they didn't recognize my superiority). After so much work and effort my only reward was suspicion and ostracism. From majesty to the dust -again.

I left the priesthood and became a lawyer in which I achieved great success (I won 39/40 major trials but I succumbed to lustful desires, failure and loss of all my legal enthusiasm (humility), etc. It was a long way down even as a lawyer.

I could go on and on. There are too many of these contradictions of majesty/failure. Each time I achieved all those great goals I had set up for myself and in fact achieved them (majesty) only to have them all result in failure (humility). I achieved greatness because I was made in the image of God (hubris) but I came to failure because I mistook myself for God, to be like God not as image but as reality which was not possible for a simple creature. This explains my constant failure all through my life. The two dimensions of my being were in conflict. As for every person. The image and breath of God which gave me majesty but relying only on myself, I attempted to be my own god and therefore the constant failure in my life for something that was not possible. In my old age, I fully came to realize how I mismanaged the two aspects of my life: the breath of God and the dust which I was and to which I shall soon return. A proper balance between the two is not possible as long as we struggle on this earth in our wounded nature. It can be resolved only in God who resolves all our wounds and contradictions, as the healing wounds of Christ do not make them less wounds while they are instruments of our redemption. Only in the eyes of faith does the cross in all its agony and pain become the instrument of glorification and salvation. That cross resolves all our contradictions of God's breath from which we came and our dust to which we experience in life and to which we are destined Reaching for the stars I finally realized that I was not God and I lived a whole life of failure because of my hubris to realize that all glory passes because we are dust and not God, mystical and humility, divine breath and dust. Resolution of the two? Only in the cross of humiliation which became a glorification. Only in God are our contradictions resolved. We wait that God resolve our humiliation into its glorification.

CHAPTER 32

LIFE OR DEATH - DESPAIR OR LOVE

President Obama on 12/17/12, seeking to console the victims and survivors of the terrible tragedy perpetrated in Newtown, Connecticut with the death of twenty small children and six adults, claimed that we must do more to control guns as if guns were the source of evil and not its instrumentality. The evil resides in man just as that massacre long ago at Bethlehem when King Herod had all male children two years and under in that town killed to preserve his power against any pretended king. Herod needed no guns to do his grisly work because the sword he used came from an evil heart. It was not the swords as it is not the guns. The results in Bethlehem and Newtown were exactly the same and even if all guns in America were removed, evil men would find another way to massacre the innocent. The President almost sounded as if he were declaring war on evil which is impossible since evil is a mystery and beyond all our faculties of reason. Remove all guns yet the evil remains in the hearts of men who will find other ways to accomplish their evil intents. Were it not for the tragedy surrounding the President, its grief and sorrow, his words would have been laughable. He was like a savior who would take away the sins of the world. But he can't no matter what laws are passed and how many guns are controlled or even removed.

His words were doubly ironic coming from a man who has advocated abortion on demand for any reason and who demands that we all pay for this monstrous evil of over a million children killed in their mothers' womb which we call "a right." That social evil engulfs us all and turns us into a culture of death, even those of us who protest this killing in our midst. No one cries over the slaughter of unborn innocents just because they have not yet been born. We do not witness their deaths in the silent scream of an abattoir. We cry about the evil we see; we are silent about the pall of evil that engulfs us all in a society that kills over a million of its own children each year. How hypocritical can you get especially from a man who weeps for twenty innocents and pushes for the death of others innocent millions? We choke on a gnat and we swallow the camel. And all those who agree with the President on abortion as a right are complicit in this culture of death and who have no right to cry over the slaughter of twenty children while remaining silent over the slaughter of millions.

I suppose we have become like Noah when the flood came in the midst of evil which covered the earth engulfing the good and the evil. Everyone who is silent about this monstrous deed in our midst is complicit in the evil that engulfs us all. Every once in a while like a volcano pent up within the earth, releases poison gas and deadly lava comes to the surface to destroy all in its path. Newtown was only one of those volcanoes.

And what does Christianity have to offer the agony of the lost children in Newtown and everywhere where innocent children are killed, starved, massacred and who suffer in war, in abusive situations, in simple abuse? We console them by telling them of a future where there will be no tears, no suffering, and no agony which awaits all this suffering after death? Is the present suffering life of children really worth it because we want to uphold the notion of freedom even when that freedom inflicts so much suffering on creatures who understand nothing and who must endure? Is Newtown the price of our freedom? By no means! Is that telling of a future life of bliss really worth the suffering even of one small child? One would like to simply reject that whole scenario of an explanation. And yet! There are some attempts at concrete charity in Christian faith to lessen the agony of children and even of adults: hospitals, orphanages, schools, child protection agencies, shelters - all concrete attempts to alleviate the horror of suffering children. But the evil of suffering children remains. There are Herods of this world who are always ready to sacrifice the fate of children for economic gain, for honor and prestige, for the pleasures of domination, for sexual exploration and for greed.

But above all this suffering of children, there is the example of Jesus Christ who confronted suffering and death without curses or revenge or hatred or any other forms of violence. He even prays for his executioners. It is the totally non-violent Jesus who came to earth not to explain suffering nor to be rid of its evil which is everywhere present at every time but simply to endure it with us and to convince us that we are not alone because He has endured all this to the very end what we endure without hatred and violence so as to give us hope even in the most dire of circumstances. He descended to the very depths of our suffering to death itself and being faithful to that loving God who is his Father, was rewarded, repaid, whatever word you wish to use, by his triumph over death, man's last and final enemy. That truly is good news.

It is truly here an act of faith in the one who will accomplish all this even for and with suffering children. Faith in the one who endured all that we endure and who conquered our last enemy of death of which all suffering is a premonition of what awaits us all. As the evil that was visited upon all those poor children in Newtown, Connecticut even when they did not know what was happening to them.

The only other answer to the mystery of evil is to disbelieve, to return us to the nothingness from which we originally came. That is the great decision in life: do we believe in death as finality whose fruit is despair or do we surrender in faith to a loving God who has endured all that we endure and whose conquest is over death, our death, by his obedience and love? That choice is upon us, each one of us without exception: despair or love, life or death, a future or a final end, a Herod or a Christ. That choice is up to us to make in freedom:

> "The people who walked in darkness have seen a great light.
> Upon those who dwell in the land of gloom a light has shown...
> For a child is born for us, a son is given to us.
> Upon his shoulders dominion rests.
> They name him Wonder-Counselor, God-hero, Father forever,
> Prince of peace." Isaiah 9: 1-5

CHAPTER 33

THE TRAUMA OF EVIL AT NEWTOWN

When I was a chaplain with the 101ST Airborne in Vietnam, I noticed something strange but logical. The grunts or the soldiers engaged in combat, who did the person to person fighting and dying, were deeply affected by the aftermath in viewing the dead and wounded, the body parts strewn about and a realization of what they had done and what was done to them, both enemy and comrades. It was not commonly known then but the survivors of combat almost to a man, suffered internally with trauma about which we knew little then. It was then unmanly to show tears and heartache about what they had done and what had been done to them. They saw the results and the trauma would be with them for years and years. I know. It took me almost forty years to even speak about it and then only to other combat soldiers in talk sessions at the local VA hospital which I later discovered. To see is to be traumatized.

This was hardly the case with the airmen and helicopter pilots who saw nothing of the results of their bombs, shells and napalm precisely because they had not seen the results and so were much less traumatized. They could speak with pride of their bombing and stratifying missions while the grunts hardly ever spoke of their experiences. There was deep shame. The airmen never saw the results of their missions so there was a lot less trauma for them. Most could return to civilian life almost untouched by their experience in that war. They had little sympathy for us grunts who line the streets even today, homeless, begging and mentally ill.

I am not much of a psychologist or psychiatrist but I know what I felt for many years of suffering alone with no one to speak about what I had seen even though as a chaplain I never fired a shot in anger. I simply saw. I didn't even have a side arm forbidden by the Geneva Accords. But I saw as I picked up body parts trying to find identification of the dead soldiers after a fierce fire fight in the jungle putting the parts we could find into body bags. Most were beyond recognition. That was a duty of mine after trying to console the living. It was the dead and their images that traumatized me for years: nightmares, cold sweats, wake up screams, sleep walking, constant images of all this in my soul, my impotence in the face of death about which I could do nothing. Then and now. And finally a deep sense of shame. After all those years, I am still not the same nor will I ever be. But talk therapy with those who had experienced the same trauma helped immensely so that now I can speak of what I saw. That helped my heart and mind to be more calm and less full of trauma. For that I am terribly grateful.

Yet all this came rushing back to me as I saw on television the terrible visitation of death in Newtown in the horrible murders of twenty little children which happened in our midst, something we could feel and see. It was for me like seeing the results again of the great evil of Vietnam in our very midst, the shrieking parents upon receiving news of what had happened to their babies, innocent all. It was for me a painful flash back but because they were all so utterly innocent, the pain of flashback was even more powerful as I cried and cried over the mystery of evil come to visit me again that none can understand but must be endured if we are going to continue in life. All of us are the wounded soldiers, then and now. Like the combat soldier, all those children at that school will be traumatized for years to come as will all the parents of both the immediate victims of the dead and those whose children survived this ordeal; this mystery of evil comes to touch them immediately, visually, for which they had seen and experienced in seeing or at least experienced intimately. Others can only experience from a distance. The combat soldier knows very well what those parents are experiencing.

This culture of death is pervasive in our society even if we do not actually see what is really happening. Every day, every year, hundreds, thousands and then more than a million each year, innocent children are killed and murdered in the name of a constitutional right called abortion. It does not affect us too much because we do not see their slaughter as in Newtown. Yet it goes on each day in our very midst. But what such slaughter does do is create an aura or pallor of death that surrounds us even if we do not see or even approve of what is happening to millions of innocent children. Like the airmen in war, we do not see until we do see and are horrified. I am not a fanatic. I know that abortion is sometimes necessary when a mother's life is endangered but that is not what is happening in our society. What is happening is that most choose death of their children for convenience as a backup for failed contraception. The culture of death remains and it engulfs us all as a society even if we do not see the slaughter.

I was also struck by the emotion of President Obama who almost broke down in his address to the nation. But I could not help but be saddened by a man who advocates the evil of abortion and wants us all to pay for that horror in his Obamacare bill passed by the Congress and signed by him. I go back to when he was Senator from Illinois where he twice voted against a bill that would have given medical care for the babies who somehow had survived the trauma of abortion. Then he accepted their agonizing death without medical help to insure the right to abortion by women. He did not cry then because he did not see those maimed children who survived the trauma of an unsuccessful abortion. The medical community solved this real problem by cutting up the child in the womb to insure that the child would be born dead. Now the President has the audacity to cry over the murder of twenty innocent children but not a tear over the agonizing deaths of those who received no medical treatment from the trauma of a botched abortion. It was Obama's negative vote in the legislature of Illinois that consigned other babies to agonizing death. Is this not an example of gross hypocrisy? The pallor of death surrounds us all.

To see is to be horrified; not to see is to accept the horror every day because we do not see. But the evil even of what is unseen comes to affect us time and again in places like Newtown and it will continue because evil does not know visibility/invisibility. Only humans do. God help us all in our culture of death increased in our midst by examples like Newtown, Connecticut. Only the God who has experienced pain and suffering can console all these victims in a way only he can console.

CHAPTER 34

THE GOD WHO SUFFERS

THE ABSURDITY OF THE CHRISTIAN FAITH

Of all the arguments given against the existence of a personal and loving God, suffering is the most powerful because it is emotional. The mind is important but it is the heart that reveals our truth. Emotions go to the heart and the heart gives us the truth about who we are. If we remain at the rational-intellectual level, we never go beyond the surface, the superficial as explanation. Not that reason is not important; only that we really think with the heart. In the final analysis, there is no rational explanation of suffering.. As Dostoevsky said, the world is not worth the suffering of even one child.

There are all forms of suffering: mental suffering, physical suffering, loneliness, spiritual emptiness, boredom, feelings of futility and failure/loss, love lost and never found, emptiness for what we do not know loss of loved ones. There is always the spiritual emptiness of the soul that seeks fulfillment in material things: power, wealth, diversions, sex, good times, fine food, etc. but the heart or the soul is never satiated, never satisfied. It is principally from this suffering that we feel wounded and grieving which nothing seems able to fill or satisfy. Material things cannot satisfy precisely because they are finite. The suffering of a child brings this to the fore most poignantly because we know what he/she does not know; namely that there is no answer to his suffering which has escaped the minds of the most brilliant of our race. We do not understand why this child must suffer. Suffering has become such a stumbling block, that many have opted either for the nothingness and futility of human freedom (atheism) or have sought to overcome desire/suffering by surrender to the oneness of all things in compassion and peace (Buddhism). Therein the individual person disappears which is hardly consoling. The thought of our absorption into the oneness of the universe may itself lead to peace or to further suffering. I find no consolation here.

Then it comes to suffering, the monotheists (Judaism, Islam, and Christianity) have the most formidable tasks of reconciling the reality of suffering with a personal, compassionate, loving God who is unconditional in his love as revealed by the central religious figures of Moses and Christ. I speak here of the Christian response to this reality of suffering in our lives.

Clearly, the very act of our creation made in the image and likeness of God as Genesis holds creates in us a dimension that can be satisfied only in reference to the one in whose image we have been created. That simply means that our hearts are restless until they rest in the one in whose image we have been created. That flows from the very nature of our creation and is, in that sense, the foundation and reason for all human suffering. There is no substitution for the reality in whose image we are created except the very one who created us. Until we are united to the one in whose image we have been created, that spiritual emptiness occupies our souls night and day and each hour of every day. No material things can ever satisfy that void. We try and fill that spiritual emptiness with that which cannot satisfy: material things, sex, power, wealth. Even spouses, family, children. All individually or taken together cannot fill the void of our being. "You have made our hearts for yourself and they are restless until they rest in you" as Saint Augustine put it. In fact, all these substitutes end in death because they are finite of their very nature. They satisfy only for the moment and so must be replaced ad infinitum. Only love is made for the eternal but love is always a relationship. How to relate to God? How is God, God in relationship? This is by Father, Son, and Spirit. But that is another story. Suffice it to say simply that there is relationship within the Godhead itself of Father, Son and Spirit.

The Christian religion holds what Jesus has revealed to us something about God who is the unspeakable, unutterable mystery who is our origin and who created others to love him freely and intelligently because he is love itself. Jesus' revelation is that God is Father, Abba and is love through and through. This mystery who is God has created us not out of necessity but freely (there can be no love without freedom or without a relationship) in function of whom and what he is: love. In other words, love is not a characteristic of God but is his very being, his essence, his reality which we cannot fathom or measure. Jesus who is the very Son of God incarnate has revealed to us in his words and actions that this unutterable mystery is a benevolent Father, Abba, whose love is unconditional because that is his nature and that he desires all men and women to share that love for all eternity. There was not a time when God does not love us from all eternity and there will not be a time when God shall have refused to love us. Even if we in freedom reject him. The prodigal son in the gospel has only to turn and recognize what was there from the beginning: the father's unconditional love and forgiveness. It is impossible that that love in God one day was and another day was not. Love is eternal because God, who is love, is eternal. We can only relate to God in love, return this love by which we are saved. Saved from what? Saved from our nothingness in death. That is why Christianity holds that all men are saved by the love of God in Christ who died to overcome death and rise to a life of eternal love with God. That is so beautiful that one is tempted not to believe it - it is too good to be true!

The revelation of Jesus consists simply in this: God is Father, Abba, who loves us absolutely and unconditionally. Forgiveness for our hatred and hardness of heart to each other is always at the ready precisely because of who God is. He is love not just one who has love for us. Love is not a characteristic of God as is his creativeness, his knowledge, his power; he is love in his very being so that forgiveness is the other side of the reality of that love. The gospels constantly come back to that theme: God is always at the ready to receive the prodigal son because God already loved without condition. The son had only to turn to recognize what was always there, never absent. It is this relationship that caused us originally to be and whose love seeks us always to unite us with him. This mystery is so powerful that we are tempted to not believe it because it is too good to be true.

Thus the creative act of God freely made man out of and for love. In that is his image and likeness and our hearts are empty until we love and are united by love to God and to our neighbor. That is our journey to return from whence we carne, the origin of love. We are one family united in God for eternity who is love. God creates to share his love freely with all men and women. Man's vocation therefore must be, like that of God, an absolutely free response. Love can be nothing other than free or it cannot be love.

God suffers therefore in an analogical sense because his creative love is never fully requited by the created creator. When that divine love is rejected, we can say that God's intention is frustrated and his love rejected. That is what we call 'sin' or abandonment of God's love. In this sense, we can say that God suffers because his very creation, his very love, is rejected. The rejection of this love causes God to suffer because of his inability to force his love on man who is free to return that love or not. God can force no one to love him because that would no longer be love. When that love is not returned, God suffers. God therefore risks in creating man. He risked in the nature of his very creation who is man who was created free to accept or reject God. This risk may therefore result in suffering because his love has often not been returned. To love is to suffer when that love is not returned. Therefore from all eternity God has willed his Son to become one of us to show us concretely that face of love and forgiveness and to share the suffering from man's violence and unrequited love. That is the meaning of the cross of Jesus.

Man's violence is not only his refusal to love God but the willingness to destroy those whom we should love who also are made in God's image. That image is destroyed and perverted by man's violence who seeks to destroy what was created to be loved and to love. In that very real but analogical sense, God suffers in his love and in and through the suffering Christ accepts freely and lovingly all the violence of men into his being without rancor or vengeance or hate; but returns forgiveness and reconciliation. Reconciliation is the very love by which we were created and destined. We are reconciled in the love of Christ on the cross who goes to the very source of love. That makes us sons of God in the unique Son of God. God therefore can love us because we have become adopted sons and daughters of God in Christ.

Jesus has come not to explain suffering or to take it away but to endure it with us because we do not love enough or even (God forbid!) not at all. That is the real core of human suffering because it reflects who we are as images of God, the suffering God in the face of the suffering Christ who is the Son of God and the perfect reflection of the Father and who is now present to suffering humanity until the end of time. He came to be like us in all things but sin, that we never be alone, that we know that we are loved to the very end and we have only to turn to him to realize this mystery of love. This is the mystery of God and therefore our own story.

Jesus as the Incarnate, suffering Word is the great scandal of the world. How could God be crucified and humiliated on an infamous gibbet? This is mockery for intellectuals, a stumbling block for Jews and Muslims. That is utterly unworthy of God, a scandal, unacceptable to many people and religions. As far back as the second century the great pagan intellectual Celsus held that it was impossible for God to feel such pain and suffering. He is beyond all suffering because God is completely transcendent and can feel nothing of our suffering. Christ the crucified one is dismissed as simply absurd. The whole notion that the inimitable and ineffable God who created the universe out of love could somehow be born, be hungry, cry, bleed, suffer and die ignominiously die as a criminal on a Roman gibbet Christ is a scandal to Jew and Muslim as well as to intellectuals. Yet God did not disdain participation in our sad realities and in Christ come to share our solidarity with death, companion of our suffering, going down to hell, that is, to the pure hopelessness and domination of violence and death, who gave all in love for his spouse who is the church and potentially the human race who are saved by loving as God has loved. It is God who feels to its dregs all the crucifixion and suffering of human existence in flesh and blood of Christ and in Christ made it God's own. He suffered all this to the end and defeated death in and by his resurrection.

There is no way to rationally understand any of this. None of us can. But God did it to be one with us in Christ to the very core of our death so he can raise it to glory with him for us. That is why the gospel of John can see the triumph of Jesus on the cross itself. At the very moment of his death in loving surrender, God raises him up as the response of love thus putting to death, death itself, man's last enemy now risen in glory. There is the answer to our suffering one with Christ to raise us up from that suffering and death.

If none of this is true, then Christians are the most miserable of all men, of all religions. Christianity stands or falls on the very notion of this human absurdity: a suffering God who suffers because of his love manifested on the cross of his beloved Son by which and in which God shares his love with all men and women for all time and conquers death by his resurrection. That is the key to understanding suffering. That is why the church can cry in the darkest moment of the liturgy while Christ is liturgically still in the clutches of death: "Oh happy fault of Adam that has merited for us such a Savior." My life. My failure.

ABOUT THE AUTHOR

Mr. Riga was for many years professor of philosophy, law and theology at many institutions and universities around the nation. he has studied in Europe at Louvain, Munich and Rome as well as in the United States at cathlic University and the University of Berkeley where he earned two doctorates in theology and law. A third doctorate was earned at the University of Louvain, Belgium in philosophy. he has taught at seminaries, University of Notre Dame, University of Berkeley, University of Florida ta Gainsville. He has written over thirty books and over five thousand articles on theology scripture, law both domestic and foreign. He has been a priest in New York and California and was a decorated chaplain in Vietnam with 101st Airborne division receiving the purple heart and the silver star for bravery in the field. He presently practices appellate law in Houston, Texas.